LOVE, LAUGHTER
and
LEADERSHIP
The Ministry of Wayne B. Smith

By
Rod Huron

The writer of Proverbs asks, "Who can find a virtuous woman?" I did — a beautiful young school teacher who played the piano in my first church.

After 53 years of marriage, including two daughters, Judy and Jana, two fine sons-in-law and five grandchildren, I must quote the Biblical writer again. "Many women have done noble things, but you surpass them all."

Whatever I have accomplished in ministry, much credit goes to a wonderful partner, mother and grandmother. Her name is Marge.

— Wayne B. Smith

Chapter Headings

Chapter Headings

"Do you have the one where he...?"

When people learned that I was writing a book about Wayne Smith, every one of them had a story. "Do you have the one where he...?" If everything were included, this would resemble the Manhattan phone directory, which is understandable considering that when *The Herald-Leader* surveyed their readership asking for "The 100 Most Influential Citizens in Lexington," Wayne B. Smith ranked near the top.

Two names in particular stand out: Susan Nelson and Virginia Warner. Susan's work at the beginning and Virginia's work at the end, proved extremely helpful. This book might never have been written without their contributions.

Joe Cooper and Fred Mitchell had the onerous task of sorting through more than 200 typed pages — almost all single-spaced — of Wayne's jokes. Well, somebody had to. The finalists are in chapter 7.

Charles Lees systematized the list of Wayne's speaking dates and we wanted to include it, but it ran to 30 pages even with type too small to be readable. The list was omitted.

Wayne's oldest daughter, Judy Speakes, logged the name of every person named in the book (almost 500), and proofed the manuscript for accuracy. "I paid her handsomely," Wayne insists.

Mike McGinnis and Williamstown (Kentucky) Christian Church provided a Sunday school room where Wayne talked and I typed.

Ann Nelson, Roy and Beth Mays, Brewster McLeod, Christine Clough...so many whose names are included and many whose names are not, have participated in this project. We've all had fun.

Brad Johnson, Chanda Veno, Dana Bart, Pat Henderson and the entire team at Host Communications deserve commendation for their patience, competence and professionalism.

Where the book is good, credit Wayne. Where it has faults, blame me. I hope you enjoy the reading as much as I have enjoyed the writing.

— Rod Huron

"The Man Who Couldn't Save"

By Edgar A. Guest

He spent what he made, or he gave it away,
Tried to save money, and would for a day,
Started a bank account time an' again,
Got a hundred or so for a nest egg, an' then
Some fellow that needed it more than he did,
Who was down on his luck, with a sick wife or kid,
Came along an' he wasted no time till he went
An' drew out the coin that for saving was meant.

They say he died poor, and I guess that is so:
To pile up a fortune he hadn't a show;
He worked all the time and good money he made,
Was known as an excellent man at his trade.
But he saw too much, heard too much, felt too much here
To save anything by the end of the year,
An' the shabbiest wreck the Lord ever let live
Could get money from him if he had it to give.

I've seen him slip dimes to the bums on the street
Who told him they hungered for something to eat,
An' though I remarked they were going for drink
He'd say: "Mebbe so. But I'd just hate to think
That fellow was hungry an' I'd passed him by;
I'd rather be fooled twenty times by a lie
Than wonder if one of 'em I wouldn't feed
Had told me the truth an' was really in need."

Never stinted his family out of a thing:
They had everything that his money could bring;
Said he'd rather be broke and just know they were glad,
Than rich, with them pining an' wishing they had
Some of the pleasures his money could buy;
Said he never could look a bank book in the eye
If he knew it had grown on the pleasures and joys
That he'd robbed from his wife and his girls and his boys.

Queer sort of notion he had, I confess,
Yet many a rich man on earth is mourned less.
All who had known him came back to his side
To honor his name on the day that he died.
Didn't leave much in the bank, it is true,
But did leave a fortune in people who knew
The big heart of him, an' I'm willing to swear
That today he is one of the richest up there.

"When you're riding the fire truck you can't let go."

Sweating, clutching a bucket of chicken in one hand and a box of Old Kentucky Chocolates in the other, the preacher mumbled to himself as he groped for the doorbell. Wayne B. Smith, senior minister of Southland Christian Church, Lexington, Kentucky, was making a call.

"What am I doing in a place like this?"

Off in the distance, thoroughbreds grazed peacefully. Homes of tenants who maintained the estate were visible here and there. The front lawn stretched along the tree-lined driveway to the entry gate down by the road.

Would the maid even let him in? Wayne swallowed; hard.

For Smith this was not just another pastoral visit. The gentle roll of the land prevented him from seeing the structure of his church building a half-mile away.

Yes, Southland Christian Church was growing. Yes, Southland had just bought more land. But could they use it?

For a conditional-use permit, the matter had to go before the Jessamine County Board of Adjustment. Last night's meeting was a disaster. It was the first hearing, and several spoke against the permit. Among those questioning the matter was Barbara Hunter, owner of Brownwood Farm, which ran alongside Southland's newly acquired acreage.

The moment the meeting was over, the church's lawyer, Billy Miles Arvin, hurried to Smith. Arvin was emphatic. "Go visit Barbara Hunter. She has money. She is well thought of. If she objects to church buildings near her thoroughbreds, it could really hurt our cause."

Now, standing on Barbara Hunter's front porch, Wayne swallowed again.

He had prayed on the way, prayed as he drove up the lane; he had prayed most of the time since last night's meeting.

In his pocket Smith had a photograph of the day the church signed the deed for the 42.5 acres. What he was going to do with the picture he

11

didn't know. But it was something, at least. That, and the chicken and the candy.

"Lexington's the horse capital of the world," Wayne said later. "I like horses, but in Lexington it's easier to attack motherhood and the flag."

He tried the doorbell once more. "Lord, I cannot handle this. I'm not that smart. This can't be me, Lord. It has to be you."

A woman in her late 40s opened the door. This was not the maid; this was the lady of the house.

"I'm Wayne Smith," her visitor said, "the preacher of the church over there."

"Oh, yes, I know who you are," she told him, her manner refined, gracious. "I've seen you on television." She glanced at the items Smith was carrying.

"You're supposed to beware of Greeks bearing gifts," he said cautiously.

She led him into the sitting room, and after they were seated, Wayne tried again. "You know why I'm here. We want to do anything we can to make you our friend."

"Yes," she said. "I see."

As they talked, she referred to the hearing the previous night. "Some of those objections were rather silly. I've been considering the matter, and the only thing I would like for you to do is to make a berm along my fence line and plant trees about every 20 feet. That will protect my horses. And that will be fine."

The photo stayed in his pocket as he thanked her and left.

The permit was granted, and Southland's expansion continued.

"She is a great lady," Wayne said. "She didn't want us to scare her horses." Then he added, "I made a trip or two after that just to thank her. I wanted her to know we were grateful. We still are."

No wonder Smith was thankful. Southland's growth did not come overnight, nor did it come easily.

Lexington needs a new church

IBM and Wayne Smith both hit Lexington in the 1950s. Fortunately for Smith, IBM came first, bringing an influx of new families.

Seeing the new developments on the city's south side, Ard Hoven, minister of Broadway Christian Church on the corner of North Broadway and Second Street, thought it was time to plant a new church. Hoven was speaker for *The Christian's Hour* nationwide radio broadcast and past president of the North American Christian Convention. Broadway was the largest Christian Church in Kentucky.

Where to find a preacher to lead the proposed venture?

Gayle Denny, president of Transylvania Printing Company and an elder at Broadway, knew. "Wayne Smith's your man," he said.

Denny's home church was Elizabeth Christian Church in the Grant County community of String Town. His family attended there and had kept him informed of the progress that the String Town and the Unity Christian churches were making under Wayne's leadership.

Wayne had come to Unity Christian Church while a student at Cincinnati Bible Seminary (CBS) and had stayed following graduation. Unity was near Cynthiana, the county seat of Harrison County. Under Smith's leadership, attendance at Unity Christian had increased five times over what it was when he first came, and the church had completed a new building.

Because Elizabeth Christian Church, later called String Town Christian Church, was across the county line and in another time zone, Wayne preached there first, then drove to Unity. The String Town church started to grow, too.

"We ought to try to get him," insisted Mr. Denny.

"I had received several offers," Wayne said, "but I promised Unity I wouldn't leave until the building was paid for."

But Denny and the elders at Broadway kept pressing.

"I met with them," Wayne said. "They all looked to be about 80. That frightened me. I told them no."

Several weeks passed, and the men contacted Wayne again. Again he drove down to Lexington, and this time he recommended a fellow gradu-

Words From Wayne

If you wait 'til all the lights are green to go downtown,
you'll never go downtown.

ate from CBS.

"They said they didn't want him," Smith explained. "They said, 'We want you.' So I said O.K." Broadway Christian Church agreed to provide land and a building and a nucleus from their membership and to pay Wayne's salary for one year.

This was December 1955. Groundbreaking services were held December 29 on a one-acre lot that Broadway had purchased at 371 Hill 'N Dale Road on Lexington's south side. Wayne continued at Unity until the end of February 1956, making numerous trips to Lexington and laying the groundwork for his new work there.

"On my last Sunday," Wayne said, "I fulfilled my promise. The mortgage was burned, the new preacher introduced, and I left for Lexington."

Unity had called Eugene Wigginton, who later became vice president and publisher at Standard Publishing. Reflecting, Wayne said, "The church had a healthy growth under Wigginton's leadership; in fact, attendance grew beyond what it had been while I was there."

Wayne's wife, Marge, finished out the school year at Buena Vista, an elementary school in Harrison County where she taught second grade. This would be her seventh year and her last. When the Smiths moved to Lexington, Marge gave up teaching so that she and Wayne could begin their family.

Making a start in the city

In Lexington, Wayne spent his time calling at people's homes. "From March 1 to July 8, I did nothing but knock on doors with a pamphlet, inviting them to a church being built on Hill 'N Dale Road to be called Southland Christian Church," he said.

"Going door to door is one of the hardest things you can do. When the weather warmed up, it was especially intimidating, people sitting in their chairs in the yard looking at you coming down the street. I kept thinking about that verse, 'Nevertheless, not my will, but thine, be done.' "

He visited each house up and down every street in the subdivision, then went to the next subdivision and did the same thing, then the next. "I had to," Wayne said. "It was essential."

Once a month Wayne reported to Broadway's elders. During this time, the new church building, a 30-foot-by-60-foot structure that would cost $28,000, was going up. Ard Hoven personally laid the cornerstone. The site was central to the developing area, and Hill 'N Dale Road was expected to become a major artery.

"Broadway gave us 92 members," Wayne said, "which was very generous. One was an elder, one a deacon."

The elder was Dr. E.M. Emmert, head of the Department of Horticulture, University of Kentucky.

"I'd heard he was coming," Wayne said, "and it made me nervous. When I met him, I told him I didn't know what a horticulture was and for sure couldn't spell it."

Wayne still remembers the older man's reply. With a deep voice, gentle but firm, Dr. Emmert said, "Now, Brother Smith, you just preach the Bible and don't worry about those of us from the university."

"So I tried not to worry," Wayne said. "But I was concerned."

The deacon was Frank Wilford, head of the Trust Department of First National Bank. Frank was hard-working and faithful, very sober in his demeanor. "Our constitution and bylaws were written in his office," said Wayne.

Opening day and crowded already

One hundred fifty-two people attended opening day, July 8, 1956, with five persons baptized. Would this building be big enough?

The Mays family lived across the street, and Wayne had been in their home often before the first service. Thelma Mays was a member of Sadieville Christian; her husband, Roy Jr., was an Episcopalian. On Wednesday evening, July 11, Wayne baptized Roy and two others.

Roy's son, Roy H. Mays III, became a leader in the youth group and quarterback for Lafayette High School, and he went on to Cincinnati Bible College and a notable career in Christian service. In 1985, after serving 12 years on the faculty of his alma mater, Roy III became Wayne's executive assistant, and he continues to serve Southland Christian Church today.

Wayne hired Ola Marion as church secretary, but Broadway's elders said the church wasn't large enough for a secretary. Until December they were footing part of the bill, so Ola was dismissed. Wayne found a lady in the church who was willing to serve without pay. Her name was Velma Francis. Her husband, Bill, became a deacon and later an elder. After two years, the church began to pay her. Velma would serve for 16 more years.

"She was a jewel," said Wayne.

He's My Best Encourager

Hebrews 3:13 says: "Encourage one another daily as long as it is called today so that none of you may be hardened by sin's deceitfulness." Wayne Smith is the former minister of Southland Christian Church in Lexington, and for many years it was the biggest church in the state; but then God began to bless this church, and the numbers here were more.

But do you know who has been my best encourager? Wayne Smith.

He has written me dozens of notes of congratulations.

He has given me phone calls and plaques.

When we had our fund-raiser for the building, Wayne Smith made a $3,000 donation to our building fund saying, "I'm so excited about that. It's the greatest thing in our movement."

Do you know what that is? That's Christlikeness. That is so special, so rare. No wonder I'm his biggest fan. And it's no wonder, hands down, that he is the most popular preacher in our movement. Wayne knows how to rejoice with those who rejoice and weep with those who weep.

Someone wrote, "Flatter me and I may not believe you; criticize me and I may not listen to you; but encourage me and I'll never forget you."

— *Bob Russell, Senior Minister,*
Southeast Christian Church, Louisville, Kentucky

Southland bought an organ, paying $1,350, a considerable step forward for a new church. When Broadway's elders heard about it, they told Smith to take it back.

This time Wayne sought help. Cecil Harp, a consulting engineer and a deacon at Broadway, was liaison between Broadway and Southland. Wayne told Cecil about the organ.

"Keep the organ," Cecil told Wayne. "I'll pay half, and W.U. Turner will pay the other half." So Southland had a new organ. Wayne didn't know anyone named W.U. Turner.

Three weeks later Wayne learned that two lots adjoining the church were to be sold, and he made a phone call to Cecil again.

"How much are they?" Cecil asked.

"$2,750 apiece."

"I'll buy one," Cecil promised. "W.U. Turner will buy the other one."

W.U. Turner was a member at Broadway and owned the dairy farm that had become Southland Shopping Center. Cecil was a close friend of Turner's and had had a significant part in developing the shopping center.

Wayne continued: "I didn't meet Turner for several months, but I sure liked him."

Later, Turner's son Charles and daughter and son-in-law, Christine and Charles Cassity, would become members of Southland.

Sunday-school space was a problem for the growing church. The homes of two church families bordered the church property, and they opened their basements for classrooms. Wayne went to the other houses on the street — people who did not attend Southland — and three "home loaners," as Wayne called them, agreed to open their basements to the church for Sunday school.

"They feel sorry for people like me," Wayne explained.

When attendance reached 200, the church began dual services. "I preached the first service, taught Sunday school, preached the second service. Did this from 1958 to 1963 and didn't think anything about it. And

Words From Wayne

It's not how many are in the army; it's how many are in the battle.

had Sunday-evening and Wednesday-night services, too."

Wayne and Marge provided their own additions to the growing congregation: Judy Lynn was born June 15, 1957. Marge's last name was Judy before she became a Smith. A second daughter, Jana Sue, was born May 8, 1961. Sue is the name of Marge's only sister.

The church was less than two years old when the leadership decided to extend the side walls to make the building 60 feet by 60 feet, doubling the space.

While at Unity Christian, Wayne had often held Sunday-school contests with other churches. Now he challenged churches such as Broadway, Trinity Baptist and Southeast Christian in Louisville. Everyone benefited. New people kept coming faster than they could be accommodated. By 1963 the solution was obvious: a building that would accommodate 600.

The bank says no

First National Bank turned the church down, saying, "Your membership is not sufficient to support borrowing $300,000."

Wayne was indignant. "I told them you can't go by membership," he said. "You go by average attendance."

What was the church to do now? He consulted three other banks, and they, too, said no.

"When you're riding the fire truck, you can't let go," Wayne said. "I asked myself, 'Who is the most influential person in our church?' I determined it was the head of the water company."

Ernest E. Jacobson was vice president and general manager of Kentucky American Water Company, which supplied water for central Kentucky. Jacobson Park, Lexington's largest with 386 acres, is named in his memory.

Jacobson's secretary, Theresa Saunders, was a member at Southland. Jacobson had stopped going to church in recent years, but at her invitation, he started attending there.

"Jacobson and I were good friends," Wayne said. "One day some of the men were standing outside between services talking. The weather was dry, like a drought, and you couldn't water your yard as much as you'd like. I wanted to needle Jake in front of those men, so I asked him, 'What do you do when your water pressure is weak?' "

Jacobson didn't flinch. "See your doctor," he replied, his voice loud. "There was great laughter at my expense," Wayne said.

Maybe Jacobson could help. Wayne phoned and made an appointment.

"I went to his office," he said. "I'd never been there before. I said, 'Mr. Jacobson, we've got a problem. We need $300,000, and we can't get it from anybody.' "

Jacobson was surprised. "Our bank won't give us a loan?"

"We tried, and they said no."

This was 1963, and Wayne had never seen a hands-free phone before. He was surprised when the man behind the desk made a call without picking up a handset. Smith could hear the entire conversation.

Jacobson called his friend, Dan Brock, chairman of the board at First National and a veteran power broker.

"Brock? This is Jake."

"How're you doing?"

"Not doing so well."

"What's wrong?"

"You turned down my church for a loan."

"I didn't know you had a church."

"You're d___ right I do," Jacobson said. "Brock, I'll tell you what I'm going to do. We need $300,000. If we don't get that money, I'm going to move the water company's account to Central Bank."

"Now Jake, don't even think about that."

Within a week, Southland Christian Church had the money.

Wayne said, "We're the only church I know built on blackmail."

"Do you think I can be a preacher?"

What is it that has made Wayne B. Smith so successful? Were you to ask him, part of his answer would be, "My mother." Remembering her, Wayne said, "She thought lying was wrong and stealing was wrong and a lot of other sins were wrong, but the worst thing that can happen to you is laziness."

Lillie Elizabeth Barron sold shoes for 19 years for Marks & Goldsen in Scottdale, Pennsylvania. Among Lillie's customers were the Smith family, whom she fitted on numerous occasions. Vernon Smith, his wife, and four children — Dorsey, Don, Bill, and Ruth — had moved to Scottdale from Frankfort, Kentucky, where he worked in a distillery.

Mr. Smith's brother, Joe, had moved to Pennsylvania and encouraged Vernon to come to the Keystone State, because work was plentiful. Vernon found a job in Scottdale at the United States Pipe and Foundry Company. Before long he was promoted to foreman, even though his formal education did not extend beyond the third grade.

Vernon's wife died of complications while attempting to give birth to their fifth child. Some time later, he married the shoe lady. He was 32; she was 39 and had never married.

Although Lillie was active in the Church of God and her minister, a woman, performed their ceremony, she and Vernon decided to align with the Scottdale Church of Christ, which was the largest Protestant church in this largely Catholic town.

On January 21, 1929, at Frick Memorial Hospital in Mount Pleasant, four miles from Scottdale, Wayne Barron Smith was born.

The Smiths come to Ohio

That year marked the beginning of the Great Depression. Scottdale, 70 miles south of Pittsburgh, was particularly hard hit. By 1931 nearly everything in the town was closed, including Vernon's workplace.

Because he was a foreman, the company offered Vernon a job as a night watchman. He would be paid $20 a week, but the family would have to move to Birmingham, Alabama; Newark, New Jersey; or Cincinnati, Ohio, where U.S. Pipe and Foundry plants were still open.

Vernon and Lillie opted for Cincinnati.

"Had they gone to Birmingham," Wayne said laughing, "I'd have been a Baptist. Had they gone to Newark, I would have been in the Mafia."

The Smiths settled in Sayler Park on Cincinnati's western outskirts, renting quarters on Rockaway Avenue, close to Vernon's work in Addyston.

They had hardly unpacked when Dan Eynon, the young minister of the Delhi Church of Christ, came calling and visited with the newcomers. As Dan stepped off the porch, the Methodist preacher walked up. There were only two houses between the Smiths' and the Methodist church, so Wayne's parents joined there. The Church of Christ was farther and considerably smaller.

The Smiths' house was half a mile from the Ohio River, and though she had five children to raise, Lillie took in boarders. Men working on the riverboats needed a place to stay, sometimes for a week, sometimes for a month. Lillie ruled with an iron hand, but word got around about her homemade bread, and she had no trouble getting tenants. Though these were Depression years, Vernon had a car, and there was always plenty to eat.

Lillie's background was rock-solid Church of God — no work on Sunday except for her sumptuous meals; strong convictions about deportment, morals and responsibility; and faithful adherence to Scripture.

Wayne was the only child Lillie and Vernon had together, and she doted on him. Coming home from kindergarten, Wayne would climb onto his mother's lap for a comforting kiss, and she would always sing a couple of hymns. He was a happy child, loved and loving, and Lillie was determined that he would follow her standards.

She lived by the motto that she taught to her son: If a task is once begun, never leave it till it's done; Be the task great or small, do it well or

Words From Wayne

Both me and the Great Depression started the same year.

not at all.

When Wayne was 9, the Methodist Church held dinners and sold tick-ets. Wayne was determined to sell the most. "I won most of the time," he said. "My mother encouraged me."

Lillie was firm, but she could have fun. "I get my boldness from her," Wayne said. "Probably my sense of humor, too."

One afternoon Lillie took the kids by streetcar to the Albee Theater on Fountain Square in downtown Cincinnati to see Red Skelton in *Whistling in Brooklyn*. Wayne said, "She laughed so loud an usher asked her to quiet down." Then he added, "I'm very much like her."

Wayne's mother forbade the boys to play near the river, though many Sunday afternoons the family would visit Dam 37 and watch the boats go through the locks.

Baptism and a decision for ministry

Wayne was 10 when his brother Dorsey, the oldest sibling, invited Wayne and Don to a revival at the Delhi Church of Christ. Dorsey, in his teens, had already left the Methodist Church.

This was the first time that Wayne had ever been in a Christian church. Bill Boice was the preacher, and after the sermon, the song at invitation time was "All things are ready; come to the feast." Both Wayne and Don went forward to accept Christ.

Delhi had no baptistery, so several days later, Boice baptized the two boys at Westwood-Cheviot Church of Christ in Cincinnati. Soon the whole family transferred to Delhi.

The Church of Christ at Delhi made an indelible impression upon the boy: "It was there on October 5, 1939, that I accepted Jesus. It was there at a Saturday-morning Bible club that I learned many Bible truths."

Wayne was 12 when Howard Lowe, an elder at Delhi, asked him if he would like to go to a Christian service camp.

"I'd never heard of a Christian camp before," Wayne said. Lowe, a regional manager for the Kroger Company and the only executive in the church, was much respected. "Had it not been for Howard Lowe, I doubt Delhi could have survived," Wayne said. "Lowe often paid the minister's salary out of his own pocket."

Lowe had a new Oldsmobile, so when he offered to take the boys from the church to Kentucky to the camp, Wayne accepted.

Just south of Williamstown, the car turned off Highway 25 onto Highway 36. A few miles down the road past Mount Pleasant Church of Christ, at the bottom of the hill, they turned left onto a gravel road, and there was a handwritten sign "Camp Northward" and an arrow.

Lowe's new Olds scraped bottom more than once. After fording a creek, they came to a farmhouse. Mr. Lowe said, "Wayne, get out and ask those people where the camp is."

"Right down there," came the answer.

Camp Northward was Raymond and Belle Oder's farm. A footbridge across the creek gave access to the makeshift ball field; a swimming hole served for recreation. Two tents borrowed from a funeral home had been erected, one to eat in, one to cook under.

The boys slept in the barn in the hayloft; the girls slept on the pews of an abandoned Baptist church. They had an outdoor privy; the boys were less fortunate.

"I thought it was great," Wayne said.

The next year Wayne returned, and during the fireside service the closing night, when they asked for recruits for Christian service, Wayne B. Smith, 12 years old, walked forward and dedicated his life to the ministry, as did his brother Don.

Ambition and early setbacks

In 1942, when Wayne was 13, there was a drive in town to see who could gather the most scrap iron to help in the war effort. Success was determined by the number of pounds collected. Wayne was in first place until a classmate's father found an anchor down by the river.

Wayne was not happy about losing.

Despite being neither scholar nor athlete, Wayne went out for football. One of his treasures is a picture taken when he was on the Hughes High School football team during his sophomore year. Hughes is across the street from the University of Cincinnati.

Wayne said, "I was on the third team and got in only four plays the whole year. We were playing Woodward, and those boys came from a rough part of town.

"I played left tackle. Their quarterback ran all four plays through left tackle, and the Lord spoke to me. He said, 'Wayne, you're going to die.'

"That was the end of my athletic career. You'll never hear me boo people who play sports. Most have no idea what athletes go through to even make the team."

The family, with Lillie at the helm, gave the same allegiance to the Delhi Church of Christ that that they had given to the Methodists and the Church of God: Sunday morning, Sunday night, Wednesday night, choir practice, and Saturday-morning Bible Club.

I Knew Him When . . .

I remember your family with such happiness. Your father was a gentle, patient, and faithful man and a good elder. Your mother, stern, opinionated, was nevertheless a stalwart defender of what she believed to be right and necessary, and what a good cook she was! Your brothers were genial and fun; Ruth was a dear, with a smile that would melt a glacier.

But little did I know what a dynamo we would be loosing on an unsuspecting brotherhood when I baptized a loving, special boy who became a great and noble man of God! What a privilege I was accorded and without any such expectation on my part.

There are special men in our brotherhood who were and are dear to me — Russ Martin, the Auctioneer; Bob Weaver, the Orator; Harold Ward, the Man Who Never Gave Up; and Wayne Smith, who made an entire brotherhood chuckle and then roar, and who loved people right into the arms of God after they stopped laughing.

— *William S. Boice, Phoenix, Arizona, now deceased*

Vernon became an elder. Lillie taught Sunday school. Ruth played the organ, and Bill was Sunday-school superintendent. Wayne's brother Don enrolled at Cincinnati Bible Seminary to prepare for the ministry.

In passing, it should be noted that some congregations, such as Wayne's home church, prefer the name "Church of Christ;" others, such as the one Wayne served for nearly half a century, prefer the term "Christian Church." Yet both are within the same fellowship.

In high school Wayne failed freshman algebra; he took it in summer school and passed. In his sophomore year he failed geometry; he went to summer school and passed. The same year he failed Latin. Not even summer school would do this one.

"I told Dad I wanted to quit Hughes High School to join the service," Wayne said. "It was during the second World War, and I wanted to go. My dad was an elder, and I never heard him say a cuss word, but when I said that, my dad told me, 'If you do, both of us are going to the hospital to remove my shoe from your _____.' "

Wayne tries a new school

With two years remaining of high school, Wayne forged his parents' signatures to transfer to Western Hills High School. "It was closer," Wayne said. "My friends were there. Sometimes you've got to do what you've got to do."

His academic record began to improve. He scored 94 in dramatics his senior year, 82 in public speaking, 82 in American history, 86 in Woodwork III, 92 in choir, 74 in gym.

"History was the only class with homework," said Wayne.

One day Smith borrowed the family car. Vernon had set a limit on how far the boy was permitted to go, but Wayne disconnected the odometer and headed for Indiana. "I was sick when Dad found out," Wayne said. Sore, too. His dad still believed in corporal punishment.

Words From Wayne

If you're not the lead dog, the scenery never changes.

Plus, he was grounded for 30 days.

During his junior year, Al Winholt, the church choir director, told Wayne, "One more trick from you and I'm quitting."

Wayne took that not as a threat but as a challenge. Before long Smith pulled another prank, and the man quit. When Vernon heard about it, he took off his belt and went to work. When he was finished, he told Wayne, "You go talk to him and pray that he comes back as choir director, or you'll get the same thing when you return."

Wayne said, "I felt like telling Dad, 'Let's just meet at the funeral home and save time.' "

Wayne rode the streetcar to Eighth and State and got on a bus, praying all the way to Mr. Winholt's house. Fortunately for Smith, Winholt relented, and Delhi Church of Christ retained their choir director.

The church needed a minister and called James Walters, whom Wayne remembered from Northward Christian Assembly and recommended highly. "He was our preacher during my junior and senior years, and we liked him a lot."

Even Wayne's mother liked Walters. Some called her "Lillie B." Walters called her "The Mayor." She had the habit of telling young preachers what to do, but she and Walters hit it off, and Lillie became one of his strongest supporters.

One Sunday night Wayne asked his father for permission to skip church and go to a party hosted by Mary Dornette, whom Wayne dated his last two years of high school. Dad didn't even answer; Wayne should have known better than to make such a request.

Students from Cincinnati Bible Seminary rode the streetcar out to the little church, knowing that several families took college students home on Sunday afternoons for a good meal, Wayne's family among them. Professors R.C. Foster, George Mark Elliott, and others often preached.

"I got a good taste of the ministry at Delhi," Wayne said. "I was hearing the best there was and making friends too."

Things continued to open up for Wayne at Western Hills High School. During his senior year, he was elected president of the Safety Club, which promoted safe driving.

"That was a joke," said Wayne, "considering the way I drove. But I enjoyed it and was later elected president over the seven Cincinnati public high schools. I went to PTAs, schools, clubs, and other places to give talks about safety.

"I spent a lot of time in police cars covering accidents, then giving speeches about what I had seen. When I graduated from Western Hills, the school gave me the oratorical award."

Early success and a crucial decision

During his senior year, Wayne took an afterschool job with The Fair Store, fifth floor, corner of Sixth and Race in downtown Cincinnati. The Fair Store was a subsidiary of McAlpins.

At first Wayne did odd jobs, but soon he was selling carpet, padding, asphalt tile, and linoleum. Wayne did well. One of his customers was Ruth Lyons, at the time Cincinnati's best-known media personality.

After graduation from Western Hills, Wayne went full time with the store — $35 a week plus commission. "I always got a commission." The church's new carpeting was paid for by Smith.

He enrolled in Miller School of Business, taking classes at night, and completed a course in salesmanship.

One day the boss came with an offer, and Smith hurried to his preacher with the good news. "Mr. Thunning hinted that he might give me more authority in the department," Wayne said, "and would pay accordingly."

That wasn't good news to his preacher.

Walters calmed the excited 19-year-old and told him, "You have too much talent to spend the rest of your life selling rugs. Do you really think that's what the Lord wants you to do?"

By this time Wayne had another girlfriend, Martha DeHart, from Butler, Kentucky. He saw her on weekends most of the time. Martha's father was a Baptist preacher. When her dad led singing at a revival in Dry Ridge, Kentucky, she asked Wayne if he would take her.

Wayne accepted, and when they gave the invitation that night, 19 people walked forward.

"I'd never seen anything like that," Wayne said. "I just stood there and wept. I did not move physically; I knew I was saved. But it had a tremendous emotional impact."

On the way home, neither Martha nor Wayne mentioned what had happened during the service, but Wayne felt that God was calling.

"I knew it was a recall to my commitment to the ministry I had made at Camp Northward," he said. "There was never a doubt in my mind that I should do what I said I would do seven years earlier."

It was now June 1948. Wayne had been out of high school for a year. He was beginning to make good money and had bought his first car, paying $200 for a 1931 B Model Ford.

Though Don was nearer to Wayne in age, Wayne felt closer to his older brother, Bill. Bill was almost 30 and working for United States Pipe and Foundry, the same company as their father.

"Bill," Wayne asked, "do you think I could be a preacher?"

Bill said yes, and two months later, Wayne B. Smith enrolled in Cincinnati Bible Seminary. "And I never looked back."

When he told his boss, Mr. Thunning said, "I think you'll make a good one." Thunning did more. "I'll give you a raise, 10 cents an hour, and you just come in whenever you want to."

"Then I told my parents," Wayne said, adding, "and they were thrilled."

But how would he ever handle college?

"Most people say the preacher makes the church; here's one preacher whose church made him."

"Would I make it at CBS?" Wayne said, explaining how he felt as he considered the commitment before him. "Studying was not my thing. Besides, I'd always thought of the ministry to be very sober. I knew part of my personality was not like that."

Yet there was that campfire at Northward Christian Assembly. And the Baptist revival. "I really felt called," he said, "but I never felt adequate. I determined to compensate with hard work for the skills I lacked." After all, Hughes had kept him on the football team simply because he tried so hard.

In September 1948, Wayne enrolled at Cincinnati Bible Seminary.

Partway through his freshman year, his brother Don invited Wayne to preach one Sunday at a little church in Gallatin County that has since closed, then a second time at Lystra Church of Christ in Grant County.

Wayne had never written a sermon and needed help. He had been in college only four months. He turned to a fellow student and one of his best friends, Robert Shannon. Bob had preached frequently while still in high school, and Wayne went home with him for the weekend.

Shannon's home was Corinth, in Grant County near Williamstown. With the help of Bob and Bob's sister, Ruth, Wayne wrote his first sermon at their dining room table. Wayne's title: "The Ark and the Church."

He said, "I spent 14 hours on that sermon, and it lasted not more than 10 minutes."

Wayne takes first place

Smith heard about the annual oratorical contest to be held in December. The rules were simple: write a 10-minute speech, memorize it, and deliver it before the student body.

Wayne entered and won.

His speech was titled, "Who Is My Brother?" Since the school's founding in 1924, only one other freshman had won this event. That student was Louis Detro, who later lost his life in an automobile accident while serving as president of Great Lakes Bible College, Lansing, Michigan.

In 2004, Cincinnati Bible College and Seminary completed a $4 million Worship and Ministry Center. A part of this complex is a chapel where young men will learn to preach. That chapel, lined with mementos of his ministry, bears the name "The Wayne B. Smith Oratorium."

Following the contest, Ralph Dornette, his speech teacher, suggested, "Wayne, you ought to find a church where you can preach regularly."

Wayne liked the idea, but preparing eight sermons a month looked like an impossibility to a boy who had not yet completed his freshman year. Dornette suggested a half-time church.

"What's a half-time church?" Wayne wanted to know.

His professor explained that a half-time church has a preacher the first and third Sundays only. On the second and fourth Sundays, it has Sunday school and the Lord's Supper, but no sermon.

Wayne wrote to a church in Indiana and one in Kentucky. He listed his qualifications: 19 years of age, had preached twice, taught a Junior Boys' Class, had a 1937 Chevrolet.

He never heard from the Indiana church. "That sure was a good thing," Wayne said later. "One day I might have been cheering for Bobby Knight and IU instead of UK's Blue and White."

Trial sermon and first church

The Kentucky church answered: Robinson Christian Church in Harrison County, it was in a village of a dozen homes, a country store, railroad tracks, and the Licking River.

Vic Shadd, an elder, wrote and asked Wayne to come and preach a trial sermon the first Sunday of January. Wayne preached Sunday morning and Sunday night. Attendance was 51; no decision on the preacher.

The church asked another candidate, then another.

Finally, Wayne received a letter stating, "We would like for you to be our preacher. We'll pay you $25 for the first and third weekends."

Which meant $50 per month to drive 60 miles one way, visit all day Saturday, preach twice on Sunday, and drive back to college. Accepting Robinson's offer would mean quitting his job at The Fair Store.

Wayne accepted.

Income had gone down; expenses had gone up. "Monday through Friday I delivered dry cleaning after school in the Delhi, Addyston, and Cleves area."

He lived at home, studying when he could. "I never spent a night on campus," he said, "and it's a good thing. If I had and someone said, 'Let's go to White Castle or Skyline Chili,' I would've gone. I wasn't very disciplined along that line."

From his first days at Robinson, Wayne wasted no time, driving that Chevy over those dirt and gravel roads and up the lanes to the people's homes. This was turning out to be fun. He liked the people, and the people liked him.

The families in his church were farmers. In that era, few had cattle crossings — logs or railroad ties spaced side by side just far enough so that a car could drive over but a cow would not cross.

Wayne still remembers his visits to the White family: "Every time I called, I had to stop the car, get out, swing open the gate, get back in the car, drive 20 feet, stop the car, get out and close the gate, and so on. The Whites had four gates. That meant I had to get in and out of my car 16 times."

Later, Smith said, "One of the best things about Lexington was no gates."

Wayne wasn't aware that Marjorie Judy, the pianist at Robinson Christian, knew him already. Marge was a student at Georgetown College, 20 miles north of Lexington. She was studying to become a schoolteacher.

Marge roomed on the fourth floor of Rucker Hall at the college, and across the hall was her good friend Martha DeHart. Martha was the Baptist preacher's daughter whom Wayne had dated.

On the Sunday the Robinson elders read the letter introducing their new 19-year-old preacher, Marge said to herself, "Why, I know him. That's Martha's boyfriend."

An invitation from a second church

Wayne began, preaching the first and third Sundays. A month later, another Harrison County church, Unity Christian, contacted him. Unity customarily found their ministers at the College of the Bible, which later became Lexington Theological Seminary, and had never had one from a conservative school like Cincinnati Bible Seminary.

When the elders at Unity asked him to come on the second and fourth Sundays, Wayne wasn't sure. The two churches were five miles apart, and if the people were to visit back and forth, this would mean a new sermon every week.

"I turned them down," he said.

He did promise to send someone from CBS, but when the prospect canceled at the last minute, Wayne had to fill in.

"They asked me again; again I said no."

Wayne lined up someone else to come and preach, but this one, too, backed out.

Unity Christian Church is south of Williamstown on Highway 36, seven miles north of Cynthiana. The congregation, founded in 1872, met in a one-room structure heated by a pot-bellied stove, with the facilities out back. The church attendance averaged 29. The oldest elder, W.H. Berry, said to Wayne, "Brother Smith, we haven't agreed on anything for

He Believed He Could

Wayne B. Smith has faithfully served the Lord with gladness of heart, has ministered to my family, and is a treasured friend.

Wayne believed that he could build the Lord's church with shoe leather, automobile tires, and an abundance of genuine love. And he was right!

— Jack H. Ballard, for 44 years senior minister of Mount Carmel Christian Church, Stone Mountain, Georgia, now minister of Northside Christian Church, Marietta, Georgia

years. You're the only thing we have agreed on."

"So I went," Wayne said. "I found out the people only visited back and forth during the annual two-week revival every summer. I was relieved."

Unity paid $17.50 per weekend for Saturdays and Sundays. "The people at Unity were so great," Wayne said. "All of them were farmers, most of them tenant farmers. They weren't accustomed to my style of preaching, but they were receptive and encouraging. Those people were dependable. The communion bread was not bought; it was made. The church was clean, and though the numbers were small, we built on commitment."

Attendance the first year averaged 31.

He was surviving and more at CBS. While going to school four days a week, delivering dry cleaning every day after class, and visiting and preaching on weekends, his grade average for four years was B- or C+, Smith the competitor loved a challenge.

During Wayne's sophomore year, he entered the annual debating contest. Each side had two debaters and an alternate. He and Bob Shannon teamed up to speak on the proposition, "Should the electoral college be abolished?"

"I didn't know what an electoral college was," Wayne said, "but I was against it, and Shannon and I won." When the Bush-Gore presidential election was decided in 2000 by the electoral college, Smith decided he was for it.

Of the three speaking contests at Cincinnati Bible Seminary, Smith placed first in two of them. The third contest had to do with dramatics. He was not interested and chose not to enter.

Wayne scrambled for sermon ideas, always on the lookout for good material, often preaching sermons he heard in chapel or using notes from class or books from the school library.

"If you plagiarize long enough," Smith said, "it's research."

Nearly every Friday night, he drove to the Delhi Church of Christ, locked the front door, and practiced his sermon. "I gave some of my best sermons to those empty pews," he said. "What's on paper doesn't always preach too well. You have to try it out. Those Friday nights were a necessity."

Saturday mornings, he headed for Kentucky. The fifth-Sunday weekends were a welcome breather.

"Visiting was my long suit," he said, speaking of his work at the two churches. "I wore out my car, got another one, and wore that out, too."

Before long he had been in the homes of all the members of both churches and most nonmember homes in the two communities.

The preacher meets his match

Numerical growth came from Unity; Robinson stayed the same. Even so, Wayne found something very appealing at Robinson: the pianist, Marjorie Judy. The only problem was, "Could she possibly be interested in me?"

Marge's parents had a 120-acre farm, her brother co-owned a lumber company, her cousin was sheriff. One more problem: "I'd heard the Judys had money."

Wayne explained, "My folks never owned a home. My mother took in boarders. I had no illusions about my looks, and here's this beautiful girl from a prosperous family. I just didn't know if it could happen."

Finally, he got up the nerve and asked her out.

There were complications. The field was crowded. Marge was dating a banker and a salesman, and she was writing to a boy in the service.

Wayne was only at his church on Saturdays and Sundays, and no matter how hard he tried, she set limits on her time.

"Marge is very independent," he said. "She would date me one night, but not both."

Wayne said he would rather have Saturday night — obviously more time — but if he took Saturday night, she would come to church Sunday night with a date.

Wayne pounded his fist: "It's very difficult to stand in the pulpit and preach the love of God when you want to kill that guy sitting out there in the audience with Marge!"

He added, "I kept trying. I remembered the law of the harvest: 'If you don't sow, you don't reap.' "

After a year and a half of dating, Marge accepted a ring. "The dating could have been better," Wayne said, "but the marriage has been great."

When people ask Marge why she chose Wayne, her standard answer is, "He was the best salesman."

Revival at Unity makes headlines

At the end of two years, Robinson averaged 53, a gain of two from where they were when Smith came. Unity averaged 45, up from 29 when he started. Wayne left Robinson and began preaching at Unity every Sunday, continuing to drive back and forth to college.

"I felt so honored to be in the ministry," Wayne said. "I felt the same way when I was preaching there with 45 people as I did later when I was preaching to 4,000."

The highlight of each church year was the July revival, "The protracted meeting, as it was called," Wayne said. "Two weeks in length, involving two Sundays and 14 continuous nights. I would preach for 50 Sundays without anyone coming forward. Everybody waited for the revival."

For his first revival, Wayne invited Professor Dornette, his speech teacher, to preach. "It was a fine meeting," Wayne said. "The building was filled every night."

The next year Wayne asked the minister of his home church, James Walters, to preach the revival. Walters was already known in the area, having preached there in his early ministry.

Commenting on the meeting, Walters said, "Most ministers don't know how to prepare for a revival. Wayne had really prepared that little church. He has such a passion for the lost. He had been calling in all their homes, and he took me visiting the very first day. Those people were ready before I preached one word."

The first night of the revival, no one came forward. The second night, 18 people responded to the invitation.

"There wasn't room at the front for them all," Walters said. "Even Wayne was astonished."

Words From Wayne

Big doors swing on small hinges.

Forty-five people came into the church during those two weeks. The Cynthiana paper ran a photo of Wayne Smith baptizing 29 people August 20, 1950, nearly all of them adults, in the creek near the iron bridge in front of Norman Taylor's farm, a half-mile below the church.

Before the revival started, Unity Christian Church averaged 45. In two weeks, the congregation doubled. Wayne smiled when he recalled that one of those baptized was his competition, Marge's boyfriend, whom she was with at the baptizing.

"Several suggested," Wayne said, "that I hold him under and send him to a better place immediately. I sure was tempted. If you'd told me that one year later I would marry Marge, I wouldn't have believed it."

Preacher Smith takes a wife

On August 28, 1951, the summer between Wayne's junior and senior years at CBS, he and Marge were married. Neither Robinson nor Unity could hold the guests coming from both communities and from Cincinnati, so the wedding was held at the Christian Church in Cynthiana, a town of 6,000 and the county seat.

"Minister T.J. Mattingly was so gracious to us, insisting we use their facilities," Wayne said later.

Just before the wedding, Wayne held a revival for his brother Don at Lystra, near Williamstown, and stayed at the home of Mr. and Mrs. Willie Adams.

During the revival, a man came from Chattanooga and painted a sign on the roof of Willie's barn, "SEE ROCK CITY." The painter provided the barn owner two passes to the wondrous attraction. Willie gave them to Wayne.

The revival closed Sunday night. The wedding took place the following week. "I used the money they gave me at Lystra to go on my honeymoon," Wayne said. The newlyweds traveled to Chattanooga and the top of Lookout Mountain to see the famed Rock City. Later, Wayne complained, "I was not impressed by all those rocks." Marge's rejoinder: "That's because your mind wasn't on rocks."

The couple set up housekeeping at Fourth and Pleasant streets in Cynthiana. Marge still had 11 hours to finish toward her degree but could teach so long as she remained in college. She taught second grade at Buena Vista Elementary, seven miles out in the country.

Cincinnati Bible Seminary had no Monday classes, so Wayne left home at 4 a.m. Tuesday mornings for a 7 a.m. class, spent the nights with his parents, and returned to Cynthiana Friday afternoons.

He graduated with the Class of 1952 with a Bachelor of Sacred Literature, a degree for which the catalog said, "foreign language not required."

"I was in Greek class two days," Smith said. "That was enough."

Upon graduation, Wayne became Unity Christian Church's full-time minister, their first since 1872.

"The most I did for Robinson," he admitted, "was to steal their pianist."

A new building for Unity Christian Church

No longer burdened by schoolwork and driving back and forth to Cincinnati, Wayne was able to concentrate on the church. What to do about Unity's building?

"The only money available was $400 in the Ladies Aid Society," he said.

But he went to work, enlisting people to sponsor the stained-glass windows he envisioned, taking bids from contractors, drumming up enthusiasm among the congregation, raising dollars. "We sure needed that new building," Wayne said.

Carlyle Whitaker submitted the lowest bid. The bank required every board member to sign the note. One man signed with an X because he could not write.

The church met in Renaker High School during construction. Lumber from the old structure was used in the new. Men in the church helped with the labor.

Wayne said, "There was never an issue during the building program that we did not decide unanimously, because we had to stick together."

The new sanctuary, with a full basement partitioned into Sunday-school rooms and those stained-glass windows the preacher wanted, was dedicated September 7, 1952, three months after Wayne's graduation from CBS. Final cost: $24,500.

The first person baptized in the new baptistery was the contractor, Carlyle Whitaker.

Smith challenged the congregation to a three-way attendance contest. Wayne Spangler, a friend of Wayne's from CBS, was preaching at Indian Creek, and William R. Nash, from Kentucky Christian College, preached at Ruddles Mills. All three churches were of similar size.

"I hate to admit it," said Smith, "but Ruddles Mills won."

Wayne continued to spend time with the families in the community, often handing up tobacco off the wagon or helping in the field. For a time, he assisted at the Smith-Rees Funeral Home in Cynthiana and at the Cynthiana stockyards.

Looking back, Wayne said, "There was never a doubt in my mind that I was where God wanted me. I loved the ministry and those wonderful people. Farmers are the most gracious people on earth. They really live by faith. If it doesn't rain, they're in the red. They love their neighbors, because they help each other with their crops.

"As a young preacher, I could easily get off on a tangent. Usually, G.T. Ritchie, a godly elder, or Ruth Berry, a grand old saint, would take me aside and calm me down. She would tell me, 'Now Wayne, everything's going to be all right.' Most people say the preacher makes the church; here's one preacher whose church made him."

On March 23, 1953, Wayne Barron Smith was ordained to the Christian ministry. Elders from Delhi came down from Cincinnati. Burris Butler, head of Standard Publishing, delivered the sermon.

Unity Christian Church continued to grow, but money was tight. "The most they ever paid me was $50 a week." Weber's Sausage Company was located three miles from the church, and during Wayne's last year at Unity, the company mailed him a check for $10 each week. "They felt I was doing some good for the community," Wayne explained.

Once a year the leaders discussed salary, asking the preacher to leave the room while they deliberated. "When they called me back into the room, they told me, 'Honestly, we're in debt on the new church building, and we can't give you a raise.' "

Herbie Casey was their spokesman. "He was a farmer and so quiet, with such a sweet spirit."

Wayne continued, "I asked them if I could hold more revivals. 'Hold as many as you want,' they told me. That year I held seven two-week meetings. Marge did not accompany me, as she was in Georgetown College attempting to finish her degree."

Marge's income was important. "Her teaching went a long way in keeping us afloat," Wayne said.

Looking back, Wayne said of the folks at Unity, "I could never adequately express how much love I have for those people and what they've meant to my life."

He is convinced that these first seven years prepared him for his ministry at Southland.

"There are probably more preachers out of the ministry than in," Smith said. "Most of us who graduate from Bible college are idealistic. It doesn't take many unfortunate board meetings or 'no raise this year' or gossip or something else, and Satan whispers, 'There's a better way.'

"When I arrived in Lexington in 1956, I had no scars and no war stories. I remember some concerns, but nothing major that wasn't overcome by a loving wife and a body of people that I know appreciated my efforts. If every church — especially at the beginning stages — could treat their preacher like he was their son or, even better, their grandson, there would be fewer what ifs."

Taking care of "The Mayor"

The year after his graduation, Wayne's father died at the age of 57. Wayne's mother was in her mid-60s. Marge and Wayne invited Lillie into their home, where she immediately took charge, rearranging the furniture, offering advice in the kitchen, and so forth. "They didn't call her 'The Mayor' for nothing," Wayne said laughing.

"After 13 months," he said, "I called Don, who now ministered to the

Words From Wayne

Climbing the ladder of success is easier
when your father owns the ladder.

Christian Church in New Richmond, Ohio. I said, 'Don, why don't we share the blessing? She's been with us over a year.' "

Don agreed.

Some time later, Wayne called New Richmond to see how things were going.

"We're all O.K."

"How's mother?"

"I moved her to Wyandotte," Don said.

Lillie had a brother who was divorced and a widowed sister who lived together in a house in Wyandotte, Michigan. "They were laid-back compared to her," Wayne said. "They needed someone to tell them when to paint the house and weed the garden and manage their lives — things like that."

In Wyandotte, Lillie immediately began attending the Christian Church. She enjoyed the years in Michigan and did not return to Lexington until shortly before her death. Looking back, Wayne said, "James Warfield was her preacher and always went the second mile for my mother. Some of my mother's greatest friends were in the Wyandotte congregation."

New venture and new adventures

Wayne was full time at Unity and going strong when Elizabeth Christian Church in String Town, 11 miles up Highway 36, asked him to hold a two-week revival. String Town was on the same highway but across the county line, and Grant County was in a different time zone.

Elizabeth Christian Church was half time and without a preacher. Wayne had an idea.

"I said, 'Let me make a proposal. I'll come up here every Sunday morning and preach, then have nothing Sunday night. That way I won't miss anything at Unity. However, you'll have to have church first, Sunday school afterward.' " They agreed.

He continued this arrangement for two years.

Sunday mornings Wayne was out of bed early. After a quick breakfast, he drove out Pleasant Street, crossed the bridge, and turned right on Kentucky 36. Marge stayed home and came later to Unity in her own car.

Once out of Cynthiana, the highway began a gentle climb between the hills, with an occasional house set far back from the road. Wayne passed the turnoff to Robinson. Then came the curve in the road and the wide place in the creek where he'd had all those baptisms. Then half a mile farther was Unity Christian Church. Already there were cars parked and people gathered.

On the other side of Renaker, the road narrowed, still gradually climbing until it followed the ridge, twisting, turning, an occasional dip only to climb again, now hemmed in by brush and trees, or the open stretch with its view of the valleys below veiled in the morning mist.

Then came the Grant County sign and, a mile farther on the hilltop, Elizabeth Christian Church.

Smith parked the car so that he could get out easily, then started shaking hands and greeting his flock. He knew each member by name; he'd been in nearly every home.

This preservice time was important; afterward, he had to head back to Unity.

A careful driver might cover the 11 miles in 20 minutes. Smith took considerably less. "I like to go fast," he said. "That gave me an excuse."

The last notes of "Softly and Tenderly" had hardly faded when he was in the car and on the way, in second gear before his tires hit the pavement. Smith had no time to enjoy the redbud in the spring or the golden colors of the fall; he was more concerned with staying on the road. There were several places where it was a long way to the bottom.

Despite the preacher's divided attention, things began happening at Elizabeth Christian Church. Attendance went from 50 to 111. Old members came back; new ones were added.

One August revival was particularly memorable. Bob Shannon was the evangelist, Robert Jones the song leader. Wayne had designated certain nights for special emphasis. Old-fashioned Night came toward the end of the second week.

Wayne had gone to Goldberg's in Cynthiana and rented a tux, complete with tails. He did not realize that the ends of his split-tailed coat formed two little pockets. Nor did he know that in each pocket, Arnold Faulkner had placed a dollop of limburger cheese.

Sitting on the platform in the non-air-conditioned building, Wayne sweated, and not altogether from the heat. Those in the congregation fortunate enough to be in the know could tell by the sidewise glances and tensing of the jaw when Brother Smith got a whiff of Faulkner's gift.

At one point, Smith, unsure of the source of this most unwelcome fragrance, surreptitiously turned his right shoe to inspect the underside. Nothing there. He tried the left, with no better success.

Announcements were particularly difficult, because by this time, the congregation was uncommonly attentive to the preacher's every word and gesture, but Smith was at a loss to figure why his most ordinary pronouncements were so hilarious.

Not until the benediction and the service was over did he learn the truth.

Wayne said of the String Town folks, "I loved that church. Those were great people."

Yes, indeed.

Their building was heated by two pot-bellied stoves. Some wanted to get rid of them. Some wanted the stoves to stay.

A good-quality cast-iron pot-bellied stove is indestructible. Unless, somehow, one might be dropped. Cast iron can crack.

Two clumsy deacons — Stanley Gill and Eugene Ogden — came into the building to do some work and, as they prepared to store the stoves for the summer, unfortunately dropped them. Nobody wants to spend money on a broken-down stove. And if you're replacing two old stoves, maybe you want to make some other improvements as well.

"We put in new seats, put in a floor furnace, and remodeled the church," said Wayne. The preacher's part in this drama remains obscure, overshadowed perhaps by what happened soon after.

"When we dedicated all the improvements there, I asked Ard Hoven, minister of Broadway Christian in Lexington, to be the dedication speaker in the afternoon. We were counting on a good crowd and a good offering.

"I had also invited a former minister, A.S. Dowd, to bring a word of greeting. He was a big man, up in years and heavy-set. His wife and two sons were in the audience. The place was packed, and it was hot. Dowd stood up to speak and had spoken about six or seven minutes when he said, 'I think I'm going blind.' His knees buckled and fell to the floor, dead.

"Brother Hoven took the white cloth from the communion table, put it over him, and we sent for the coroner.

"While we were waiting, we decided to dismiss and not have the rest of the service. Brother Hoven knew we needed that offering. We had bills to pay. Hoven said, 'I'm going to ask everybody to stand, and we'll pray. But before we do, deacons, put offering plates by the door.'

"Whew," Wayne said, relieved. "We got a big offering."

Smith had never met Hoven in person before that service. Little did he know that four years later, Dr. Ard Hoven would invite Wayne B. Smith to become the founding minister of Southland Christian Church.

"Climb a big mountain one step at a time! And pray as you go."

When Wayne left Unity, James Wilson, editor of *The Log Cabin*, the Cynthiana paper, published a lengthy editorial Friday, February 24, 1956, under the headline, "A Tireless Worker," from which the following excerpts are taken:

This young, human dynamo has not only fought sin in Harrison County with a vigor that beggars description, but he has radiated peace of mind and happiness that makes his presence welcome wherever he goes.

As pastor of Unity Christian Church at Breckenridge in this county, Bro. Smith has brought this church to the forefront as one of the most progressive in the county if not in the state. During his stay there a new edifice was constructed, and many worth-while programs started, not the least of which was a basketball team for the youth of the church. . . .

Obviously, one with such vigor could have gone to a well established, financially strong congregation after having gained a wealth of experience here. But he didn't choose to do so. He was challenged by the thought of starting a new church — one that, when he accepted the call, didn't even have a building in which to worship. If his future performance may be judged by what he has accomplished in the past, we may be sure that Lexington is going to get a good, stiff shot in the arm, so to speak.

Part of that "shot in the arm" was Smith's long standing practice of ringing doorbells.

"He loves to call," Marge said, "most of the time in the evenings, when people are home. He went in the daytime to see where they lived, because it's nearly impossible to find an address after dark."

Smith explained his devotion to making house calls: "Andrew Blackwood said it and I believe it: 'Churches are held together with worthy preaching and are built by shoe leather and automobile tires.' People would give me names, and I made sure I was in those homes before next Sunday, because somebody would ask if I'd done the call. If nobody was home, I'd go back a time or two."

Wayne found Saturday afternoons a good time to find people at home, calling from noon until after dark. "I love UK sports," he said, speaking of the University of Kentucky. "But I never saw the games, unless it was on somebody's TV when I was in their house."

Many times on Sunday morning he rose at 4:00 to finish his sermon before facing the congregation.

Paul J. Bryant was chairman of the elders that first year. Wounded on Omaha Beach, D-Day, 1944, Paul was one of 10 survivors out of the 300 on his ship. He came home determined to show his appreciation to God through Christian service. He taught Sunday school; worked with the youth; helped with Hearts Harbor, a food and clothing ministry; and kept up a constant flow of letters, phone calls, and personal visits for the church.

One of Smith's innovations was a men's quartet begun in 1960. "I challenged my sister-in-law and her husband to form a quartet," Wayne said. "And I wanted it to be a good one."

The Messengers were an instant hit. With Marge's sister, Sue Johnson, playing the piano and Sue's husband, Larry, singing lead, the quartet sang nearly every Sunday for the next 35 years. The other beginning *Messengers* were Bill Brumfield, Jerry Beard, and Kenny Evans.

Marrying into the family was not without its disadvantages. Referring to Smith's constant requests to help some unfortunate, Larry complained, "I could have been a rich man if my brother-in-law had not been a preacher."

Larry, president and owner of Thermal Balance, a company that he built from two employees to 40, was called home July 13, 2002. Wayne said, "Larry was generous with his income, and gospel singing was his first love. I've said often, 'If a man couldn't preach after *The Messengers* sing, then he couldn't preach.' "

Smith discovers Kentucky Fried Chicken
During the early days, Smith invited Ben Merold for a revival. The two

Words From Wayne

Some of the sharpest pictures are developed in the darkest rooms.

preachers stopped for lunch at the Starlite Restaurant to try the new Kentucky Fried Chicken. Owner Andy Rasmussen was the first KFC franchisee in Lexington, adding to an already successful carhop and dining establishment that he and his father-in-law opened in 1954. The next year, Kentucky Fried Chicken was added to the menu and became a popular item.

Waitress Sharon Cole accidentally spilled a soda on Wayne. Instantly, he was on the floor kneeling. "Lord," he said, eyes raised toward heaven, "please forgive this Catholic for this act of unkindness."

Everybody laughed, and not long afterward, Wayne baptized her. This restaurant would figure large in Wayne's ministry.

Contests, revivals, calling: Wayne kept the heat on. Reporting on the monthly meeting of the Bluegrass Christian Men's Fellowship, his church paper crowed: "MEN WIN BANNER. In a most convincing and satisfying manner, the banner was returned to its rightful place Monday night when the men of Southland devastated all opposition with some 39 men present. A sister church very near had the next highest figure with 24 present ...Wayne said of his men: 'God gave us good leaders.' "

William "Buddy" Mossbarger grew up in a rural church at Cecilia, Kentucky, near Glendale in Hardin County. He and Martha were married in 1957 and visited different churches for the first year or so. Buddy describes his first time at Southland: "The first day we visited Southland, we came out and said, 'This is the church for us.' " The year: 1959.

Jack Burdette, vice president of Kentucky Utilities, was on the board of another church in Lexington when Billy Graham held a crusade in town. Greatly moved by the crusade, Jack went to the next leadership meeting at his church with requests that he felt would help the spirituality and mission of the congregation.

Disappointed by the response, Jack stood up in the meeting and resigned. "I'm not leaving you," he told the group. "You have left me."

Jack and his wife decided to try other churches, and Southland was the first. The Burdettes stayed. They have two sons and a daughter, now grown. Rick Burdette is senior minister of Fern Creek Christian Church, and their son-in-law, David Johnson, is senior minister of Fairdale Christian Church, both churches in Louisville.

Those who selected the Hill 'N Dale site expected the unfinished street to become a major artery. City planners changed their minds, and Wayne found himself landlocked and isolated on a side street.

Maybe if he gave people directions. Wayne commissioned a designer and a carpenter and went to work. After he was finished, Smith thought perhaps he'd better get permission, so he contacted the city engineer.

On the way to the man's office, Smith kept praying: "Like Nehemiah of old, I pray you will give your servant success today in the presence of this man."

Wayne tried to remain calm as he went inside to explain what he'd done. When Smith told his story, the official asked, "Well, how many signs did you put up?"

Wayne swallowed. "Sixteen."

"Sixteen? You put up 16 signs?"

After the official had calmed down, the two talked a while longer, and Wayne left. He said later, "They only made me take down two of them."

When Wayne saw a new home going up, he was often there before the family moved in. He bought the Lexington newcomers list and called on every home within a mile radius of the church and many homes farther away.

"There was an anesthesiologist," Wayne said. "He was Methodist. Every time I saw him in the hospital, he apologized to me for not coming to Southland. 'You were at my house first,' he would say."

Smith personalized the "Go" in the Gospel. "If God wanted these people to come to Southland," Wayne said, "it helped that I bought the list and knocked on their doors."

Wayne was not the only one doing the calling. His church paper, which he called *The Voice of Southland Christian Church*, frequently listed by name those who participated, as in this midwinter report:

"Tuesday night was a great night here at the church. Eleven went out calling on behalf of the Lord. As a matter of fact, two didn't return until after 11 p.m. (Swartz-Caywood) — they went the second mile. Thank God for women such as Barbara Byington and Dorothy Clark; and men such as Gene Hisel, Bill Francis, Stewart Wylie, Monty Byington, Bob

Swartz, Spencer Caywood, John Boyd, and Ron Summers. (I went, too.) Thanks to Virginia Parker and Frances Gerkens for coffee and dough-nuts."

Wayne holds a revival at Southeast

Wayne found time to hold revivals for other churches. In 1962 Southeast Christian Church in Louisville was in the beginning stages, and its minister for the first two years was Joe Rex Kearns.

Preacher Kearns asked Wayne to come and hold a revival for the new church. At the time, Southeast was meeting in the basement of a house, with an attendance of 70. Wayne preached Monday, Wednesday, and Friday nights; Robert O. Weaver, minister of Tates Creek in Lexington, preached Tuesday, Thursday, and Saturday.

"They gave me $75," Wayne said, "$25 a night for three nights."

Smith participated in a television program on Channel 18, *The Christian Hour*, sponsored by area Christian Churches, Southland's turn coming every fifth week or so. The format was a panel discussion, and Wayne did not hesitate to invite celebrities to appear, becoming acquainted with public figures such as Lt. Governor Harry Lee Waterfield; UK's football coach, Charlie Bradshaw; city manager Jack Cook; and others.

Bluegrass Breakfast Lions Club

Wayne had been active in the Lions Club in Cynthiana even though Unity Christian was a rural church. "When I came to Lexington," he said, "I visited four Lions Clubs. They were all so big I didn't feel I could make a contribution. So I didn't do anything."

Wayne had been in town seven years when a call came from Lions International: "We're thinking of a new approach. We'd like to have you help us form a breakfast club."

"I told them yes, I was interested," Wayne said.

"Headquarters called 15 other people. We got together and organized. I was elected founding president. Our Bluegrass Breakfast Lions Club met Tuesdays at 7:20 in the morning. Ours was the first one like it east of the

Mississippi River."

Southland kept growing. Many of those who had come into the church in the early days were advancing in their careers as well. William Bechanan had moved to Lexington from Elizabethtown and was one of the original members from Broadway. Bill was a rising young engineer for Kentucky Utilities.

Wayne and the elders had determined that Southland needed a youth minister. After a long search, they settled on a young man from Phoenix.

"He came and met the elders and me and we were sold on him," said Wayne. The church flew the man's wife to Lexington, and the couple suggested colors for the redecoration of the house being provided.

The newly hired staff member returned to Arizona to make arrangements for the move to Kentucky. Two weeks later, Wayne received a call from the minister and chairman of the elders at the church the man had served until his recent resignation: "At least one girl, maybe two, have become pregnant by this man."

Southland had no lawyers within the membership at the time, and engaged the services of an attorney from outside. After carefully reviewing the situation, the attorney advised, "You have to pay him 60 days' severance, plus moving expenses, plus incidentals."

Wayne phoned Arizona, but the man's furniture was already on the way and he and his family were somewhere between Phoenix and Lexington.

"I told our secretary," Wayne said, "when his furniture comes, don't let them take it off the truck."

When the truck arrived, the driver of the moving van had a message of his own: "As long as that furniture is on that truck, it's $10 an hour more."

The secretary said, "It stays there." After 24 hours on the truck, Southland put the furniture in storage.

Wayne finally tracked the man down at a relative's house in St. Louis. "We didn't accuse him, because we didn't have evidence," Smith said. "We just told him the arrangement was off, and if he wanted to learn why, to call the church in Phoenix."

Southland began to add up the dollars: $840 for moving expenses; $10 for every hour the furniture remained on the truck, two months salary,

The Messengers Quartet

Speaking of the Messengers, Wayne said, "I don't have words to adequately describe how they inspired me and the congregation each Lord's day."

A.T. Moreland, an elder in those early years, named the group. Listed below are the names, years of service, and present locations of those who have been part of this unique quartet.

Larry Johnson, 42 years. "Called home," Wayne explained.
Sue Johnson, 42 years. Nicholasville, Kentucky. Sue is Marge's only sister.
Wally Schmidt, 32 years. Lexington, Kentucky. Still singing.
Bill Brumfield, 28 years. "Called home."
Dick Carpenter, 15 years. Lives near Raleigh, North Carolina.
Roger Wellman, 15 years. Lexington, Kentucky.
Ron Beckett, 10 years. "Called home."
Ben Rainwater, 8 years. Nicholasville, Kentucky. Still singing.
David Waits, 7 years. Lexington, Kentucky.
John Leinbaugh, 7 years. Wabash, Indiana.
Ralph Chinn, 6 years. Lexington, Kentucky.
Paul Hill, 4 years. Lexington, Kentucky. Still singing.
Jerry Beard, 3 years. Lexington, Kentucky.
Jess Barnett, 3 years. "Called home."
Kenny Evans, 3 years. London, Kentucky.
Joe Wright, 3 years. Wichita, Kansas.
John Lowery, 2 years. Waynesburg, Kentucky.
J. D. Miller, 1 year. Shelbyville, Kentucky.
Bob Abbott, six months.

Eighteen men in all, plus Sue Johnson, have been a part of the group. "Four are singing in heaven," Wayne said.

and the cost for renovating the house where the newcomer was to live. The total came to almost $5,000.

Next board meeting the matter came to the floor. "We've wasted $5,000," someone said.

Bill Bechanan spoke up: "If we've saved one girl — and if it had been my daughter — this is some of the best money we've ever spent."

That ended the discussion.

Looking back on this incident, Wayne said, "Bill was quality. When leaders who have quality speak, other people listen. You're always standing on the shoulders of your leaders. Sometimes they can take a position you can't take and one that is best for the church. I've been thankful I've had strong men."

Area Christian Churches planned a combined sunrise service for Easter 1963. What if they could offer free coffee and doughnuts?

Smith talked with Mr. Rasmussen at the Starlite KFC. "Andy, I can help your business," Wayne proposed. "Why don't you give me a little coupon so that anyone who comes to the service can get a free cup of coffee and a doughnut at your place."

"How many are you expecting?"

"A couple hundred; maybe 250."

Six hundred eight people showed up from 14 churches, 128 of them from Southland. Everybody was happy except Andy. "You and your idea nearly ruined me," he told Wayne. "I was giving out eggs, bacon, and everything else. We ran out of doughnuts the first 10 minutes."

Easter services at Southland totaled 814 in worship and 522 in Bible school. This, in a building 60 feet by 60 feet and on a most inadequate lot. Between services, Jake Jacobson and Wayne were standing outside looking at cars in the parking lot, on the grass, on the sidewalks, out on the street, down the block.

"If this sight doesn't make a preacher happy," said Jake, "nothing will."

Wayne's vacation that year totaled eight days at Myrtle Beach — slight-

Words From Wayne

Geared to the times; anchored to the Rock.

ly less when you consider four and one half of those days were spent driving down and back.

"I never felt that God is lucky to have me," Wayne said. "I remember that little incident where someone asks, 'Why does your boy like Christmas so much?' The mother answers, 'He's never gotten over it.' I feel that way about the ministry. I've never gotten over it. It's an honor."

Like everything else at Southland, Wayne's church paper did the usual and did it well but always included something extra, as in this article about the September picnic:

Well, vacation time is over, the summer is past, and the King's business is upon us...

I am really looking forward to the picnic Sunday. And, may I give you fair warning, I'm wearing my bermudas. Why don't you plan to attend? This is the time that you really get to know each other and you can let the kids run wild... A word of welcome is in order to our newest minister in town, Brother Sherwood Evans (coming to Northern Heights).

"Bro. Evans and I have often been mistaken for each other because we look so much alike. We did until Sherwood put on so much weight."

Building expansion and start of Southern Acres

Folding chairs, multiple services, crowded hallways — these were finally eased when Southland dedicated its new building November 8, 1964, on that same one-acre plot. Jack Ballard, from Mount Carmel Christian Church, near Atlanta, was the dedication speaker. Southland set another record: 947 in morning worship and 743 in Bible school, and 416 came back that night.

Jake Jacobson's arm-twisting of his banker friend was vindicated.

Guest speakers and missionaries asked for and were given opportunities to visit the growing church. When Operation Evangelize, a singing group fresh out of Kentucky Christian College, came through, Wayne was shocked when he saw their old van.

"Those people were Christian Scientists," he said. "They just thought they had tread." Smith replaced OE's bald tires with four new ones, and the young people went on their way.

Wayne's brother Don accepted a call to Berea Christian Church in Lexington, across from where the Kentucky Horse Park is located now. Lillie moved back to Lexington to be near her sons, living with a family named Johnstone.

One Sunday night on the way home from church, Wayne stopped at Kelly's Ice Cream Store in the Southland Shopping Center. Marge and the girls were in the back seat; 77-year-old Lillie was up front. As Wayne opened the car door, she asked, "Where are you going?"

"I'm going to buy some ice cream."

Lillie asked, "Since when do we buy on the Lord's Day?"

Wayne replied, "We don't, Mother."

He got back in the car and took Lillie home; then he and Marge and the girls returned to Kelly's and had their ice cream.

About a year later, Lillie died. When he learned of her death, Bob Shannon sent Wayne the following letter, dated April 11, 1967:

"Heaven is a little neater than it was a few days ago. If I know Lillie Smith, she is dusting off the pearly gates right now. And if any of those white robes ever wear out, she will turn the collars. And none of those angels had better drop out of the heavenly choir.

"No one ever fed more preachers than your mother. No one was ever more zealous at chasing dirt, or in chasing the devil. Now she has moved her operation to a better climate. Rest? Not her. And just think, there is no night there! Somehow, I cannot be sad."

For the first 17 years, Southland Christian Church averaged 140 additions per year. By 1971, Sunday-morning attendance stood at 970, and the building could hold no more. The solution: start another church. Smith knew who he wanted as the preacher.

Wally Rendel was leading a successful work in Florence, Kentucky, and Wayne had dedicated their new building.

"Wayne pointed to me," said Rendel, "but he didn't go over or around his men. He sent a committee up, and they recommended me to the elders."

Southern Acres Christian Church began June 4, 1972. The charter was kept open for one month, and by the end of June, Southern Acres had 132 charter members, most coming from Southland. Counting children, this represented more than 200 people. "If you're going to have a baby," Wayne said, "try to have a healthy one."

Rendel said, "He encouraged people to leave and help us — seven elders, two deacons, and other leadership-type people. It's an example of Wayne's magnanimous spirit. Most preachers aren't like that, which is one reason there are not more new churches."

"I wanted Wally to know we were with him," Smith said. "I gave him a yoke, like those for oxen, to be a symbol that we were together."

Southern Acres flourished under Wally's leadership. He and Wayne have stayed close. When Wally's daughter Jill was killed in an auto accident, Wayne B. Smith conducted the funeral.

Twentieth anniversary and a celebration

Wayne held a revival meeting in Elizabethtown in 1976 and needed better transportation than his battered Oldsmobile. The thing wouldn't start, and when it did run, it kept going even after the switch was turned off.

He happened to mention his predicament to Billy Kerr, the co-owner of a funeral home that had served many Southland families.

"Take one of our family cars," Kerr suggested.

"No, I can't do that," Wayne said. But Kerr insisted.

"Few people have been more generous to the Smiths than Billy and Wilma Kerr," Wayne said, then added, "She and Marge were best of friends, too. We stay in touch with the Kerrs' daughter, Becky, who is married to horseman Jim Plemmons. Becky and Jim are a fine couple."

Back home after his week at Elizabethtown, Wayne confided to a friend, "Driving down Bluegrass Parkway in a 10-passenger Cadillac, eating chocolate peanuts, I said, 'If I have a wreck and die, it won't be any different because this is heaven.' "

Little did Wayne know that better transportation was on its way. Southland went all out for Wayne's 20th anniversary.

During the Sunday-school picnic, held on elder Charles Cassity's farm, the barn opened up and out came a new Cadillac, with 20 pounds of chocolate peanuts on the front seat, a new fridge for Marge, bicycles for the girls, and more.

Wayne kept knocking on doors. Buddy Mossbarger asked Wayne to call on his friend, Craig Avery. Avery's background was Methodist, and he described Wayne's visit: "He came to our apartment. Dori had made a plate of fudge. Wayne ate fudge and talked; ate fudge and talked some more. We started going to Southland and have been there ever since."

Though he gives credit to his leaders, Smith does not always recognize the part he himself played in developing them. When Brewster McLeod came to Southland in 1979 as youth minister, Smith poured himself into his new staff member's life. "What are you doing for lunch?" "Come go make this call with me." For years, Brewster went with the Smiths on their vacation. Wayne Smith did "mentoring" long before the word became fashionable.

Not everything went smoothly. "I had a back operation in 1981," Wayne said. "I went to Central Baptist Hospital. Don't ever go to a Baptist hospital. They believe 'once sick, always sick.' I thought I'd never get out."

Southland's new building was soon overflowing again, with worse parking problems than ever. If a home adjacent to the church came up for sale, Southland was first in line.

"But," Wayne said, "unless we wanted to buy the entire neighborhood, I knew it was time we started looking."

"You are the best, and you deserve the best."

Wayne is emphatic: "A team cannot rise higher than the quality of its players. A church cannot rise higher than the quality and commitment of those who make the decisions."

Roy H. Mays III, Wayne's senior associate for 10 years, said of his boss, "One of the keys to Wayne's success was that he could influence the influencers. Wayne made his mark in central Kentucky in the business community, in education, athletics, the political arena — all because he was able to stimulate strong men."

Southland's growth forced one major decision after another, decisions that would have defeated lesser leaders.

"After 25 years on Hill 'N Dale, we considered relocating," said Wayne. "We'd talked some about leaving a church in that location, but would anyone want to stay?"

Southland had a firm offer of $600,000 for the Hill 'N Dale site from the branch of the Church of God headquartered in Cleveland, Tennessee. Wayne felt that this was a good offer.

He and his family were on vacation in Myrtle Beach when he received a phone call from the chairman of the church board: "Wayne, you probably should come home. Bill Bechanan wants to talk to you about the proposed move and our present building."

"So I got on a plane and flew home," Wayne said.

Bechanan had continued to rise in the ranks at Kentucky Utilities until now he was president. Smith had never been to his office.

Bechanan went right to the point. "Wayne, are you going to leave a church on Hill 'N Dale?"

"No, I don't think so," Wayne answered.

That was not how Bechanan had understood the move.

"He didn't say that I lied," Wayne said, "but he came close. And he was probably right."

While Smith was still in town, the chairman called a special board meeting. Wayne outlined the plan: "Men, it would be a hollow victory if we disenchanted some of our people who want to stay."

So Wayne returned to Myrtle Beach and vacation, pondering how to manage a move and plant a daughter church at the same time. "I wanted to do this right," said Wayne.

Smith had never been a sound sleeper. Thinking about what lay ahead shortened his nights even more.

"Still," he said, "I felt it was the right thing to do. We had only one acre of ground plus five houses and no room to build. Parking was bad. Moving seemed like the only way out."

Wayne and his leaders selected a 20-acre site 4.2 miles south of New Circle Road and 5.5 miles from the Hill 'N Dale site. The property was part of the old Headley farm at Harrodsburg and Brannon roads, "so far out in the country nobody will come," according to one critic. Even worse, the proposed site was across the county line, which, in Kentucky, may as well have been in another state.

Smith never considered taking a religious census. "There wasn't anyone out there to survey," he said.

However, he did commission an aerial photo of the property, and later, as hundreds of new homes went up, that photo was leverage against those who wanted to curtail the growth of the church. "We were here first," Smith could say, pointing to his photo showing acres of empty land and only three farmhouses.

Wayne learned that Kingsway Christian Church in Indianapolis had raised a record offering for its new building, so he and three of his elders met with minister John Caldwell. "John was very gracious and informative," said Wayne.

Based upon what he had learned, Wayne presented this proposition to his leaders: "Let's set a goal of $200,000."

"No," they told him, "$250,000."

The offering totaled $314,000.

Like the Pope Giving You his Blessing Among the Catholics

In the fall of 1981, I conducted a prophecy conference in Lexington sponsored by a group of premillenial Churches of Christ but held at a high-school auditorium. Wayne Smith attended the last night of that conference. A few weeks later, he called and asked if I would conduct a prophecy conference at his church.

The meeting was scheduled for April 1982, exactly two years after the founding of Lamb and Lion Ministries.

He met me at the airport. Driving to the motel, I asked, "Wayne, how long have you been studying prophecy?"

He started laughing as only he can laugh: "HO, HO, HO." He laughed and laughed, and I couldn't figure it out. I asked him what was so funny.

With tears of laughter rolling down his face, he replied, "David, I don't know *anything* about Bible prophecy. I just heard you speak, and you sounded convincing."

I asked how much his church knew about prophecy, and he laughed all over again.

"Your question," he explained, "reminds me of something that happened to me when I got married. My wife came to me and asked, 'Go buy me a cookbook,' and I said, 'Honey, what kind?' and she replied, 'One that says, Number 1: Stand facing the stove.' David, my congregation doesn't know anything about Bible prophecy. Start with the fundamentals."

God blessed that meeting and many more that I held at that remarkable church. When Wayne Smith wrote about my prophecy conference in his church paper in glowing terms, it was equivalent to the pope giving you his blessing among Catholics. I suddenly started receiving invitations from churches all over America.

— *Dr. David Reagan, Lamb and Lion Ministries, Princeton, Texas*

Hill 'N Dale Christian Church launched

The church that stayed would be called Hill 'N Dale Christian Church. Wayne Holcomb was called as minister. To ease the transition, Holcomb preached Sunday mornings, Smith preached Sunday nights, rotating each week for two months.

"I arrived in June 1981," Holcomb said. "We completed the transition at the end of August. Brother Smith was very gracious. He would come and give me names: 'These people plan on staying; if you want to give them a call.' I was using the choir practice room as a temporary office, and when Brother Smith went on vacation he said, 'Here's my office. Use my desk. Make yourself at home.' "

Those who stayed wanted to buy the building. Many of them had helped pay for the church. Were they to pay for it a second time?

Southland had nine men on the finance committee. The chairman suggested, "Write down what you think is a fair price. We will throw out the high number and the low number and average the other figures and that's what we will ask."

The figure was $254,000, and everybody was happy.

"We've always had a great relationship with Hill 'N Dale," Wayne said. "The church did well. There were at least 200 to 250 who stayed behind. Hill 'N Dale kept growing and reached over 1,000."

When Hill 'N Dale outgrew the building, rather than relocating, Wayne Holcomb and 30 families started the Wellington Christian Church in 2001 and erected a new building on Nicholasville Road. Smith was there for Wellington's opening day. "Brother Smith was celebrating with us in our new facility," Holcomb said.

Hill 'N Dale called David Welsh, who had been in Holcomb's youth group when Holcomb worked with Gene Welsh, David's father, and the church is doing well with an attendance of more than 700. The influence of those visionary elders at Broadway Christian Church in the 1950s continues to grow and multiply.

Words From Wayne

We have a vision, and with his (God's) help we shall have a victory.

Holcomb is an unabashed admirer of Smith, but that is no protection for the latter during a roast, as evidenced during one downtown event when it was Holcomb's turn. Holcomb took the mike, looked at the crowd, then at Smith, and began. "Brother Smith has more friends than anybody I have ever known. In fact, he has friends he hasn't used yet."

When the laughter died down, Holcomb showed a photo of Smith taken in an outdoor setting at Gatlinburg, commenting, "Here is a man who loves nature, which is amazing considering what nature has done to him."

The next day the *Lexington Herald-Leader* published a photo of Smith waving his white handkerchief in surrender while the crowd roared.

New building for Southland and more worries for the preacher

"When our building went up," said Wayne, "it frightened me. I wasn't worried we couldn't pay for it. I was worried we couldn't fill it. I would go to the Starlite and ask Carol if I could use the rear dining room. They closed at 9:00. I went in the back room; the lights were out. Sometimes I just had to be alone. There was never a time that I didn't think I was dispensable."

Southland's attendance dropped with the move but quickly came back up and continued to increase. The church had grown to become a political force not only in Lexington but across the commonwealth.

The *Louisville Courier-Journal* carried an article October 10, 1982, which closed as follows:

"The realities of power in Lexington are best illuminated by a glance at the Southland Christian Church. Its towering new building sits on the southwest edge of the city, on land that once nourished horses. It's minister, the Rev. Wayne B. Smith, is a favorite on the local civic-club, rubber-chicken circuit and the city's top clergyman-politician.

"He has demonstrated many times that he can produce the votes in a showdown over the soul of Lexington. And in the enlarged, more complex, schismatic Lexington of today, that's something none of the people on the society page and none of the diners at the Idle Hour* could do."

Such sentiments looked good in print but failed to consider the anxiety Wayne felt behind the scenes. When the elders interviewed Roy Mays III, Tom Fields asked Roy, "What do you see as the future of this church?" Roy said, "I see 4,000 coming to Southland."

Smith had not expected that: "It scared me to death."

Wider outreach through TV

Soon Wayne Smith had a bigger platform than ever. Tracy Farmer, a highly successful entrepreneur from Lee County who moved to Texas and did well there, had returned to Kentucky and was living in Lexington. Tracy's sister went to Southland. Tracy started coming, and Earl Swank baptized him.

After church one Sunday, Tracy approached Wayne: "We ought to be on television."

Smith agreed. "I'm for it, but TV costs money."

"We'll see what we can do," Tracy answered.

God was working in another heart as well. One Sunday night, Roy preached a sermon on "Service." After the benediction, attorney Pat Moores approached Roy and gave him his card. "I told Roy that I wanted to get involved," Pat said. "I knew because I'd been divorced that I couldn't be an elder or deacon, but I still wanted to do something." (That exclusion has since been changed at Southland.)

Two months passed without a word from Roy, so Pat made a phone call.

"Roy," said Moores, "I haven't heard from you. I want to get involved."

Mays' response was immediate. "Would you know that just this afternoon, Wayne, Tracy, and a couple of us from the staff were out at Channel 27 talking about going on TV. What do you know about television?"

Pat's response was less than encouraging: "I know how to turn one on." Pat headed for Atlanta to spend a weekend at First Baptist watching

Idle Hour, founded by Col. E.R. Bradley, owner of Man O' War, was turned into the most prestigious Country Club in Lexington after it was no longer operated as a horse farm.

Charles Stanley's team as they broadcast their service. "It was incredible," he said.

This was the mid '80s. Tracy wanted to put Wayne on Channel 27 because of the potential audience, but Channel 27 was locked into *The Early Show* with Harry Smith and Charles Osgood.

Tracy next approached WTVQ, Channel 36. The manager of the station, Bill Service, had been to Southland. Tracy owned Citizen's Union Bank in Lexington, First National Bank in Falmouth, and the National Bank of Cynthiana. Tracy did a lot of advertising over WTVQ and knew Bill through these contacts.

Tracy approached the station's management and settled on a time slot and a weekly rate, then came to Wayne: "I'll pay the first year."

Smith was not about to take this to the elders alone. When the time came to explain the offer, Wayne had Tracy wait outside, then brought him into the meeting.

The Southland Hour — a half-hour, actually — went on the air in 1983. The TV audience grew until it was estimated at 50,000 minimum.

"Tracy had a lot of business interests," Wayne said, "and was head of the state Democratic Party." Smith cringed at the latter, adding, "The water wasn't hot enough when he got baptized."

"We started with one camera," explained Pat Moores. "Wayne never moved from the pulpit; he couldn't."

As ratings grew, so did the broadcast. "We went to an hour program," Moores said. "We bought our own equipment, added cameras, trained our own people. We even let Wayne move around."

The Southland Hour continues today on Channel 36 at 10 a.m. and is rebroadcast at various times during the week on the cable network Insight.

Tracy Farmer speaks of Wayne: "He is one of the finest individuals that I know. He has a pure heart. I had a bank in Harrison County when Wayne was minister over there, and I knew the Judys, Marge's family. Wayne Judy, Marge's brother, was on my board of directors."

A keen judge of character, Tracy continued, "Wayne is an original. He has a heart of gold; he doesn't know how to say no. We've been on opposite sides of the political spectrum and several other issues, but we've always been friends. He will always be my minister. He didn't get all of that from Cincinnati. Somewhere along the line, the Lord touched Wayne in a wonderful way."

Southland and Southeast: Wayne Smith and Bob Russell

The *Courier-Journal* was also carrying stories about the phenomenal growth of Southeast Christian Church in Louisville, and no one was more enthusiastic than Wayne Smith, even when Southeast began to match, then surpass, Southland's attendance.

"I told Russell," Wayne said, "I'm with you till you get 6,000. Then I'm out of here."

"Wayne rejoiced with us," said Bob Russell, senior minister at Southeast. "To be able to joke with me about it — that's an incredible trait."

Even more so when one considers the intense rivalry between Lexington and Louisville. As a long-time UK fan observed, "When Louisville won the NCAA men's basketball championship in 1980 — it was their first time — we said, 'Louisville: No. 1 in the nation; No. 2 in Kentucky.' "

When Wayne read in Southeast's paper that the church had received $350,000 in a Special Day offering, he sent a note to Bob: "Years ago yours truly held a revival for your church and for my services received $75. With all that money from your special offering, perhaps you feel now is the time to correct an injustice of 40 years outstanding, perpetrated upon a young preacher."

A note came back from Southeast, signed by Russell's secretary, Barbara Dabney, and a close friend of Smith's: "You're lucky you got $75."

"Barbara's got a lot of good qualities," Wayne said, "but compassion isn't one of them."

Russell went on: "I'm embarrassed to tell you what he would give me

Words From Wayne

If you lead a good life, go to Sunday school and church,
say your prayers every night, when you die, you'll go to Kentucky.

at Christmas, with a note inside saying something like, 'This is small compared to what you have meant to my ministry.' I would say, 'Wayne, I can't take this.' He'd say, 'Please, I want you to have it.' "

When Southeast announced their plans to build, one of the first commitments came from Wayne B. Smith.

"He pledged $3,000 toward our new building," Russell said. "You would have to know preachers and how guarded we are with our own territory in order to realize how unbelievable that was. No. 1, Southland was about to launch their own finance campaign, and No. 2, Wayne's church was the biggest church in the whole region until Southeast got bigger. Most people's reaction would be jealousy, but not Wayne."

Marge was aghast when Russell's church paper mentioned Wayne's $3,000 gift. Smith had not told her about what was to him "a small item."

Smith and his leaders

Wayne relied upon his men. "I have led," he said, "but I was cautious about it. I suppose my beginnings had a lot to do with it; I never was very sure of myself. A lot of times I didn't attend finance meetings. I couldn't read the chart. We never got into any problems financially, because the men took care of the money."

Wayne added, "If you're going to take the time of your men — and it takes time — you need to respect them and honor them."

A church across town threatened to split and called on Wayne to see if he could help.

"I went to Buddy Mossbarger," Wayne said. "He said, 'Tell each side they can bring five.' I had four other elders present, but Buddy was the spokesman."

When the estranged brethren arrived at Southland, someone apparently had miscounted. "One side had 37," Wayne said, "the other had 17. We only let five from each side come in."

Wayne described what happened: "After everybody had their say, Buddy stood up and got the leaders from each side together. He told them, 'I want you two men to come here. I want you to shake hands. No,

I don't want you to shake hands. At Southland we hug.' So they made up."

Later, Smith commented, "It lasted about as far as the parking lot."

During an elder's meeting, one man said, "My wife went to King's Island with our young people, and our bus broke down. We had 30 kids on the side of the road."

Mossbarger asked, "How many buses do we need?"

John Langley said, "We need three."

Mossbarger made the motion: "I move that we buy three buses."

Someone asked, "Can we afford them?"

"We can't afford not to," Buddy replied.

Smith often went to Mossbarger. Wayne explained: "It's hard for a minister to get advice. He was honest with me. Some of our presidents have surrounded themselves with yes men, and it hurts their administration. Buddy was always kind, but he was always honest, and I needed that."

Southland expands again

During 1991, Southland's long-range planning committee spent many hours addressing the church's needs for the immediate and distant futures, culminating in the purchase of the adjacent property to the south. "We bought half the farm, 42.5 acres," said Buddy Mossbarger, an elder involved with the negotiating. "Three years later we bought the other half."

On April 1, 1992, the church signed a contract with Mr. and Mrs. Billy Oaks, an agreement that extended the church's land all the way to Barbara Hunter's Brownwood Farm.

Wayne wrote in the *Voice*, "We are spending $1 million over 10 years to protect the $7 million value of our current property and buildings. The reason we left Hill 'N Dale was because we were out of space. Thus, this new property should care for our needs in the foreseeable future."

Wayne's encounter with the Jessamine County Board of Adjustment over rezoning has been described earlier. His labor resulted in more than

Words From Wayne

The church at her worst is better than the world at its best.

permission. Sam Sternberg, vice president and later president of Farmer's National Bank in Nicholasville, his wife Ceil, and Sam's two sons became deeply involved in the life of Southland Christian Church. Sam was on the board of adjustment and had seen Smith in action at the zoning meetings.

As he so often did, Smith gave credit to his leaders. In his newsletter, *The Voice of Southland Christian Church,* July 1, 1992, he wrote:

> A word of thanks to Board Chairmen and committee members who have worked hard and sought God's will relative to this purchase. . . . We give God the glory for making this possible. However, Chairmen Avery, Doggett, Mossbarger, and Moore would say this article is incomplete without a word of thanks to Len Aldridge . . . His negotiations had a great deal to do with the final victory . . . In closing, permit this writer to commend Lloyd Moore, Chairman of the Planning/Building Committee and his men for an unbelievable amount of time invested in this project. The committee consists of Eugene Peel, Sherman Davis, Don Fugette, Bob Lyons, Bill Mossbarger, Ron Ray, Roy Mays III, and yours truly. Attorneys Jim Ishmael and Jim Hodge and Business Consultant Butch Locklar were also major contributors in this acquisition. Thanks, men! You have served Him and the cause well.

Preacher Smith: Mentor and encourager

Roy Mays III said, "He knew who to talk to ahead of time and did." Wayne knew his men, because he spent time with them.

He seldom drove anywhere alone, often taking an elder or prospect or new Christian with him to a speaking engagement. Lunch and even breakfast were opportunities to invest time with present and future leaders. Smith spent more face time with people than most counselors.

Even so, board meetings were not always harmonious. Southland Christian Church gave Smith a new Lincoln for his 30th anniversary as its minister. Not long after, things heated up during an elders meeting. Wayne protested, "Aren't you the same guys who gave me the Lincoln?" Mitch Cooper responded, "Yes, and right now we wish we had it back."

Everybody laughed and the tension eased.

Nearly every *Voice* carried a note from Smith naming those who had led in one project or another: arranging the church picnic or directing Vacation Bible School or caring for the army of preschoolers and infants week after week.

"I called in a doctor's home," Wayne wrote, "and he said their choice of Southland was largely due to the beauty and efficiency of our nursery. Director of Nursery and Early Childhood is Michelle Wash. She has two assistants: Julie Begley and D'Ann Blankenship. Michelle informs me that on any given Sunday we have 500 children under school age. We are indebted to past Directors, Betty Jo Friskney, Kim Barton, and Kim Goodman."

Then Smith added the expected surprise: "I discovered that it takes eight coordinators, six teachers, and 250 caregivers each month to operate our nursery. Of course, the Bible explains the reason for that in 1 Cor 15:51: 'We shall not all sleep, but we shall all be changed!' "

Smith was still not finished: "I also understand we have at least 27 expectant mothers, so more growth is on the way."

Wayne constantly doubted his own abilities, but Southland kept growing, with many coming from a distance. In the *Voice* for November 11, 1992, Wayne revealed that "Patty and Huff Snyder drive 47 miles one way." The Snyders observed, "For the worship service and warm fellowship. This is a short trip when you think about the journey to Calvary."

Wayne told of Douglas and Sue Beck, who came 60 miles one way from Owingsville, where Doug was president of the Farmer's Bank; of the Baber family, "a family of four who found Southland through the TV ministry," and who made a 70-mile round trip; of Thomas Sinclair, 43 miles one way; of William and Joann Jett, and Dorothy Wills, 38 miles one way; of Roger, Alicia, Chris, and Scott Arnold, 61 miles one way.

Easter in Rupp Arena
Southland's attendance in 1993 averaged 3,071; average attendance in 1994 was 3,472.

Easter, however, had leveled off. The building simply would not accommodate all those who wanted to come. In a post-Easter staff meeting in 1994, someone suggested, "Let's go to Rupp Arena." Every citizen in Fayette County knew of Rupp Arena.

The arena, in downtown Lexington, is home court for the UK Wildcats and named for Adolph F. Rupp, legendary coach of the Wildcats 1930-1972. Rupp retired having won 874 of 1,064 games, one of the most successful coaches in the history of intercollegiate basketball.

Wayne's Secretaries

In addition to mentions elsewhere, Smith talked about his secretaries. "Velma Francis was the first," he says. "She loved the Lord and served 18 years, the first two without pay. Velma had a unique personality and was a tremendous blessing. Her sense of humor was one of a kind."

He continued: "Velma and Bill have two married daughters, Mrs. Marylin Singer and Susie Jones."

Between Velma's 18 years and Ann Nelson's 17 years there were others: Theresa Saunders, former secretary to Jake Jacobson, head of Kentucky American Water Company; Betty Vandepool, who, like the others, served with zeal and dedication.

"My last secretary," Wayne said, "was Diana Taylor, a receptionist whose office was at Corporate Center. Diana was very willing and helpful."

Due to lack of space on the main campus, several church offices were located in the Corporate Center on Harrodsburg Road, four miles north of Southland Christian Church. When he retired, Smith kept his office in his basement at home, and Corporate Center was closer.

One more: "I need to add the name of Linda Tackett," Smith said, "who was very helpful during the writing of this book."

Rupp Arena seats 23,500.

Yes! The possibilities excited Wayne. Butch Locklar was put in charge of the business aspects of the venture, such as the contract for the building, parking, and so on; Todd Tyler was put in charge of the program.

The congregation had not worshiped together as a family since 1982 because of its multiple services. Wayne knew that many from his TV audience who would not enter a church building might come to Rupp Arena.

Smith began promoting the giant service weeks in advance. "We want to reach new people with the Gospel," he said. "This will help us do that."

Anticipating the crowd, Southland reserved parking for 2,000 cars in lots to the south and west of Rupp Arena, for 270 under the Kincaid Towers and for 600 in the Kentucky Parking Garage, plus shuttle buses from Turfland Mall. Special arrangements were made for the handicapped.

One afternoon Wayne dropped in on one of his favorite haunts, Old Kentucky Candies on Southland Drive. Owners Don and Pam Hurt greeted him with, "We'll see you at Rupp Arena. We're driving a truck."

"A truck?"

"Yes," Don continued. "We're putting the communion juice in our refrigerator truck."

Attendance on Palm Sunday was 4,375. What could they expect next Sunday? Southland's previous record for Easter was 5,870. Wayne hoped for perhaps 7,000.

8,350 showed up!

Former deacon Tom Holland and his wife, Gayle, drove from Mauldin, South Carolina, and sent Smith a letter expressing their gratitude for the privilege of being there.

Southland's empty building? Not empty at all. Weeks earlier, First Assembly of God's church building had been torched by an arsonist. By unanimous vote of Southland's elders, First Assembly of God had its Easter service in Southland's building free of charge.

Smith gave the credit to others. "None of it would have been possible," he said, "without the dedication of everyone."

After he announced his retirement, Wayne wrote in the *Voice of South-*

land Christian Church for November 1, 1995:

Ministers are honored more often than not based on the size and influence of the church they serve. I doubt if several high points in my life would have taken place had I not been the Southland minister (president of North American Christian Convention, trustee Cincinnati Bible College & Seminary, and honorary doctorates from Kentucky Christian College, Louisville Bible College, P.V. Alexander's Kerala Christian Bible College in Kerala, India.). Regardless of one's talent, a minister rises no higher than his elders and deacons.

Who approved and supported five building programs? Who voted to buy 105 acres? Who voted to give birth to Southern Acres, Hill 'N Dale. . . . and provide funds for other new churches? When buildings were built and land purchased, the minister is recognized for great accomplishments. However, I know who built this Church and upon whose shoulders I have stood for four decades — Godly men and women, boys and girls, and a dedicated staff. Some ministers make a church. In my case, a church made a minister. Thank you for being so good to me and my family. You are the best and you deserve the best.

"She was called to be a minister's wife."

"Marge would drive across town to buy gasoline from Satan if it was a penny less," Wayne said. "From the day we moved to Lexington, she was in charge of the money." Then he admitted, "She has good reasons."

During their first months together, Wayne served at both Unity and String Town. Smith became concerned over the benches used by the latter congregation.

"They were made out of two boards," Smith said. "One for the seat and one for the back. Now, they would probably be historic; then, they were just uncomfortable."

He learned that the high school in Owensboro was selling its old theater-type seats for a dollar apiece. The year was 1952, and a deal like that was not to be missed. Smith borrowed a truck and drove to Owensboro, where he was told that if he would take the entire lot, he could have them for 50 cents each. Wayne needed only 120, but this was too good to pass up.

What to do with the extra seats? Maybe Northward Christian Assembly. No, its chapel had a cement floor, and these seats had to be screwed down. Smith tried several other places, but no one wanted them. Not even a few. Not even for free.

Borrowing the truck again, Smith donated the seats to the Licking River.

Shaking his head, he said, "When they had flooding at Falmouth, I wasn't just worried about the water getting too high. I worried about the water getting too low."

The press was unaware of Smith's contribution to Pendleton County's water supply, but a short time later, his momentary inattention behind the wheel in Cynthiana made news all the way to Lexington.

On Saturday, April 7, 1956, under the headline "Minister's Wave Costs

$400," the *Herald-Leader* reporter told of Wayne's "driving down Pleasant Street this morning when he saw his wife, Mrs. Marjorie Judy Smith, in a car with Mrs. William Lyons, en route to the Buena Vista school where Mrs. Smith teaches." The article continued:

> As he pulled up behind the Lyons car at an intersection, he tooted the horn to gain his wife's attention, so that he could wave goodbye to her.
>
> Mrs. Lyons misunderstood the toot and slammed on her brakes.
>
> The minister tried to do likewise but, as he described it to police who investigated the resultant crash, he was wearing a larger size shoe than usual and "I just seemed to be all feet." So much so, in fact, that he couldn't get his feet on the brake quick enough to avoid hitting Mrs. Lyons' car and a telephone pole.
>
> Nobody was hurt, but total damage to the two vehicles was estimated at $400.

Investor Smith finds another bargain

Shortly before leaving Unity, Wayne learned of an auction featuring used school buses. "I took the rent money and bought a bus," he said. "I got a real good deal. I knew the church would buy it."

The elders turned it down.

Wayne panicked: "That was our rent money."

He called Sammy Penn at Porter, Kentucky, a little town near Georgetown. Sammy bused schoolchildren for Scott County with his own fleet, and during a revival, Wayne had stayed at Sammy's parents' home.

"I've got a great bus over here I'd like to sell you," Wayne told his friend.

After hearing the description, Sammy offered Wayne $150.

"No," Wayne said. "It's a better bus than that."

Sammy wanted to see for himself, so they set a time. Sammy looked the bus over, took it for a test drive, and inspected the motor and interior. Despite Wayne's best efforts, Sammy never offered a cent more than $110, and it was a struggle for Wayne to get him that high.

"But you said $150 over the phone."

"Maybe I did," said Sammy, "but it's $110 now."

Finally, Smith gave up and accepted the $110. At least he could pay the rent.

The following week Wayne went to get a haircut and had hardly sat down in the chair before the barber commented, "Sammy Penn was here last week. I asked him what he was doing in town."

Smith sat up straighter.

"I told him about them selling the school buses," the barber continued. "He asked what they went for. I told him the highest was $110."

Marge makes a decision

During his weekly visit to Cincinnati in his last year at college, Wayne chanced upon a sale of old church furnishings. "I saw church lights, church pews, and other things," he said. "The fellow said if I would bring a truck I could have the whole lot for $35. I got a truck. Thirty-five dollars was a bargain; there was so much stuff we couldn't use it all."

That was the last straw for Marge: "I will handle the money," she told her husband.

"That's how we survived," Wayne said. "After that I gave her the check, and she put it in the bank and gave me an allowance, and that arrangement continued until I retired."

Grinning, he added, "She never gave me what I was worth."

Marge explained, "As long as I was teaching, I wasn't concerned. But when we moved to Lexington, I said I just have to handle the money."

Marge not only had to keep the family finances; when the girls were born she raised them largely by herself. "Marge never complained," Wayne said. "She was called to be a minister's wife."

Marge is as predictable as Wayne is the opposite. "Marge is steady," Wayne said. "She is even. She doesn't favor me, either. She doesn't compliment my sermons, although she has done so with funerals."

Words From Wayne

The heart of America is not Washington, D.C.; the heart of America is the living room. As the living room goes, so goes the nation.

Different, yet firmly together

Marge and Beth Mays go walking together several times each week. Beth, the wife of Roy H. Mays III, knows Marge as well as anyone in the church would know her.

"She is one of the most well-balanced women I've ever known," Beth said. "Wayne tells funny stories; Marge finds fun in everyday life. She enjoys things but nothing to excess. She knows her limits and is comfortable with that. Marge would help you do anything, yet she doesn't feel guilt when she says no about something."

Beth continued: "She knows what she believes; she has not moved very far from the faith she developed as a girl. Events cannot shock her or upset her. She is not envious; there's no jealousy about her."

Marge will drop by the Mays' house, knock, and go in, bringing cookies or other treats. "There are times we walk for six or seven days straight, then miss a day or two," said Beth. "Some friends can wear you out; Marge is not like that."

Marge talks freely about her life and speaks of the advantages. "Our girls didn't have the life of most preachers' kids . . . moving every few years . . . having to change schools. We never moved. This gave them stability."

The Smiths did move, however. They rented a house at 608 Sheridan Drive for six months, then purchased a home at 282 Hill 'N Dale for $12,500 and lived there for 11 years. "We walked to church," Marge said. "It was so handy."

The house next door came up for sale for $21,500. It had a two-car garage, two baths, a fireplace, and a basement, and it was larger, so the Smiths decided to move. The girls complained, "Couldn't we at least go someplace farther than this?"

The girls often walked to the Saturday weddings at the church. "Whether we knew the people getting married or not," Judy said. "We always enjoyed the reception with cake and punch in the basement."

Wayne and Marge still live there, nine houses from the Hill 'N Dale Christian Church, where Southland used to be. How many ministers have lived on the same street for 47 years?

A woman watching the telecast of Southland's service wrote a letter criticizing Wayne as "just another televangelist." But there was a note at the bottom of her letter: "P.S. I drove by your house and at least you live in a humble dwelling."

Jana said of her dad, "Nothing material really means that much to him. You could give him a brand new Lexus and he'd say, 'You got any peanuts?' If it's a car, he drives it. If it's a house, he lives in it."

The joke's on the preacher

Wayne is a Republican, Marge a Democrat. "When I was dating her," Wayne said, "I had this poem about how FDR went to hell, and I was reading it to her and her parents. I got through about two paragraphs, and her dad stopped me: 'Wayne, do you know who put these lights in our home?'"

During the Great Depression, President Franklin D. Roosevelt introduced the New Deal. One of FDR's projects was the Rural Electrification Administration in 1935. Before that, Marge's home, like many others, was lighted by coal-oil lamps.

Wayne continued: "Her dad said some other things, too. There were no more poems about Roosevelt from me."

Their political differences have caused few problems, though Wayne often teases Marge in his sermons. Midway into his sermon, Smith stops, looks at the audience, and chuckles. People know something is coming.

"Last Sunday night after church, I was worn out. I preached three times Sunday morning, another time Sunday night, and I came into my own home and went into my den and started to say something to my wife, and she held up her hand: 'Shhh, I'm watching Charles Stanley.'"

Charles Stanley pastors a large Baptist church in Atlanta.

The audience laughed at that, but laughed even more at Smith's punchline: "After preaching all day, when I go home, the last thing I want to do is watch Charles Stanley preaching on TV; I need to watch Clint Eastwood kill someone."

"I knew people expected it," Marge said. "They would come to me after church and tell me, 'Oh, Marge, he was on you today.'"

Person to Person

May I use my column this week for a rare purpose, to talk about the one whom I love very much. Much credit has been given to me for my labors here at Southland. I appreciate this more than I can tell you.

However, in all honesty, it would be very revealing to know how much less would have been accomplished on my part had it not been for the complete cooperation of Marge.

The majority of nights I am away from home; the meals prepared that I can't consume because of an unexpected visitor or emergency. All these things she seems to take in stride. When I have been called out in the middle of the night or the vacation or outing plans have been changed or cancelled, I have yet to hear her complain.

She does her share of the work in the church: V.B.S., keeping the nursery, playing the piano if needed, and "preacher" in Primary Church. If in these years in Lexington she ever had a misunderstanding with a church member I am not aware of it.

She has never had an unkind phone call from any of our fine people. Words cannot express my appreciation for your love and kindness to her.

When God looked the world over to give her a husband, I thank Him that He chose me. I am unworthy; I realize this, and for that reason try feebly to prove my love in labors of love.

Marge has no knowledge of this article…. I thank God daily for a God-given wife, two lovely children, and the privilege of serving the finest Christian Church in the world.

— *Wayne B. Smith, in* The Voice of Southland Christian Church, *on the occasion of his and Marge's 15th wedding anniversary*

They were with friends when Wayne asked Marge, "Would you like some ice cream?"

"I don't think so," she replied. "I'm cold."

"I didn't ask for a weather report," Wayne said, grinning at his friend. "I asked if you wanted some ice cream."

Jake Jacobson presented Marge a baseball bat with this note: "To Marge: We have realized for several years your disadvantage to a husband who makes rash statements to a semi-captive audience regarding your past, present, and future life, without affording you equal time for rebuttal. Therefore we, your friends, present you with this effective 'persuader.' "

It did little good.

One Sunday morning during the first service, Wayne decided to introduce Marge. A listener to the TV program had made the request.

During the service, which was not televised, Wayne turned to Marge in the choir and made the presentation: "Many of you do not know my wife, my companion along the way and mother of our daughters. My ministry would not be possible without this gracious lady. Marge, stand up."

So Marge, never one to seek the spotlight, got to her feet, to a hearty round of applause.

During the second service, Wayne did the same thing. One of the women in the church — no one will admit responsibility — knowing full well that this service was being televised, enlisted collaborators, and at the point where Wayne asked his wife to stand, at least a dozen women stood. One version says they were only choir members; others say that women stood all over the church.

What everyone remembers is that this is the only time anyone can recall when Wayne B. Smith was at an absolute loss for words, despite the gales of laughter from the congregation.

Usually, Wayne is quick with the comeback. His nightly practice was to kneel by the side of the bed to pray. One night he fell asleep. About 2:00 a.m., Marge woke up, and seeing her husband's form kneeling in the darkness, she asked, "Wayne, are you asleep?"

"I waited a bit, then said, 'Amen,' and got into bed."

Family life in the Smith household

With her husband gone so often, Marge was a stay-at-home mom. "When the girls were growing up, I had full responsibility," she said. "Thank goodness they were girls. If they were boys, they might have been juvenile delinquents."

Asked about being a preacher's kid, Jana said, "I always thought it was more of an advantage than a disadvantage because of who he was."

Judy added, "It sure helped, because Southland is such a great church."

Jana continued: "When I was little I didn't know any different, but by the time I got older, I realized he was well-known. It was like, 'Oh, this is your dad.' They would start telling me 'We just love your dad' and go on and on. That made me feel good."

Did the girls feel neglected?

"Mom was always here," Jana said. "I never felt neglected or left out. It was 'Bring me something when you come back. See you later.' I didn't grow up with Dad here, so I didn't know any different."

Judy asked her dad more than once, "With all the preachers in the world, how come everybody wants you? Why can't somebody else go?"

On one occasion he told her, "They think your daddy's the best."

She replied, "Well, I've heard a lot better."

Wayne would often take one or both of the girls with him when he went hospital calling. "He was never ashamed of what you had on," Jana said. "I might be out playing and he would say, 'Come go with me,' even if I looked like some poor orphan."

He would give money to the girls and leave them in the coffee shop at Central Baptist or St. Joseph's hospital, telling the waitress, "These are my little girls," and be on his way.

"I met Joe Hall at the basketball banquets," Jana said, speaking of the renowned head coach of the University of Kentucky Wildcats. "I would sit right up there with him, because Dad was the emcee. Mom didn't care about going, so when Dad asked me, I'd say, 'Sure, I'll go.' "

Marge, not her husband, was the disciplinarian. Wayne came home one day to find the girls upstairs and their radio on. "That's too loud," Wayne told Marge. "Tell them to turn it down."

"What's wrong with your telling them to turn it down?" Marge asked.

So he went to the foot of the stairs and shouted, "Kids, your mother says to turn down that radio."

"He could get steamed up," Marge said, "but I was usually the one who had to be the bad guy."

Wayne kept an office at home as well as the one at the church. Noticing the contrast between his office and her house, Marge waited until Wayne was out of town and enlisted two women in the church, Bev Williams and Barb Turner, to help her clean the place.

Wayne happened to get home the night before garbage pickup, and when he pulled into the driveway and saw the brown bags lined up at the curb, he made an inspection.

There, on the top of the first trash bag, was a sermon book by his hero, Clovis Chappel. Those bags — every one of them — were back in the house before his suitcase was out of the trunk, and suitable instructions delivered to Marge.

Only rarely did Marge accompany Wayne on speaking trips. "I didn't want to hinder him," she explained. "He would be zeroed in on what he was supposed to do that night, and he didn't need to divide his attention with me."

She added, "Then he goes from table to table, talking to people, saying hello, shaking hands and all that. Everybody knows him. He's thinking about what he's going to say. I'd just as soon not go; it's like going alone."

Vacations and then some

With Marge's eye on the dollar, vacations for the Smith family were modest. Of the 40 state parks in the Commonwealth of Kentucky, Wayne, Marge, and their two daughters have stayed in 22.

"We would get to New Circle Road," Wayne said, "and the girls would start: 'Are we there yet?' " New Circle Road is the inner beltway around Lexington.

When the girls grew older, they wanted to go to Florida, so in 1972 the Smith family headed south in the family Chevrolet. Judy, then in high school, took her friend, Jan Barnette.

"Three girls," Smith said, throwing up his hands. "Don't ever take three girls to Florida."

Judy and Jan innocently took an automobile ride with two boys they met on the beach without informing anyone as to where they were going or when they would return.

"When we came back," Judy said, "wow — that's another story."

"I thought we'd never see the girls again," Wayne said. "The next year we tried Florida one more time, but that was the last. My nerves couldn't stand it."

So the Smiths started going to Myrtle Beach. "Myrtle Beach was better," Wayne explained. "One day's journey from Lexington."

"Dad loves the scenic route," Judy said. "This means not taking the interstate, but going through the kind of small towns that have a gas station with pickled eggs on the counter. That always took longer."

Brewster McLeod, Wayne's youth minister for 22 years, often went along. He explained the delays: "He was ready to stop at Jerry's Big Boy before we got on I-75. Then, we'd get to Knoxville or some place down the road, and he would say, 'This preacher needs some encouragement,' and so we'd stop again."

Myrtle Beach boasts many posh hotels, not one acceptable to Marge. "Lida's Motel," said Brewster, "that's where we stayed. Twenty-four dollars a night. Some rooms had carpet, but these cost more. Ours had linoleum. No phone, either, except one at the office."

Vacation for Wayne was not sand and sun; it was flea markets and food. The more of both the better. Everybody else hit the beach, with instructions to meet on the porch at Lida's at dinnertime. Sometimes the girls would go with Wayne to the flea markets, knowing he was an easy touch.

Wayne learned of a new church being started in Myrtle Beach and became interested at once. A company from Lexington was engaged in construction in North Myrtle Beach, and Joe Lewis, an elder at Broadway Christian Church, had moved to Myrtle Beach in connection with the project. Wayne used his contacts to help his new friends. Lewis soon became deeply involved in the new church.

Joel Wilson, minister of The Christian Church in Myrtle Beach said,

"While Joe was here, he drew the plans for our building and helped us in a lot of ways. He even worked physically on the building."

Architect Royce Bourne was an elder at Southland who had played major roles in the construction of Southland Christian Church and the Wayne B. Smith Center for Christian Leadership at Kentucky Christian College. He, too, gave considerable expertise to the construction of the new church.

Myrtle Beach Christian developed into the Smiths' "vacation church."

Wayne credits minister Joel Wilson for the success of the new work and for founding The Promised Land, a home for homeless persons of all ages. Said Smith, "Joel and Sheri gave new meaning to the word 'sacrifice.' "

Wayne continued: "Some of our greatest experiences were in Myrtle Beach. Another great couple there were Phil and Lora Spruill. He was an elder and a hard worker in the church."

Wayne added, "He had connections, and made it possible for us to stay in a condo right on the beach. When we stayed at Lida's, the ocean was only a rumor. Plus, the condo even had carpet and a phone."

Looking back, Smith said, "These two couples made a difference in our lives, and we will always love them."

Dad the protector and encourager

When Jana started to date, Dad swung into action. "It was an eighth-grade Friendship Banquet at our church," Jana said, "my first official date." Tommy Todd, a boy from the church, was taking her. James Todd, his father, was a Southland member and vice mayor.

Wayne was prepared. He had gone across the street to Marshall Fugate's house and borrowed a shotgun. Smith was sitting with the gun across his lap when Tommy came for Jana, ready to walk her to church.

"Come in here, boy," Wayne demanded.

"Son," he told the wide-eyed eighth-grader, "I want to know if your

Words From Wayne

Marge doesn't cry much; I cry when they cut the ribbon at Wal-Mart.

intentions are honorable. I want her back here by 10. I want you to be sure and behave yourself."

"Tommy is a lawyer now," Wayne said. "He's doing well, and I'm proud of him."

Smith, known for his generosity to others, is generous at home, too. Marge kept telling him that he couldn't buy the children's love, so Judy sent her dad a card that said, "Dad, remember you can't buy my love, but keep trying."

Dad gave notes or cards to the girls, many of them signed, "Sure am proud of you."

"He was and is such an encourager," Jana said. "He always tries to see the good."

While working at the phone company, Judy met Kenny Speakes.

"I told her to marry him whether she loved him or not so we could get some looks in the family," Wayne said.

Kenny and Judy have two children: Amanda, 17, and Barron, 12. Kenny has a daughter, Lyndsey, by a previous marriage. Kenny is now the preacher at Mount Zion Christian Church in Clark County. When Lyndsey, who is in her early 20s, got married during the summer of 2003, her father was the minister she selected to perform the ceremony.

Jana and her husband, Tim Thore, have two boys. Landon, Tim's son by a previous marriage, also is in his early 20s and lives in Cincinnati. According to Wayne, "Landon will tell you he was thrilled at 6 years of age to get a mother named Jana." Austin, 11, is in the fourth grade at Lexington Christian Academy.

The week after Wayne's retirement, Jana went to the house to do some typing for her father. At the time, Austin was just a toddler.

"It was hurry, hurry, hurry," Jana said. "He had to be somewhere to speak at 6:30 and kept telling me, 'I got to get this done. Got to.' Then, Tim drove up and Austin came down the basement stairs to Dad's office. 'Papaw, Papaw! I want you to come upstairs.' "

Smith dropped everything and followed the boy upstairs, listening as his grandson told him a long, windy story. Wayne, a stickler for time, was late to the dinner.

Marge and her husband's schedule

Ann Nelson, Wayne's secretary for 18 years, tells of a surprise Smith gave his wife. "Marge called to find out what time Wayne would be home for supper. She asked if she could speak to him. I just looked at the telephone, trying to think of what I was going to say. Then I told her, 'Marge, he left this morning for Arizona and won't be back until Thursday.' "

Some wives have killed for less. Marge took that — and more — in stride. Much of the time she had no idea where he was, with whom, or what time he was coming home.

"Marge laughed about his Arizona trip," Ann said. "She and Wayne have a wonderful relationship in a unique way. She continues to allow him to be his own person."

For perspective, the Arizona trip was in 1977, the year he was president of the North American Christian Convention. "I spoke in 22 states," Wayne explained. "Being out of town was the norm that year, not the exception."

In later years Wayne has kept Marge better informed, providing her with an itinerary complete with church and hotel numbers. "However, when he's home," Marge said, "he'll write me a note and lay it on the kitchen floor and put five or six cans of food around it to get my attention."

She laughed, then continued, "He doesn't give me any credit for being able to come in here and see a note somewhere other than in the middle of the floor."

She and her husband spend more time together now, often going for dinner with friends or to places such as The Greenbrier at White Sulfur Springs in West Virginia for their 50th wedding anniversary — the latter part of a $3,000 gift certificate from Shockey Tours. "They are the best," Wayne said. "We've been on five tours with them."

"One of the reasons I respect Dad is that he truly lives his faith," Judy said. "Picking up chicken at the Starlight KFC for some needy family or getting people a room at a hotel or finding them a job at the car wash — he was always helping someone.

"Several times Dad would ask people who called him for financial help where they got his name or number. Their response: I called such and such church, and they told me to call Wayne Smith. Is he a modern-day Good Samaritan or what? But on the other hand, behind every good man is a good woman, and my mother is that and more."

In 1995 Wayne published a grade-school photo of Marge in the Southland *Voice* with the caption, "She was married 44 years ago on August 28. A jewel! Looked great even in the third grade."

And she still does.

"He is easy to locate . . . . You can hear that laugh."

Wayne loves telling a good story, he loves hearing a good story, and, even more, he loves a good story on himself. He tells a story about Hazel Ogden of Grant County, when he was just starting out. Hazel's husband was a deacon; she taught Sunday school, played the piano, and liked that new young preacher. One of Hazel's sons later became a minister, the other a high-school principal.

"Her aunt got sick," Wayne said, "and I stopped to see her and had prayer, but the aunt died. A year or so later, Hazel took sick, and I stopped to see her. Before I left I said, 'Let's have a word of prayer.' 'Oh, please don't,' she said, 'the last one died.' "

At Northward Christian Assembly one of the chores for the dean of men was getting the boys settled for the night. One week, Smith filled that role. After lights out, he sneaked a pan of water into the room and managed to get into bed without spilling anything, then flung the water across the beds down the row.

"They yelled, and everybody got up and turned on the lights, and I stood all the boys in a line and kept demanding, 'Who did this?' Nobody owned up, of course, so I went after them again."

He added, "I was accused so many times of doing things, I thought, this time, I'll do it before they accuse me."

Smith's friendship with fellow minister Ben Merold goes a long way back. Wayne complained, "Ben doesn't tell a lot of jokes. He uses a lot of Scripture instead. A real deficiency there."

Then, "Ben is much deeper than I am."

Ben had the last word. When Smith spoke for Merold at Eastside Christian Church in Fullerton, California, Ben rented a replica of an army tank from a prop lot in Hollywood, had the tank waiting at the airport, and told Smith to get in. After a few blocks Ben transferred his passenger to more customary transportation.

The folks at Southland looked forward to Wayne's humor. "I tried to have a good story every week. That meant I had to really dig."

Smith does not use joke books. People are constantly telling him stories. "I can remember jokes," he said. "It's scripture that I can't remember."

Cameron Mills was a key player on UK's championship basketball team; after college he entered the ministry. One Sunday morning, Wayne called on him to have the benediction. While Mills was coming to the platform, Smith kept talking: "I have to say that I don't like tall, thin people with hair, especially good-looking ones." Then to Cam, "If you're going into the ministry, you need to put on some weight. You need to look like you've been blessed."

Several of Wayne's friends are bankers. Tom Bloemer told about the time he was in his office at Bank of the Bluegrass when Wayne came in.

"He walked right by the people standing in line for the tellers, walked past the people in the waiting area, came into my office — and I had a customer sitting there on the other side of my desk. Wayne knelt and clasped his hands and said at the top of his voice, 'Please, please don't repossess my Bible.' "

Several years ago, when both churches were running about 1,200, Southland had a Sunday-school contest with Southeast in Louisville. The losing preacher was required to preach Sunday night in the winning church.

Wayne lost.

People at Southeast still remember the Sunday night Smith came to pay the penalty. When he got up to preach, Wayne referred to a story in the *Courier-Journal* about a recent front-page crime in Louisville.

"I hear what goes on in your town," Wayne chided the congregation. "You kill people over here. We don't have that in Lexington; our churches are stronger. To be sure I was safe, I brought some protection." Wayne then called to the platform two men he had brought with him from Lexington: Sam Hawkins, a Kentucky state trooper in full uniform, and Larry Long, an agent with the FBI.

Smith then launched into his sermon, his "bodyguards" at his side. He stopped the sermon after a few minutes and made a great show of removing a bulletproof vest he was wearing. "This thing's too hot," he told the crowd as they roared with laughter.

When Wayne accepts a speaking engagement, those who introduce him often prepare a special introduction, as at First Christian in Phoenix, Arizona, where John Greenlee introduced Smith during a conference as follows:

"Wayne Smith is from Kentucky, a very poor state. His dad was a tenant farmer. His mother was pregnant, and his dad came in from the field one day and there she lay in the bed, having given birth to two boys. The dad says, 'This is phenomenal, but we're poor people, so we're going to have to drown the ugly one. Fortunately for us today, Wayne Smith could swim.' "

Wayne can poke fun, too. Someone asked if he and H. Sherwood Evans, former executive director of Christian Benevolent Outreach Inc., in Lexington, were related. "You and Sherwood look alike," the questioner said. "Are you brothers?"

Wayne leaned over as if he were sharing a secret: "Yes, but Sherwood is illegitimate. That's why our names are different."

Evans laughed at that one, telling Smith, "I'll go along with this, but next time it's you that's illegitimate."

The North American Christian Convention, an annual gathering of Christian Churches and Churches of Christ, was perpetually broke and more than once called upon Smith to loosen the crowd's pocketbooks.

One year he came to the platform, approached the microphone, and started chuckling. No words; just the body-shaking, audible chuckle. A warmth swept across the room. Wayne's image, magnified on the big screens, grinned at them, and he chuckled again and laughed, then started his appeal.

He hardly needed to. People already had their checkbooks out. An observer remarked, "Look at that. He can move a crowd without saying one word."

At the 1997 North American Christian Convention in Kansas City, the convention held a "Roast of Wayne B. Smith" fund-raiser that drew more than 500 people. When Dan Garrett's turn as a "roaster" came, one of his lines was, "I thought it might be fun to tell all of Wayne's jokes, but since

Smith Loses His Memory

On the last day of the 1997 North American Christian Convention, held in Kansas City, Wayne spoke for a Christian Seniors Fellowship Breakfast. After breakfast he was talking to Ben and Pat Merold and to Cotton and Betsy Jones, two minister friends, and telling them how badly his leg hurt.

"What do you think?" Smith asked, pulling up his pant leg. Wayne's left leg was red from ankle to knee and very swollen.

"We're taking you to the hospital," said Ben. He put Wayne in his car, and the five of them went to the Lutheran Hospital.

Smith had spent most of his cash, but did have his checkbook and credit cards. Aware that some hospitals won't extend credit to out-of-staters, Wayne asked, "Do either of you have any money?"

Ben gave Wayne $200, and Cotton gave him $100. The admissions personnel took Smith immediately to the emergency room. Wayne was there nearly two hours while his friends sat in the waiting room.

While under treatment, Smith concocted a scheme. When he was finally about to be released, the nurse went out into the waiting area and asked, "Is anyone here connected with Wayne Smith?"

Alarmed, the Merolds and Joneses instantly got to their feet to hear the bad news. "He is going to recover," the nurse said, "but the medicine we gave him affected his mind. He does not seem to remember anything."

Just then, Smith was brought out, and he made as if he were leaving. The attendant stopped him and told him that the four people standing there had brought him to the hospital.

Embarrassed, Wayne said, "Oh, thank you. Thank you. Thank you for helping me. They say I'm going to be all right; it's just that I can't remember right now."

Ben and Cotton looked at each other. "Smith," Ben said, "We're saddened by your condition, but you still owe us $300."

there's not time, I'll just do the punch lines."

Which he did.

"Does that pet store sell birdseed?"

"Somewhere in a funeral home there's a basket of flowers that say 'Good luck in your new location.' "

"I'd become a referee like you, Mr. Bell."

"I'll take the banker's heart; I want one that's never been used."

"Nothing; it was a small mistake."

"And if you don't put anything in, it takes your picture."

"Tell me about it. I'm the UPS man."

The audience loved it, most of them having heard every story and punch line multiple times.

Though he does not use joke books, he has compiled his own, from which are these examples, taken from his notes.

• • • • • •

Long funeral procession. Large dog following the casket. About 15 men single file following the dog. A fellow approached the man who was walking along beside the dog.

"What's this all about?"

Fellow answered, "It's my mother-in-law's funeral."

"How did she die?"

Fellow: "Well, my large dog bit her."

Other fellows: "Can I borrow that dog?"

Fellow: "Get in line."

• • • • • •

"Grandpa, make a noise like a frog." Grandpa replied, "I can't really make a noise like a frog." "Yes, you can. I heard Grandma say that when you croak, she is going to move to Florida."

• • • • • •

Two men were talking at the office water cooler. One was telling the other about a fight he'd had with his wife. "In the end," he said, "I had her begging on her knees."

"What did she say?"

She said, "Come out from under that bed, you coward."

• • • • • •

Man applied for life insurance. Agent asked, "How old was your father when he died?" "47." "What did he die of?" "Heart attack."

"How old was your mother when she died?" "49." "What did she die of?" "Cancer." Application refused.

Man applied through another agent with another company. Same questions.

"Father died at 94. Fell off a horse playing polo."

"Mother died at 92. Childbirth."

• • • • • •

Couple married. Luke and Lucy. Lucy had a lot of money. Bought a nice new house. "If it weren't for my money we would not be here!"

She bought beautiful new furniture. "If it weren't for my money, this would not be here."

She bought a state-of-the-art stereo. "If it weren't for my money, this would not be here."

Luke finally responded, "If it weren't for your money, I wouldn't be here."

• • • • • •

Preacher preached for one hour and 20 minutes. Fellow got up and left. Head usher stopped him in the lobby and said, "Where are you going?" He answered, "I'm going to get a haircut." Usher asked, "Why didn't you get it before you came?" The man replied, "I didn't need it."

• • • • • •

A fellow has two obsessions in life, his sickly mother and his cat. Wasn't married and spent all of his time with mother and cat. Went to doctor himself, not feeling well.

Doctor: "You have to get away. You will end up at the funny farm if you don't take a vacation."

Persuaded his brother to take care of his mother and his cat. He would take a flying trip to Europe and then be home again, but would call every couple of days. England, Germany, France.

First day he called from London. "How's the cat?" Brother said: "Cat's dead." The man fainted and was rushed to hospital. Couple of days later he called his brother again.

I don't think I'll ever forgive you for what you said to me. You bluntly said, "The cat's dead."

"How insensitive, how cruel. You have no compassion. Why didn't you tell me when I called from London the cat was on the roof. Then a couple of days later, when I called from Paris, you could have told me the cat fell off the roof but was at the vet's and there was hope. Then a couple of days later, when I called from Germany, you could have told me the cat was dead. How insensitive and cruel to just tell me all at once: "The cat's dead. By the way, How's mother?"

"She's on the roof."

• • • • • •

The secret of our long marriage . . ."We take time to go to a restaurant two times a week. A little candlelight, dinner, and soft music and then a slow walk home. She goes Tuesdays and I go Fridays."

• • • • • •

A very successful businessman had a meeting with his new son-in-law. "I love my daughter, and now I welcome you into the family," said the man. "To show how much we care for you, I'm making you a 50-50 partner in my business. All you have to do is go to the factory every day and learn the operation."

The son-in-law interrupted: "I hate factories. I can't stand the noise."

"I see," replied the father-in-law. "Well, then you'll work in the office and take charge of some of the operation."

"I hate office work," said the son-in-law. "I can't stand being stuck behind a desk."

"Wait a minute," said the father-in-law. "I just made you half-owner of a money-making organization, but you don't like factories and won't work in an office. What am I going to do with you?"

"Easy," said the young man. "Buy me out!"

Words From Wayne

Your conscience says, "Get thee behind me, Satan,"
and a voice says, "It looks good from here, too."

• • • • • •

Rich Texas oil tycoon had a daughter who was a little on the homely side. She couldn't seem to find a boyfriend, and her prospects for marriage were dismal. The father announced he was going to give a super party and that any young man who passed a test would be given a million dollars, an oil well, or the daughter's hand in marriage.

Large crowd gathered at the wealthy man's ranch. Father announced the swimming pool was filled with alligators and any young man who would swim the length of the pool would receive the money, oil well, or his daughter. No one moved, then everyone heard a splash and saw one man begin to swim rapidly across the pool. When he reached the other side, bleeding from various alligator bites, the wealthy father shook this young man's hand.

The tycoon said, "You are a real man. Do you want the money?" "No." Do you want the oil well?" "No." "You're smart if you marry my daughter. Some day you'll get everything."

"I don't want your daughter." "What do you want?" "The name of the guy that pushed me in."

• • • • • •

Man stopped at barbershop for haircut. Was getting ready for big vacation trip to Italy. "Don't go there," barber said. "People are rude, weather is lousy." Barber asked him how he planned to travel. "I'll be flying on TWA." "Bad choice," barber said. "They have lousy service; most of the time they lose your luggage." Barber asked what he planned to do while in Italy. "Do some sightseeing and go to Rome and maybe get a glimpse of the Pope. "You won't like Rome," barber said. "The crowds are terrible. You won't get close enough to even see the Pope."

When man returned from his vacation, stopped by the barbershop to inform the barber that the trip was fantastic, weather was great, airline was super, sights were all that he expected, and even though there was a large crowd, he got within a block of the Pope. "A representative of the Pope even came and invited me to a personal audience with the Pope." "Why you?" the barber asked. "The Pope told me that he saw me about a block away and told his personal aide that he felt sorry for me because I had the worst haircut he'd ever seen."

• • • • • •

Huge oil fire was raging at a town in Texas. Owner offered $500,000 to anyone who would put out the fire. Red Adair, the famous man who put out fires on oil wells, came, looked at the fire, and said, "I can't do it. No one could ever get close enough to put out that fire."

About the time Red Adair was explaining this to the owner, they heard a siren and a volunteer-fire-department truck come tearing past. It never slowed down and ran right up to the fire. Surrounded by flames, the men of the volunteer fire department jumped off the truck and put out the fire.

Owner said to the volunteer fire chief, "That's the bravest thing I've ever seen. I guess you must have heard about the $500,000 reward for putting out the fire. What are you going to do with all that money?"

Volunteer fire chief said, "The first thing we're going to do is get the brakes fixed."

• • • • • •

A young man who worked in a grocery store was in a hurry to close the store and go home. An older lady pecked on the window. The young man opened the door and the woman said, "I just need one thing: a half a head of lettuce." The young man, mumbling to himself, went to the back of the store to see the manager. He didn't realize that the old lady was right behind him when he said to the manager, "I was ready to leave and some dingbat wants half a head of lettuce." Then he noticed that the woman was hearing everything, and he added quickly, "But Boss, we're in luck, because this nice lady wants the other half."

The woman paid for the lettuce and left. The boss complimented the young man for his quick thinking and asked him, "Where are you from, my boy?" "Kentucky, sir, the home of great basketball teams and ugly women." That made the boss mad. "Now wait a minute. My wife is from Kentucky." Without a moment's hesitation the young man said, "Which team did she play for, sir?"

• • • • • •

Preacher went to visit a man who never attended church or gave any indication of faith. During the conversation, the preacher asked him a question. "Do you ever think about the hereafter?" "Oh, yes," was the reply. "I think about the hereafter all the time. I go upstairs and think to myself, 'Now what am I here after?' I go to the basement and think to myself, 'What am I here after?' "

• • • • • •

Three expectant fathers were in the fathers' waiting room at the hospital. The nurse came in the room and informed one of the men that his wife had just given birth to twins. "That is amazing," he said. "I am a pitcher with the Minnesota Twins and my wife has twins." After a while, the nurse came back and informed the next man his wife had just given birth to triplets. "That's really weird," the man said. "I work for the 3-M company and my wife has triplets." The third man got up and started for the door. The other two men asked where he was going. "I'm getting out of here," he said. "I work for Seven-Up."

• • • • • •

A preacher brought his car to a garage to have it repaired. When the repairs were completed and the mechanic was adding up the bill, the minister said, "Remember, I'm just a poor preacher." "I know," the mechanic said. "I heard you preach last Sunday."

• • • • • •

Getting back at someone for a bad introduction.

When I was a small boy I used to torment an old donkey that Dad had in the back barnyard. I would throw corncobs and small stones, etc. Dad finally caught me one day and said, "Quit that! If you don't stop teasing that old donkey, someday he will come back in some other form of life and haunt you."

• • • • • •

"I'll need to see your license and registration," says the highway patrolman after stopping a middle-aged couple. "You were speeding."

"But officer," says the husband, "I was way under the speed limit."

"Sir, you were doing 70 in a 55-mph zone."

"I was not speeding," insists the man. "Your radar gun must be broken."

At this point, the wife leans over. "It's no use arguing with him, officer," she says apologetically. "He's always stubborn when he's been drinking."

• • • • • •

A nun ran out of gas. Walked back to a station about a mile down the road. Attendant did not have a gas can but scrounged around in a back shed and found an old discarded bedpan. The nun said that would work. So the attendant put a couple of gallons of gas in it and she very carefully carried it back to her car. As she was pouring it in, a trucker passed by, slowed down, and shouted, "Sister, you sure have more faith than I have."

• • • • • •

A man slammed down the book he was reading and looked over at his wife. "I'm sick and tired of sitting around here with you all the time," he yelled. "I want to find someone I can have fun with. I'm going to shower, shave, and use some of that cologne I just bought. I'll put on my best suit. After that, I'm coming back down and guess who's going to knot my new silk tie for me."

The woman looked up from her magazine and replied, "The undertaker?"

• • • • • •

Two couples who've played cards every month for years are taking a break from their game. After the wives go into the kitchen, Joe says to Frank, "I usually have to remind you what cards have been played, but tonight I don't have to. How come?"

"I went to memory school," says Frank.

"Really?" asks Joe. "What's the name of the school?"

"Let me see…what do you call that flower that's red with thorns on the stem?"

"A rose," says Joe.

"Yeah, that's it. A rose. Hey, Rose!" yells Frank toward the kitchen. "What was the name of that memory school I went to?"

• • • • • •

Lost on the back roads in the state of Vermont, a tourist collided with a local man at an intersection. He and the local got out to examine their bent fenders.

"Well, it don't look like much," observed the local. "Whyn't we just take a little nip to steady our nerves." He grabbed a jug from his battered pickup, removed the stopper, and handed it to the tourist. After taking a good slug, the tourist handed the jug back to the local, who banged in the stopper and set the jug back in his truck.

"Aren't you going to have some?" asked the tourist.

The local shook his head. "Not till after the trooper comes."

The Joke Is on the Jokester

I came to know Wayne while in law school in Lexington 1957-1960. I was a member of the old Maxwell Street Church, served by one of Wayne's contemporaries, E. Ray "Cotton" Jones. Cotton and I would play golf, and Wayne would come out and walk two or three holes and try out some of his new jokes on us.

He would tell the story and no one in the foursome would laugh — not a smile, not a snicker. Finally, he would give up and go about his way.

For the first time, I confess that it was all conspiratorial and predetermined. No matter how funny the story — no one was to laugh. We would simply exchange looks of bewilderment: "Did you get that?" It was brutal.

Wayne B. Smith is a legend in his own time. The man can preach. He can't sing a lick. He knows how to win souls to Christ.

He knew exactly what to say to convince Marge to walk along beside him over the years, and you know that she has to go to heaven.

He can make you laugh. He can make you form a lump in your throat and start a flow of tears. Over the last 45 years, I count it one of my greatest blessings (and I have had many) to have known Wayne Smith and have him call me his friend.

— *Henry R. Wilhoit Jr., Senior U.S. District Judge,*
Eastern District of Kentucky

• • • • • •

A young husband came home from the office one day and found his wife crying profusely. "Honey, what's wrong?" She said, "We have only been married two weeks, and I am not a good cook. But, I did my very best. I made a cake from scratch, and the dog ate it." He said, "That's O.K. honey; we'll get another dog."

• • • • • •

A man was told by his physician that he had only six months to live. "Doc," he said, "is there anything I can do?"

"Yes," replied the doctor. "First, give all your possessions to the poor. Next, move to a cold-water shack in the backwoods. And then marry a woman with nine young children."

"Will this give me more time?"

"No — but it'll be the longest six months of your life."

• • • • • •

A fellow was accused of fishing illegally by throwing sticks of dynamite over the side of the boat and then scooping up the fish with a net. The game warden invited himself to go fishing with this guy. Sure enough, the fellow lit a stick of dynamite and dropped it over the side. He scooped up several large fish. The game warden shouted, "You can't do that!" The fellow lit another stick of dynamite and handed it to the game warden. "Are you gonna talk or are you gonna fish."

• • • • • •

Two brothers from the backwoods went to the big city and watched an elevator go up and down. A very big lady stepped in and went up, and a minute later, the doors opened again and a pretty, trim lady walked out. One brother looked at the other and said, "Let's go home and get Ma."

• • • • • •

A notorious miser was called on by the chairman of the community charity. "Sir," said the fund-raiser, "our records show that despite your wealth, you've never once given to our drive."

Words From Wayne

My sermons are like marriage — never as long as it seems.

"Do your records show that I have an elderly mother who was left penniless when my father died?" fumed the tightwad. "Do your records show that I have a disabled brother who is unable to work? Do your records show I have a widowed sister with small children who can barely make ends meet?"

"No, sir," replied the embarrassed volunteer. "Our records don't show those things."

"Well, I don't give anything to them, so why should I give anything to you?"

• • • • • • •

What is the difference between a psychotic and a neurotic? A psychotic thinks 2 and 2 equals 5. A neurotic knows that 2 and 2 are 4, but it bothers him.

• • • • • • •

A lady died and went to heaven, and her husband died shortly afterward and also went to heaven. The two met and were walking arm in arm all over heaven. The wife said, "It sure is beautiful up here. It's so quiet, so peaceful, no problems, no cares, and everybody is so happy."

"It certainly is beautiful," the husband replied. "And if it had not been for you insisting we eat all that oat bran and other stuff, we would have been up here 10 years ago."

• • • • • • •

Minister out to dinner. Saw a three-legged pig. "How come the pig has three legs?"

Farmer: "Oh, we love that pig. Saved Junior when he fell out of the apple tree. We love that pig."

Minister: "But how come the pig has three legs?"

Farmer: "Oh, my, you don't know how much we love that pig. That pig saved little Susie when she nearly drowned in the pond. We really do love that pig."

Minister: "But you haven't answered my question. How come that pig only has three legs?"

Farmer: "Well, we really love that pig. You wouldn't think that we would eat him all at once, do you?"

• • • • • •

People are more violently opposed to fur than leather, because it's safer to harass rich women than motorcycle gangs.

• • • • • •

An old Jewish gentleman goes to see his rabbi. "Rabbi," he says, "something terrible is happening and I have to talk to you about it."

The rabbi asks, "What's wrong?"

To which the man replies, "My wife is poisoning me."

The rabbi, very surprised by this, asks, "How can this be?"

The man then pleads, "I'm telling you, I'm certain she's poisoning me. What should I do?"

The rabbi then offers, "Tell you what. Let me talk to her. I'll see what I can find out, and I'll let you know."

A week later, the rabbi calls the man and says, "Well, I spoke to your wife. I spoke to her on the phone for three hours. You want my advice?"

The man anxiously says, "Yes."

"Take the poison," says the rabbi.

• • • • • •

And so it goes. . . .

In 1991 the Lexington Kiwanians held a "roast" of Smith, and word of the impending event made the papers. Don Edwards, *Herald-Leader* columnist, offered his own comments under the banner, "Kiwanis to raise funds by roasting a preacher."

Edwards' article read like a joke book and closed with the following: "Look for plenty of weight jokes. Wayne B. used to have so many chins he needed a bookmark to find his mouth, but lately he's been on a diet and it worked so well that now his Chrysler air bag can inflate *inside* the car."

Well-known Kentucky humorist Carl Hurley featured Wayne on <u>Carl Hurley's Cavalcade of Comedy for Motorcoach Travelers</u> in 1994. Hurley's program carried Smith's photograph and the following description: "We call him 'America's funniest preacher.' For the past 38 years, Wayne has been pastor of Lexington's Southland Christian Church. He speaks to an average morning worship crowd of 3,200 plus 50,000 on television and radio. Known for his humor, Wayne has been referred to as 'The Bob Hope of the Ministry.' Church attendance would go up if every church had a pastor as effective and entertaining as Wayne Smith!"

About three months after Smith retired, Brad Walden, senior minister at Tates Creek Christian Church, invited him to preach. Marge knew there would be a lot of Southland people there.

"Wayne," she told her husband, "I want you to preach the Bible Sunday."

"Now, Marge," Smith replied, "I preach the Bible every Sunday."

"Yes, but not deep like Dr. Walden."

The next Sunday at Tates Creek, Wayne told this story, then asked the congregation, "Do you know why Dr. Walden gets into the Word when he preaches? It's 'cause he doesn't know any jokes."

Brad and Wayne are dear friends. Wayne often uses Brad as a positive example. "He not only cares for his own flock," said Smith, "but also the Christian Student Fellowship at UK, camp work, men's fellowship, and so on. And, he does enjoy humor."

Bob Nelson, a Methodist evangelist whose wife, Ann, was Wayne's secretary, described Wayne's laugh: "His laugh is memorable, a fun-filled guffaw that shakes all over. Smith's laugh, washed by his own tears, lifts entire congregations. Smith's laugh renews auditoriums, arenas, hearts, and homes.

"He visits hospitals after hours; is welcomed past locked doors in nursing homes. And when he enters, everyone and anyone are targets. He ministers to the sick and to the staff. He offers hope to the students as well as teachers. He is easy to locate; just listen. You can hear that laugh.

"It begins as a chuckle. The whole body shakes. The laugh starts deep within, comes rolling out. He laughs at everything, including, and most of all, himself."

"If you need anything, call me; I'll always be your friend."

Wayne B. Smith does not use a computer. He does not own a Palm®; he has blue sheets instead — an 8 1/2-by-11 inch page for each week with enough space to explain the day's commitments and enough pages stapled together to show three months.

Mornings when those blue sheets were misplaced sometimes registered as high as 6.4 on the Richter scale. The church installed a new phone system, and it took the preacher three days to learn how to use it.

Nor is Smith a friend of answering machines. "You wouldn't give one of those things to a fire department or a hospital," he said. "The church is more important than either one of them."

He continued: "I've had people call me and be crying or upset or be in some kind of emergency. It's inconceivable to me that a church would have less than a human voice answer the phone at an institution that says, 'We're here for hurting people.' You don't get that impression when something mechanical says, 'Push one for . . .' and all that.

"If I call and get an answering machine, I hang up."

Meeting people and changing lives

With Smith it's personal. He does his best work face to face.

Jack Cottrell grew up in Minorsville Christian Church in Scott County, Kentucky. Jack planned to enter the ministry, then won a generous scholarship from Farm Bureau. Jack drove to Louisville to talk with the officials at Farm Bureau, but the scholarship did not apply to Bible college, so he planned to enroll at UK.

"Then I went to Camp Northward," Jack said. "Wayne Smith was on the faculty that week. Wayne had held a meeting at our church, and our family followed him around to area revivals to hear him preach."

Jack continued: "After lights out one night, he talked to me for a couple of hours, telling me all the reasons why I should stick to my original intention to study for the ministry."

Cottrell turned down the scholarship and enrolled at Cincinnati Bible Seminary, as the school was called then. "But that's not all," Jack said. "When it came time to pay my bill, they said, 'It looks like half your bill has already been paid.' "

Through his writing, speaking, and 35-plus years teaching at Cincinnati Bible College and Seminary, Dr. Jack Cottrell has touched thousands.

In the 1960s, E.E. Jacobson, head of the Lexington Water Company and the man who influenced the bank to loan Southland the money for the new sanctuary at Hill 'N Dale, was diagnosed with cancer. Jake came to Wayne. "I want to go with you," he said. "Wherever you go, take me. When I'm with you, I'm not thinking about cancer."

Wayne told what happened. "He went with me to the Lions Club in Stanton where I spoke, and numerous other places. In 1967 I was planning on going to the Holy Land, but I knew he was close to death, so I decided not to go."

Jacobson would not permit Smith to cancel the trip. "Go," Jake insisted. "I'll be here when you get back."

Wayne said, "He died three days after I arrived home."

Bob Russell said about an encounter with Smith, "It was around 1964, my junior or senior year of college. My roommate and I went out to Delhi Church of Christ, where Wayne was preaching a revival. We asked him if he had time to visit with us, and he said, 'Sure.'

"The next morning he met us in the parking lot at Frisch's, and we told him, 'We're studying to be preachers, and we're a little discouraged about Bible college. We just want to talk to somebody who's doing it and ask some questions.' "

Bob continued: "He did not know me; he did not know Ron Eversole, but he got up and had breakfast with two college students and listened to us. I've admired him ever since."

Anyone within range of Smith soon realizes his concern for the lost and hurting.

"Girl Scouts are fine; Boy Scouts are fine; day-care centers are fine,"

Wayne said. "But our job is really Luke 19:10: 'to seek and save the lost.' "

Wayne knows people personally, because he spends personal time with them. "I felt it was my job to have people in the audience and give the Holy Spirit a chance. It's not me; I never dreamed Southland would get so big."

Smith plays Cupid

Vivian Allen grew up in Southland and married Jim Hutchison. Wayne's influence led to Jim's conversion. Mentored by Wally Rendel, Jim left a career in business to pursue the ministry and was preaching at Georgetown, near Lexington.

The Hutchisons had two little boys when Vivian entered the hospital for what was supposed to be a routine operation. Vivian never came out of the anesthetic and lapsed into a coma.

"It wasn't unusual to get a call from Wayne during her time in the hospital," Jim said. " 'Let's go to lunch,' he would say, and we would talk. The last two weeks, when she was in ICU, Wayne came every night for 14 nights straight and visited her, then would stand outside her cubicle and cry."

Jim continued: "Not long after Vivian died, Wayne called again: 'Let's go to lunch.' So we did. He hemmed and hawed until I finally said, 'Smith, what's on your mind?' "

Finally Wayne got to the point: "There's this girl. . . do you know about Elaine Casey? In Tulsa? Her husband was killed last summer in a car accident. She has two little children. I thought maybe you and she could correspond, since you've both been through the same thing. Maybe comfort each other."

"Had that come from anyone but Smith," Jim said, "I would have been miffed. But it was Smith. So I told him I would consider it."

But Wayne was not finished. "As a matter of fact," he confessed, "I

Words From Wayne

In the Bible, it's always grace and peace, never the other way; grace comes first, then peace.

wrote her a letter and told her all about you."

"That would have miffed me even more," Jim said, "but again, it was Smith."

Wayne pulled a copy of his letter to Elaine out of his pocket and gave it to Jim. He hadn't mailed it yet. "I thought it might be better, since you're the man, if you wrote to her first." Then Smith asked, "Have you seen her? She's really good-looking."

"I thought about it for two or three weeks," Jim said, "and then I wrote to her."

Vivian died in August 1977. Jim and Elaine had their first date the day after Christmas. Bob Stacy married them February 1, 1978. Jim is now the minister of Bedford Acres Christian Church in Paris, Kentucky. Elaine is an active supporter of her husband's ministry and is herself a counselor. David Casey, Elaine's son by her first marriage, is the church's youth minister.

From prison to the pulpit

Before dawn on May 10, 1984, Wayne received a call from Nolan Barger, one of his deacons. "Can you meet me at Frisch's in Mount Sterling? I'll tell you why when you get here."

Nolan's sister-in-law had awakened that morning to find two hand-written pages from a legal pad on the dresser explaining that by the time she read this, her husband, Whit Criswell, would be dead. Just as she had finished reading, she looked up to see her husband coming in the door.

"I couldn't do it," he told her.

Whit was executive vice president of the bank in Mount Sterling, a member of the school board, a city councilman, a Sunday-school teacher, an elder in First Christian Church, and a compulsive gambler. He had financed his addiction by embezzling from the bank.

"I was a wreck," Whit said. "I'd been out all night. I'd held a gun many times to my head, sweating. I looked like I had been on an all-night drinking binge."

Whit had graduated from Transylvania University with letters in basketball and golf and was a high school coach before he started his banking career.

"Sports had been my whole life," he said. "Every Saturday morning I would go to the bank, falsify records, then make my bets, mostly on sports."

By the time he had planned to take his own life, he owed $380,000.

Wayne told what happened. "We went to the back room in the house. You can't prepare for things like this. You just lean on the Lord."

"We talked a long time," Criswell said. "Then he prayed. I don't remember the words, but I remember that during his prayer, I felt that a ton of weight was lifted out of my life. From now on I was going to tell the truth, and somehow this was going to work out."

Then Whit continued: "This man dropped his schedule and drove 50 miles to be with strangers, because a member of his church had asked him. He stood at my front door, and I heard words I thought I'd never hear again: 'If you need anything, call me; and I'll always be your friend.' "

Criswell went to the state prison for two years. "Wayne came to see me," Whit said. "When I was released to St. Andrews House, Wayne came by to take me to a revival at Southland Christian Church.

"Ben Merold was speaking. I went three straight nights and the third night went forward and rededicated my life. Afterward, Wayne invited me to go eat with him and Merold and the Gospel Lads.

"After I got out of the halfway house, we went back to Mount Sterling. It was not a good decision. I had a bad attitude. I expected forgiveness; the people were not ready for that. We moved to Lexington in December of 1987 and joined Southland.

"Wayne came to the house to say hi and that he appreciated our joining. He saw that I was not working. He asked me to go places with him. He took me hospital calling, to trustees meetings in Cincinnati, to the study group in Louisville at Southeast. Four of us: Bob Russell, Wayne Smith, Dave Kennedy, and me."

Whit continued: "This was in 1989, and these preachers had started a sermon study group. They let me help, let me give my input into sermons. It became my Bible college. Wayne and Roy Mays mentored me. They put reins on me when I needed reins put on, let me loose when they thought

I could handle it, and that sort of thing. It was unbelievable what was going on in my life through Jesus Christ."

Commenting on this, Dr. David Ditto, an optometrist in Nicholasville, south of Lexington, and a member at Southland, said, "Wayne had a deeper motive than just asking somebody to drive him around. He wanted to give this man a reason for living."

Almost three years after Whit's rededication, Ben Merold returned to

You Helped Me Cope

I know you must receive hundreds of letters from people you have touched over the years, but you will just have to suffer through one more. . . .

Recently, a co-worker of mine lost his 21-year-old son to suicide. I have great empathy for anyone who is dealing with the pain this sort of death brings on the family left behind to wonder why. I was amazed and pleasantly surprised at how right to the point the message was at the funeral service. It made me remember that if it had not been for you, I would have had a much more difficult time dealing with the death of my father when I was only 19 years old. You were the only one who really talked to me about what happened. Of course, 30 years ago, most people did not discuss suicide; it was swept under the rug, and we all dealt with it internally. You may not remember what exactly you said that gave me such great relief, but I remember it like it was yesterday. . . .

I truly believe your words kept me sane over the years, but more than that, had a profound effect on me throughout my life. . . .

P.S.: I miss seeing you at the opening ceremonies of the State Games. I hope all is well with you and your family.

— Marilyn Owens, Lexington, Kentucky,
in a letter after Wayne's retirement

Southland for a speaking engagement. When Merold saw Criswell, he told Whit that he had prayed daily for him by name.

"I was blown away," Whit said, "to think that a man from California would do that for someone he had only met once."

On November 4, 1985, Earl Swank, Southland's minister of visitation, died of a heart attack. Whit offered to take his place on a volunteer basis until a replacement was hired. One day Wayne said, "Whit, you've got to put bread on the table."

"I can't find a job," Whit told him. Wayne looked at Whit, then asked, "Do you feel called to the ministry?"

Criswell did not answer immediately, but the next day he sought out Wayne and told him, "Yes."

"We'll go to the elders," Wayne said. Roy Mays made the presentation: that Southland Christian Church hire Whit Criswell as director of involvement. Wayne spoke in favor, underscoring what Roy had said. Whit told his story, then left the room.

Wayne cried when the vote was announced. Criswell said, "I think it was one of the greatest decisions Southland has ever made, to give a chance to an ex-con."

Whit continued until January 2000, when he became minister of Northern Heights Christian Church in Lexington, a church of 250. Since then, Northern Heights has moved and changed its name to NorthEast Christian Church, and attendance now runs a little over 1,000 each Sunday.

"It's just exploding," said Whit. "There are decisions every weekend; more than 50 percent of them baptisms. By the grace of God, the grace of a church, and the grace of my family, I've been restored to usefulness again in God's kingdom."

Smith and a former White House aide

Jeb Stuart Magruder moved to Lexington in 1990, and Smith was one of the first to welcome him. Magruder had been Nixon's deputy campaign director, an aide to White House Chief of Staff Bob Haldeman, and deputy communications director. Charged in the Watergate cover-up,

Magruder spent seven months in prison.

After his release in 1976, Magruder earned a Master of Divinity degree from Princeton Theological Seminary and began preaching in Ohio. He moved to Lexington to serve as senior pastor of First Presbyterian Church.

Wayne went to see him, and the two became friends.

"His wife left him when he got out of prison," said Smith. "Magruder told me, 'When you go from the White House to the jail house, that's hard to take.' He said he was having problems getting sermons, so I gave him some literature, sermons from Bob Russell, and so forth."

Magruder remarried, and according to Wayne, "he did a lot of good for the church." Later, speaking at Kentucky Christian College, Wayne quoted Magruder: "He said preaching 38 sermons a year is not easy. I said to the boys at KCC, 'You'll be preaching a lot more sermons a year than that.' I wanted them to know it's not easy."

The Fellowship of the Wounded Heart

Smith has said, "If I looked like Jim Bird, there's no telling how big my church would be." The rejoinder came back: "If you looked like Jim Bird, you'd probably be out of the ministry."

Bird, a builder, realtor, and developer, was named Outstanding Young Man in Lexington in 1973 and Outstanding Young Man in Kentucky in 1975, was president of the Home Builders Association of Lexington in 1976 and president of the Home Builders Association of Kentucky in 1983, and the same year was named Outstanding Builder in Kentucky.

Gov. Julian Carroll appointed Bird as Kentucky's first commissioner of the Department of Housing, Building, and Construction. Bird wrote the first building code for the state.

Bird had a post in state government and he and his partners owned four banks; but Bird was also a "chronic polysubstance abuser."

"I went to Charter Ridge Treatment Center and got sober," Jim said. "But I was miserable. I had money, power, acclaim, alcohol, drugs, but nothing filled the hole. I literally practiced killing myself. I put the gun to my neck, in my mouth, to my temple. But I never pulled the trigger."

Garrett Stephens was seniors minister at Southland and had met Bird in Jaycees. "I stopped by his house one day," Jim said, "and I was all messed up."

Not sure what else to do, Garrett started sending Jim the church paper.

"I'm at my wits' end," Jim said, "and they announce in the *Voice* that Whit Criswell was forming a group called HOPE: He Offers Peace Everlasting. I had not attended church in all my adult life.

"I went to the inaugural meeting. This was late summer in 1989. I went every week thereafter until December. They said, 'We can't meet in December because of the Christmas program, but we want you to have this gift. When you reach your lowest, open this gift. You don't have to wait till Christmas.' "

Jim paused as he told this, then continued: "I reached my lowest December 16, 1989. I opened my gift. It was a sheet of paper and had written on it Ephesians 1:11 from *The Living Bible*: 'Moreover, because of what Christ has done we have become gifts to God that he delights in, for as part of God's sovereign plan we were chosen from the beginning to be his, and all things happen just as he decided long ago.'

"There were some words afterward:

> What delight youngsters display when given a special gift. Joy radiates from their eyes, spreading across their faces in big happy smiles. As adults we rarely experience such pure delight, yet we ourselves are gifts that inspire an infinitely higher and greater delight in the heart of God. He accepts us with joy because of what Christ did for us. If you feel that your life isn't worth much to anyone, remember that you are a special gift in God's eyes, a precious present that brings Him great joy.

> God has offered salvation to the world just as He planned to do long ago. God is sovereign, He is in charge. When your life seems chaotic, rest in this truth: Jesus is Lord and God is in control. His purpose to save you cannot be thwarted no matter what evil Satan may bring."

Jim told what happened next. "I went to my knees and prayed the only prayer I knew: 'God help me.' And he did."

Jim had seen Smith on television, but he didn't know him. Jim says, "I think Wayne has a special attraction for those I call 'The Fellowship of the Wounded Heart.' It was like he was looking for me."

The former builder becomes a preacher

One day Smith called at Jim's house. "Do you want to go with me this evening?" Wayne asked. He was speaking at Kentucky Christian College in Grayson. "I drove him," said Jim. "During the breaks, I sneaked outside and smoked."

The "dry" forces in eastern Kentucky sought Wayne's help. He would take Jim with him, and the two would be on radio live, Smith talking

I Can Count on Wayne No Matter What

I met Wayne through my wife, Lois, in 1961. That summer I entered the U.S. Army. Through correspondence and visits to Lexington when I was on leave, Wayne led me to accept Jesus Christ as my Lord and Savior and be baptized into him. Wayne continued to write to me during my remaining time in the Army.

Although he knew I had another career in mind, I'll never forget the first time he wrote and said he felt God was perhaps leading me into the ministry and asked me to pray about it.

When I was discharged, I returned home to find that Brother Wayne had already enrolled me at Cincinnati Bible Seminary and had paid for my first year's tuition! I was thrilled and left two weeks later to begin classes.

Wayne is the most generous person I have ever known. Perhaps the greatest trait is faithfulness. Wayne is someone I have always known I could count on, no matter what.

I realize that without God's bringing Wayne B. Smith into my life, I would have never experienced the blessings and successes I've been very fortunate to have. I thank God, daily, for him.

— *Joe Wright, Senior Pastor,*
Central Christian Church, Wichita, Kansas

about the evils of alcohol and Jim giving a testimony.

Jim's wife, Eleanora, was going to Southland, too. "We were both grow-ing," Jim said. "Wayne might take me someplace with him two or three nights a week. It was a wonderful education for me.

"For Christmas he gave me an old pulpit to practice on. A man in his church had made it.

"I have it in my house to this day. There's a little metal plaque which reads, 'Presented to Jim Bird, a changed man, who has a thirst for knowl-edge and a hunger for service 12/25/91 Wayne B. Smith.'

"Eleanora and I were praying that God would use us somehow. My money's gone; my business is gone. I thought maybe I could be a race track chaplain. I love the back side of the track, the sounds and smells and excitement.

"We were in Florida trying to figure out what to do, and when I get home there was a message from Wayne on my answering machine: 'If you get home before 10:00 call me.' It was after 10, but I called him anyway. He wanted me to have the prayer in the first service.

"Between services he asked me if I'd ever thought of preaching. He said his home church in Cincinnati needed a preacher and would I be willing. I said I'd like to give it a try."

Wayne suggested that Jim speak four Sundays, to let the church become acquainted with him and he and Eleanora acquainted with the church. If nothing developed, then nothing was lost.

"I preached my first sermon July 12, 1992," Jim said.

Wayne arranged, with Bob Russell's blessing, for Jim to join the sermon study group at Southeast in Louisville, a discipline Bird continued for almost 10 years. In May 1995, while serving the church at Delhi, James S. Bird completed a bachelor of science degree with a major in biblical studies from Cincinnati Bible College, graduating summa cum laude.

He transformed the Delhi Church of Christ, then moved to George-town, Ohio, where he had another successful ministry, and today is serv-ing the historic Broadway Christian Church in Lexington.

Words From Wayne

The phone is like your parking lot; it's your first impression.

"A significant number at Broadway did not want to take a chance on me," Jim said. "Wayne, through the sheer force of his personality, insisted that they come to Georgetown and hear me."

In the five years since Jim came, Broadway has doubled in size, has completed a $1.2 million renovation — paid for, has given $100,000 to plant a church on Lexington's west side, and is funding several inner-city ministries in addition to its regular missions giving.

Jim continued: "On those trips with him, I was blowing cigarette smoke out the window. The first months at Delhi, I was blowing smoke out the windows of the church. Wayne never said a word about smoking. He loved me right where I was. I'll be forever in his debt.

"One of the greatest honors in my life was at Wayne's retirement. During his tenure at Southland, 50 Timothys have gone into the ministry. He asked me to speak on behalf of 50 Timothys. That's the greatest tribute I've ever been given."

Jim and Wayne still see each other frequently.

"The last time he was at my house," Jim said, "he put his hand on my shoulder and said, 'Sure am proud of you.' There's not many people who would have taken a chance on a guy like me, but he loved me too much to let me stay that way.

"Eleanora and I look at each other and just praise the Lord for the life we've had for the last 10 years. I'm not special; Wayne's special. He loves people. I'm just one example."

Above: "Wonderful shot of my mom (Lillie)
and dad (Vernon)."
Right: "Kindergarten in Sayler Park School.
Age 6, 49 pounds, Feb. 14, 1935."

Above: "Me (front row, second from left) in Sunday School
class at the Delhi Methodist Church, Cincinnati."

"Western Hills High School in Cincinnati is known for celebrities that graduated from that institution including Pete Rose, Don Zimmer, Jim Frey, Russ Nixon, Andy Williams and Dr. Lewis Foster. I'm not sure I (front row, second from left) made the list but I was proud to be pictured with the HI-Y Club."

Above: "I attended Delhi Church in Cincinnati every single Sunday because Mom and Dad expected no less."
Right: "Me with my brother, Don, who became a minister. He's the tall one."

Right: "I delivered for Kroger
in 1943 (at age 14)
and would get 25 cents for
each delivery within a mile.
Over a mile was worth more,
and this Dad-made trailer
made it all possible."

Left: "My first car!
So what if it was a 1931 Ford bought
in 1947, it was special to me.
Selling carpet in Cincinnati allowed
me to purchase this beauty
for a whopping $200."

Right: "I won't forget this day
and I'm sure Marge won't.
Joining us on this glorious
afternoon in 1951 (August 28)
at Cynthiana Christian Church:
Left to Right — my brother
Don; Marge's brother Wayne;
Bessie Lyons, Marge's best
friend; Marge's brother Ray;
Marge; my friend Lowell Jack-
son; me; my brother Bill;
Lloyd Stephenson, my friend;
Marge's sister Sue; Robert
Shannon, my best friend in
college; and Marge's
sister-in-law Virginia."

Above: "Me, Marge and the girls
(Judy is 4 and Jana is six months old)
in 1961."

Above: "Marge with her sister Sue and parents
Henry and Aleene Judy on their farm in 1954."
Right: "Me and my siblings, seated left to right,
me (youngest) and Dorsey (oldest). Standing
from left, Bill (third oldest), Ruth (second oldest) and Don (three years older than me)."

Above: "My three girls. . .
Jana, Marge and Judy
in 1990."
Left: "Cruisin' in Alaska
with my gal to celebrate
our 35th anniversary
at Southland."

Right: "My daughter
Jana's son, Austin,
apparently had to pull
that machine over to
watch that familiar
character on the
television screen."

Left: "Marge is pictured with grandson Barron (14 months). Barron is the son of Kenny and Judy Speakes. I wanted them to name him Wayne Smith Speakes."

"My two oldest grandchildren, Lyndsey Speakes, left, and Landon Thore, right."

"My four cousins and their husbands at a family reunion in New Alexandria, Pa., in 2001. Left to Right: Wes Westwood, Level Green, Pa.; Elizabeth Lohr, Somerset, Pa.; Dorothy Westwood; me and Marge; Don and Flora Carlson, Cortland, Ohio; Pauline and Calvin Taylor, Sun City, Ariz."

Above: "Marge and me. . . happy as can be."
Below: "My brother Bill's widow, Emalu."

"My brother
Don's widow,
Isabel."

"My brother
Dorsey's widow,
Nancy."

In front: "Amanda and Barron Speakes and Austin Thore. The older folks are left to right: Kenny and Judy Speakes, Marge, me and Fluff, Jana and Tim Thore. Christmas 2003."

Above: "At the end of a two-week revival
in 1950, I baptized 29 people, mostly adults,
in a nearby creek. The revival resulted in
45 new members."

Above: "It cost $24,500 to build
Unity Christian in 1952. It seated 144
and I was there for seven wonderful years."
Left: "E.E. Jacobson, who was a manager
and vice president of the Lexington Water Company,
had a big influence on my life."

Right: "Not only did we
introduce new minister
Eugene Wigginton (center),
but we torched the mortgage
for Unity Christian just three
and a half years after it was
built. It was my last Sunday
of a seven-year ministry."

"It's not the big things; it's the little things."

Tom Fields, who has known Smith for half a century, says of Wayne, "He'd give the shirt off his back. And if you were standing next to him, he'd give them your shirt, too."

Because Smith does so much for other people, he thinks nothing of asking someone else to go above and beyond.

Gordon Walls said, "I can't count the times Wayne called me and said, 'Go take this money down to this person.' Every bus station had his phone number. I've seen him roll down the car window and hand money to a person I would never have given a dime because of what they might do with it. But he would look at me and say, 'It's not for me to decide. Jesus said, "Nevertheless."

Gordon added, "Wayne Smith is a giant of compassion."

At 8:30 one night, Wayne got a call from a family in a rundown section of town. No food in the house. Could the church help? "I sent two deacons," Wayne said. "Kent Mays and Tommy Weaver. One carried the chicken; the other carried a brick behind his back."

Wayne loses a piece of furniture

Wayne was in his office one morning when the phone rang; Andy Rasmussen was sounding an S.O.S. "There's a family over here I've kept for three days in my parking lot. They need more than I can give. I'm turning them over to you."

When Smith reached the Starlite restaurant, he found a husband and wife, their household goods, and three children crammed into an old green station wagon. The father looked bedraggled and confused; the mother looked exhausted. Three children cast wary eyes upon this stranger.

Smith had a discount arrangement with the Day's Motor Lodge on Versailles Road and the Howard Johnson's motel. He took them to the latter. Then Wayne asked the man to follow him to Russ Marshall's tire company. "Russ, these people need tires. Send me the bill, and I'll take care of it." Later, Wayne said, "Marshall never charged me."

Rather than wait at the garage, Wayne took the father back to the motel and went home. Smith had not been in the house 15 minutes when the phone rang. It was Marshall: "Wayne, you've got to come down here right now."

Wayne jumped in his car and left, telling Marge not to hold supper. When Wayne pulled into Russ Marshall's place, Marshall confronted him: "Preacher, that car's alive. One of my men ran in here yelling, 'I'm not working on that car. It's alive.' "

Besides the human family, the other occupants of the car were a family of rabbits, complete with smell. It might be difficult to determine who was more grateful — the workers at the garage or the recipients — when the tires were mounted and the station wagon drove off.

How long did these people intend to stay? Smith called Ottis Platt, minister at Maxwell Street Christian Church. "Do you know of a place we can keep these people?"

Platt responded, "We have an old house behind the Aaron Smith Funeral Home that we're going to tear down for parking. They can stay there. But there's no furniture in it."

Wayne paid the motel and moved the family into Maxwell Street's house. Even with the discount, his finances could only stand so much.

Sure enough, the house was empty except for a couch that had seen considerable use, several stains complementing the faded yellow fabric.

Wayne left the family and was back in an hour with supper. "Tomorrow I'll find you some furniture."

Another errand took Smith south of Lexington the next morning, and he was driving north on I-75, wondering where to find beds and a table and chairs to bring his needy charges when he noticed a particular vehicle in the southbound lanes across the median.

It was the old green station wagon headed south, hunkered down under its load of dad and mom and kids and rabbits and household goods, plus the yellow couch strapped to the roof.

The second mile and more

Coming up Southland Drive in a snowstorm, Wayne saw a man on crutches trying to make his way through several inches of snow, with more coming down. Instantly, Smith pulled over.

"Get in. Where do you want to go?"

"To Winchester," the stranger answered. Twenty-five miles one way. Smith took him to Winchester.

Gordon Walls told of a gift from Smith. "I was in the car-leasing business," Walls said. "I had given my heart to the Lord when I was 16, but I didn't go to church much. I'd known about Wayne since my high school days at Tates Creek, and attended Southland off and on. This was in the old building on Hill 'N Dale.

"On my 21st birthday, Wayne showed up where I worked and produced a golf ball inscribed 'Happy Birthday Gordon WBS 1981.' I didn't even know him. It blew me away to think that he'd take the time to think about me and go to the trouble of finding that golf ball and getting it inscribed. I keep that golf ball on my desk. From that moment, the game was on."

Wayne's daughter Judy said, "There's a lot of people at Southland who think that Dad's their best friend, and they're right."

Smith explained. "You've got to press the flesh," he said. "You've got to shake hands with people. You've got to remember their names."

Wayne confessed, "Sometimes someone will come up to me and say, 'Do you remember me?' There may be only one of you, but there's many of them and it's difficult. So I lie a little. Most times I say, 'I remember your face.'"

Wayne helps the stork — and a felon

Effie West, a member at Southland, was across town in a Virginia Avenue laundromat when she heard a girl crying.

Words From Wayne

People love to hear 'Thank you' and 'I love you,'
but the most important is to hear their own name.

"What's wrong?" asked Effie.

"I'm going to have a baby," the girl sobbed. "I'm not married. I don't have any money."

"I'll have our preacher come see you."

Wayne made contact with the girl and stayed in touch during the coming weeks. He told what happened.

"I put her in Good Samaritan Hospital. Her name was Smith. They gave me a big discount, because they thought she was my daughter. She got good treatment."

Wayne knew a couple who wanted to adopt, and he contacted them. The husband was on the staff at the University of Kentucky and an elder in Southland Christian Church. Smith helped with the arrangements, and all concerned counted the days until the birth. He would have preferred that the new parents receive the child directly from the hospital, but this was not possible.

He said, "I didn't think it was a good idea for the girl to hold the baby, because she might get attached to it; so I was carrying the baby as we were leaving the hospital.

"There was this nurse," Wayne explained. "She could have been a top-sergeant. She told me, 'Reverend, you can do whatever you want to in the parking lot, but that baby goes out of here in its mother's arms.' "

Wayne sighed. "And that's what happened."

The girl's brother, Richard, was incarcerated at the state reformatory at LaGrange, Kentucky, and Wayne would take the girl to visit him about once a month.

Wayne told how he quickly became Richard's supplier: "Along about Shelbyville, she would say, 'Richard needs cigarettes,' so I'd stop and buy cigarettes. One day she called me and said 'Richard needs a radio.' "

In the closet at home, Marge had a radio that one of her boyfriends had given her for Christmas before she and Wayne were married. Wayne decided to put that radio to good use.

About a year later, Marge approached her husband. "Have you seen my radio? I've looked all over the house, and I can't find it."

Wayne swallowed. "Marge," he began, "you're going to be blessed, because you have helped a person in need."

Marge was unimpressed. "Next time keep your blessings to yourself."

An architect, a member of Southland, asked Wayne if he knew of someone who could put a new roof on his house. "I have this friend getting out of prison," Wayne said, and Richard started to work.

"He needed transportation, so I signed for a used motorcycle," Wayne said. "He did about half of the roof and quit. Then he took off. A 14- or 15-year-old girl ran off with him. Probably the happiest day of his life."

Richard defaulted on the note, so Wayne paid for the motorcycle. Marge discovered what Smith had done when another preacher asked Wayne, in front of her, how the rehabilitation program with the ex-con was progressing.

Giving money and more

There is a man in Smith's neighborhood who rides his bicycle over to the house, looking for a handout. Wayne found him a job in a storage company, but according to Smith, "he couldn't be that orderly."

Wayne advised the supplicant, "Don't stop when Marge's car is in the garage."

"I have to constantly fight to keep him from giving it all away," said Marge.

Ann Nelson was in her office one morning as Wayne was opening his mail, and she heard him say, "Well, look at this." He showed her a check for $2,500. Twenty years earlier he had co-signed a note for $2,000 so that a couple who lived in Georgetown could get a car. They moved, leaving Wayne to finish off the note, and he never heard from them again. Until this check.

In the 1980s Lexington churches went together to form a community resource center to coordinate local benevolence: If someone stopped at the Baptist church, the church would get the person's Social Security number, call the center, and determine if the applicant was "making the rounds" or not. It didn't work with Smith.

"He would always jump the gun and give them something," Ann said.

"One day he gave $100 to two men who told him they were going to their mother's funeral and needed money for gas and food."

Yeah, sure.

Southland received an average of 40 requests for help *every week,* and Smith often took care of the requests himself rather than pass them on to others.

Looking back, Wayne explained, "I'd rather be cheated than miss somebody who needs help. I guess I got a lot of it from my parents. Their house was rented, and they took in boarders. But they got a boy from the orphanage and brought him to our home for a while. We didn't need another kid, but they were generous."

He Was the Best and the Worst of a Counselor

My husband and I went on staff at Southland in the summer of 1974. Three weeks later, my brother committed an alcohol-related crime.

As our days of sorrow increased, Wayne would drop by for a daily report. In a sense, he was the best and the worst of a counselor. The worst in that he said mostly nothing. He would just sit with tears running down his cheeks as I shared the latest. The best in that his tears revealed how much he cared.

Five years later, Wayne was largely responsible for my brother's release from prison. During my brother's days in prison, Wayne was like a father to my brother's boys, touching their lives with hugs and occasional gifts during the five years and after. Today those boys are walking with the Lord, and one is the head of the counseling department at Central Christian Church.

And, through Wayne's influence, we put in a baptismal unit in the chapel at Eddyville prison from Southland Christian Church.

— *Doris Howard, Family Life Director,*
Central Christian Church, Wichita, Kansas

The boy's name was Denny Korb. "I've often wondered how he fared in later years," said Smith.

Tom Fields tells of the time he ran for city council. "As soon as Wayne heard about it, he came and brought me $100 and told me, 'I want to be one of your first supporters.' "

Leon Appel held a revival for Wayne, and when Appel died years later, Smith drove to Lincoln, Illinois, for the funeral, even though he had no part in the service.

Charlie Delaney said, "My mother lived in Florida in her later years. When she died, we had a service there. We brought her body back to Lexington and had a service at Gardenside Christian Church. Wayne came to the service. We were not all that close to Wayne, but I remember he was the only preacher who came."

Wayne held a meeting for Dean Hammond in 1980 at the Ripley Church of Christ, in Big Prairie, Ohio. "I took him to Amish country," Dean remembers. "We visited a cheese factory. Wayne bought $40 worth of cheese to take back to his elders."

Wayne frequently brought candy or other treats to elders meetings. "Dad thinks food will cure anything, even obesity," said Jana.

When Smith returns from a speaking engagement, he will send a gift to thank the person who picked him up at the airport, a gift for homes where he ate a meal, gifts for the host preacher, and so on. Wayne has an ear for people's likes and will frequently surprise a casual acquaintance by sending an item the person happened to mention.

Mike McGinnis, minister of First Christian Church in Williamstown, took Smith and a couple of other preachers to Alice's Restaurant, two blocks from the church. Wayne was astonished to find an extensive array of UK memorabilia lining the walls and filling several display cases. "This is as good as they've got in Lexington," Smith said, and he and Eddie, Alice's husband, talked for the next hour about Cawood Ledford, UK's announcer who had recently passed away, and about present and past

Words From Wayne

You can't make good decisions on an empty stomach.

coaches, players, and basketball teams.

Eddie happened to mention a particular book, and before the week was out, Wayne had found a copy in a Lexington bookstore and sent it to him.

Why does Smith go to such lengths?

Nevertheless . . .

"My motive for serving the Lord is twofold. First of all, I love him because of what he did and is doing for me. Secondly, we only go through here once, and I feel strongly if we're going to do something of any significance, it must be done now," said Smith

Southland associate minister Gary Black said, "His vision for the church is to love as many people as God puts in his path."

"You've got one opportunity," Wayne said. "Somebody dies; you have one opportunity to be at their house. Wait two or three days and it's too late. If it's the middle of the night and something's happened, they want you there right now."

Marge spoke from experience when she said, "Someone calls in the middle of the night and there's been a wreck or whatever; he'd think nothing of it to get up, get dressed, and be with them. Or to get somebody out of jail at 2:00 in the morning. That's his call; that's his call."

Wayne goes to the Bible to back up his actions. "I tell you a Scripture that's had a great impression on me: The Lord said, 'If it be possible, let this cup be removed. Nevertheless, not my will but thine be done.' I'm surprised someone has never really jumped on that word 'Nevertheless.' I think it would be a great slogan for an attendance contest. I'd rather not tithe — nevertheless. Go to church on Sunday night — but nevertheless."

He is emphatic. "You do not make extra points by preaching. People expect that. That's your job. But when you do something that's not expected — show up at the hospital where you're not expected, drive to Ohio or Tennessee for a funeral — that's where you add up points.

"Frankly, I've done some things in the pulpit I shouldn't have, but I've gotten by with it because I was there when Mother died or when their child died."

Wonder where Wayne is?

"One of the greatest compliments I've ever had was an occasion of sudden death, and the family said, 'Wonder where Wayne is?' They said, if he knew, he would be here. I've learned, it's really not the big things; it's the little things."

Tom Fields suggested that it is more than wanting to earn points.

"I've never heard him preach on the Holy Spirit," he said, "and I've known Wayne for more than 40 years. He follows the promptings of the Holy Spirit more than anybody I know. If there's a widow in need, he will go find out how things are. When someone's sick, he's there."

Wayne and several friends were eating at the Cracker Barrel in Dry Ridge, 55 miles north of Lexington, when Joyce Doyle, principal of Grant County High School, stopped at his table and thanked Wayne for going to see her father years earlier when he was in a Lexington hospital.

"Dad watched you on television," Joyce said, "and our preacher called and asked if you would go see him. Dad was in St. Joseph's Hospital. You went, and the next time I drove down to see Dad, he was so excited. The first thing he said to me was, 'I met him in person.' He didn't even tell me hello."

When Wayne goes to the funeral home to pay his respects, after greeting the people, he glances around to see if flowers from the church are there. "Just to be sure," he will say. If he expects you to do something, and you don't do it, he will find someone he can depend on.

"If there's a job to be done, I want it done," he explained.

When James Whalen, one of the church's elders, was CEO of General Telephone, he gave 31 people from Southland a job, every one at Wayne's request. The story is told of a couple of workers at General Telephone talking, and one asked the other, "Who's the new guy?" The answer came, "I don't know his name, but I can tell you where he goes to church."

Whalen finally asked people not to say that they went to Southland.

Words From Wayne

When money is in your hand, that's good;
when it's in your heart, that's bad.

An Unexpected Letter

One afternoon Smith was working in his office when the phone rang. The call came from a bar at the Imperial Shopping Center on Waller Avenue.

"Are you the minister?" It was a man's voice, probably about 35.

"Yes, I am."

The voice continued: "I just got out of jail for vagrancy, and if I don't get back to Iowa, they are going to put me back in jail. One reason I'm in jail is because I'm not mentally right."

"That struck a chord with me," said Smith. "How many people have the honesty and even the intelligence to know that they are not mentally right? I'd already decided that I'd help him."

But how? Wayne told what happened. "I knew about how much a bus ticket to Iowa cost and knew I didn't have the $80. I went around the staff and was borrowing money when the phone rang again. It was the same man."

He said, "This is my last quarter. A member of your church is here with me, and he promised you'd help."

"I sure hoped he was wrong about one of our members being in the bar," Wayne said. "I asked him, 'How did you get my number?' "

The voice explained that the secretary of another church had provided Smith's phone number.

The caller was standing outside the bar when Wayne drove up. The Greyhound bus station was on Limestone at that time, and as they approached downtown, the man told Smith, "It's closed."

Wayne said, "I thought, 'This guy is mentally off. What does he know?' "

Sure enough, Greyhound was on strike and closed.

Wayne's passenger kept talking. "I know where there's another bus station. It's in a motel on I-75 and Winchester Road."

Wayne discovered that Trailways used the motel as a terminal. "I had lived here 30 years," he said, "and I didn't know it was there."

Inside, Smith asked for a bus ticket to Des Moines. "That will be $119," said the woman at the ticket counter.

"No, lady," said the man. "That's $72."

Quickly, Wayne chimed in: "Lady, he's right." This was coming out of Smith's pocket.

The ticket agent responded, "I can give you a ticket for $72, but it's going to take you a while to get there."

"That's fine," Wayne said and handed over the money, plus $30 for food.

Several weeks later Wayne picked up the mail and saw the postmark from Iowa. Inside the envelope, he found a note from the boy's mother and a check for $100.

Tears welled up in Smith's eyes. Here was one who said thank you and meant it.

"Most people don't know what that costs."

"I'm sort of a poster boy for the man with the one talent," Wayne said. Tom Fields disagrees. He and Clara met Smith at Northward Christian Assembly at Falmouth before they were married and liked him. When Tom was discharged from the Air Force in 1957 the couple moved to Lexington.

"We visited several churches," Tom said. "We chose Southland."

Tom quickly became a leader in the church, and he has served as an elder for almost 40 years.

"Wayne Smith is probably the best friend I have, outside of my family," Tom said. "He's the most complex person I've ever met in my life.

"He's a perfectionist. At the old building, he wanted every blade of grass to be mowed just so, every bush and flower to be standing up just right. Before services on Sunday, he would go around and pick up any scrap of paper he saw on the lawn. The hallways were getting so crowded we moved the coat racks into the back of the sanctuary, but Wayne couldn't preach looking at that mess of coats. So we moved them."

Wayne's staff grew as the church grew. Roy Mays described Smith in a staff meeting: "Sometimes in a discussion he could be in your face, like coach to team at halftime. It can get hot. Then he softens it with an apology. He's strong on keeping relationships."

He brags on his staff, gives them gifts, and takes them out to eat and on trips with him. He is both traditional and innovative. The congregation at Southland has heard his phrase, "Geared to the times; anchored to the rock" almost as often as John 3:16.

New leadership style for new circumstances

Southland grew, but Smith grew with it, changing his leadership style to fit the new demands. He applied his frequent question, "Can we do better?" to himself as well as to the church program.

An intense competitor, he is not afraid to take risks, describing his style as "trial and error." Wayne said, "You will preach to empty pews unless you are flexible in your methods."

Roy continued: "For a person who had such fixed principles, he was so adaptable as he multiplied through leaders. He was at his best when he was doing direct ministry. But he built a leadership culture. He attracted strong leaders, spiritual men who had great leadership skills."

In the early days, the only way to use these skills was to make the men elders or deacons. Later, Smith and the staff opened additional channels for ministry. "You didn't have to be an elder or deacon," explained Mays, "to be responsible for a major area of service."

Staff members, too, were given significant responsibility. Wayne encouraged his staff to try new and creative ideas, with the freedom to make mistakes. Smith celebrated their successes, without a hint of jealousy. Roy said, "If any of us saw something he didn't see, he felt good about it."

Mays continued: "We built this church by allowing the staff to be strong in their areas. Each of us had our own constituency, and we worked to keep all of these pulling together."

Whether at a staff retreat at Herrington Lake or a quick encounter in a church hallway, everybody usually knew in which direction Smith was headed.

Jack Ballard, Smith's friend at Mount Carmel Christian Church in Atlanta, used the Living Christmas Tree as the centerpiece of Mount Carmel's holiday program. In 1975 Smith presented the idea to his elders at Southland, and they voted it down, primarily because of the cost.

The following year Wayne brought it up again but with a difference. Before presenting his idea to his elders, he took four of them to Atlanta to see for themselves. This time the idea passed.

Soon the Living Christmas Tree became a prime doorway for the unchurched, with seven out of 10 new members giving this as their first

Words From Wayne

If you want to see the ocean, you've got to make the drive.

exposure to Southland Christian Church. More than 22,000 people came in the course of the 10 nights in 1995, the program's last year.

Wes Moye, who was writing a paper for a college class, asked Wayne to rate himself from one to 10 on persistence. Wayne responded, "I'm a 10."

"He's always had vision," said Roy. "He had such energy to make things happen, but he did it through other people."

Besides, he made it fun. When Steve Gay, one of the church's custodians, married, he brought his new wife to meet Wayne. Wayne had not performed their marriage, and as Mrs. Gay was introduced to Wayne, she looked at her husband and said, "I have dedicated my life to making this man happy."

Wayne's response was instant: "Have you got a sister?"

Creating excitement and enthusiasm

Smith constantly looked for ways to create enthusiasm. The Living Christmas Tree grew into 10 nights at Christmas, and an Easter program became 10 nights at Easter.

Before each service, Wayne would mix with the huge crowds, shaking hands, greeting newcomers and old-timers alike.

Then he would go up on the stage and welcome the people. "You've been sitting here for an hour," he said. "You are next to people who believe the same things you do: in the Resurrection, in the birth of Jesus. Now I want you to get up and shake hands with these people. And when you hear the orchestra play a great old hymn" — he stressed *great old hymn* — "I want you to sit down."

After a minute of handshaking the orchestra launched into "On, On, UK," and the crowd went wild, laughing and clapping. "That was one of my favorite things," Wayne said later. "I got two or three letters about that being irreverent, but they ate it up."

A friend asked Wayne how it felt to be asked repeatedly to speak at the North American Christian Convention and was surprised at Smith's answer: "Most people don't know what that costs." Nothing about the honor; nothing about the recognition. Only an awareness of the responsibility and the work that goes into facing a crowd of 10,000.

"I love to preach," he said. "That's my motivation to prepare. I don't enjoy preparing."

His preparation? "I write everything down," Wayne said. "Even the jokes."

The results are apparent in his preaching, such as this excerpt from a message with the one-word title "Duty," delivered in Anaheim, Calif., July 17, 1992, at the North American Christian Convention personnel dinner.

> Moses was faithful. At 80, he led 3 1/2 million out of captivity. Caleb was faithful.
>
> At 85 he said, "I want to take this mountain." Joseph was faithful in the midst of unbelievable temptation. Daniel was faithful in a hostile environment. David was faithful, refusing to return home at the bidding of his brothers; he stayed and slew Goliath. Gideon was faithful and he proved you can do more with less if God is in it.
>
> When a brick layer is faithful he becomes a mason. When a typist is faithful she becomes a secretary. When a carpenter is faithful he becomes a builder. When a cook is faithful he becomes a chef. When a bookkeeper is faithful he becomes an accountant. When a plumber is faithful he becomes a pipe fitter. When a speaker is faithful he becomes an orator. When a boss is faithful he becomes an executive. When a painter is faithful he becomes a decorator. When a preacher is faithful he becomes a prophet.
>
> When a Christian is faithful he becomes a missionary.

In private, Wayne will rephrase a sentence over and over, carefully selecting each word in order to deliver a powerful close to a sermon or the right punch line to one of his famous illustrations.

Dr. E. LeRoy Lawson, president of Hope International University, invited Smith to participate in a seminar on effective storytelling in preaching. Wayne had a scheduling conflict and suggested another speaker. "No," Lawson said, "we all felt you were the best when it came to using stories."

Smith is always on the lookout for new material. On speaking trips he will pick up books or tapes, playing those he likes over and over in his car back home. He has listened to every tape B.R. Lakin ever made. Were he the intellectual type, Wayne could write a master's thesis on the great

The Sermon Group

For the last eight years of Wayne's ministry, he traveled to Louisville every Thursday except in June, July, and August. Bob Russell, senior minister of Southeast Christian Church, formed a group of eight ministers, who met weekly to prepare sermons. The sermons were planned a year in advance.

"Each of us was expected to bring fresh bread to the table," said Wayne. "Sermons are not easy to build. Having eight learned men of God providing illustrations and ideas weekly was a godsend to me. It extended my ministry — no doubt about it. To preach to the same people for 40 years and be interesting is a major effort. I shall forever be indebted to Bob Russell for inviting me to join the group."

Though the group usually numbered eight, there were 11 different ministers during the years Wayne studied with the group. Six of the 11 have moved to other churches. Locations given here indicate their places of service during the time Smith met with them. John Turner came from Mason, Ohio. Three were from Indiana: Dave Kennedy, New Albany; Phil LaMaster, Scottsburg; and Mark Jones, Columbus. Seven were from Kentucky: Bob Russell and Dave Stone, Louisville; Brad Johnson, Bowling Green; Dean Scott, Shepherdsville; Jim Bird, Don King, and Wayne, from Lexington.

"Phil LaMaster is one of my best friends," Wayne said, noting, "However, he has a good side and bad side. He is generous with gifts — sent me 28 pounds of chocolate-covered peanuts once. That's good. He loves Bobby Knight. That's bad."

Smith singled out another Hoosier for special mention: "Mark Jones is a great friend and a real student of the Word. Many, many times he has gone the second mile in assisting me with sermon preparation."

Methodist preacher Clovis Chappel.

"I know a great sermon when I hear one," said Smith. "It has Scripture, application, humor, illustration and ends with emotion. I like to end with emotion, because most decisions are made in the heart, not the head."

During Wayne's term as chairman of the board of trustees of Cincinnati Bible College and Seminary, the group commissioned a portrait of professor George Mark Elliott and presented it to Elliott, explaining that it would hang in the library.

After the presentation, Wayne turned to his friend Jack Ballard and asked, "If they did a painting of me, where would they hang it? In the men's room?"

"No," Ballard replied. "Over the copy machine."

Wayne taunted his friend Ard Hoven for his deep voice and elegant manner. "Brother Hoven, you could read the phone book and 10 people would come forward." Both men laughed, then Smith added, "I've got to work at it."

Leaders complain, "We love you, but . . ."

Several years ago, some of Wayne's friends approached him and shared their concerns about his preaching: "Wayne, we love you, but you're preaching old sermons. We need some fresh material."

Smith was hurt, but he knew they were right. He approached Bob Russell and asked if he could join the group of preachers who were meeting at Southeast to prepare sermons. "He had tears in his eyes," Bob said.

"I credit Bob Russell with helping my preaching and extending the length of my ministry," Wayne said. "He let me join this group of preachers who get together every Thursday. Everybody brings illustrations and materials and joins in. Bob Russell is my friend. He has gone the second mile and more to help me write sermons. I owe him a lot."

Wayne Smith started preaching when Bob Russell was 3 years old.

Out of this friendship grew a unique arrangement that has blessed both Southland and Southeast. "Our church was growing," said Bob, whose Louisville congregation has become the largest in the Commonwealth and one of the top three in the country, "and we had Wayne over to preach. I said, 'Wayne, it's always a burden to write a sermon when I'm at the convention. How about if we were to exchange pulpits?' So that's how it started. The Sunday after the NACC he would come and preach, and our people just loved it. He might bring gifts or plaques. He always made it an event."

Russell said of Smith, "He downplays his intellectual ability and lack of talent. But there's an energy when he comes into a room. Nobody wrote a better church paper than Wayne Smith. When he gets fired up about something, he can be eloquent."

What is "prosthodontics"?

In May 1992, Dr. Charles Ellinger, a prosthodontist on the faculty of the University of Kentucky, asked Wayne to speak for him. Dr. Ellinger was chairperson for a five-day conference sponsored by the Academy of Prosthodontics, which was meeting at the Marriott hotel. Three hundred doctors were in attendance.

"I didn't know what a prosthodontist was," Wayne said, "and I still can't spell it. The way I understand it is that the prosthodontist takes care of anything in your mouth that's not permanent." Then Wayne added, "But the good doctor reports that the short, funny preacher was a real hit."

Others think more of Smith's ability than he does. He is never afraid to ask for help. When the invitation came to preach at the North American Christian Convention in June 2000, Wayne was assigned a particular text for his message.

Each preacher was free to develop the selection as he saw fit. Smith wrote to 10 preachers with the question, "How would you outline this passage?" One of these letters went to Bob Shannon, Wayne's friend from college who helped him write his first sermon 54 years ago.

Staying up when he's feeling down

A fellow preacher in Lexington complained to Wayne, "There's one man in my church that I cannot please, no matter what I do."

"I didn't tell him," Smith said later, "but I thought, 'You've got only one? Man, that's pretty good.' "

He continued: "There are times when it's not easy. When we're with people we've got to be up: — 'How y'all doing? Good to see you' — no matter how we feel. We've got a lot to be thankful for; we can think about that."

Marge was asked, "Does Wayne ever get down?"

"Sometimes," she admitted. "But he keeps up a good face. And he doesn't stay down for long."

Wayne's optimism reaches beyond his church.

"The most emotional letter I ever got," he said, "was from the wife of the minister of the Christian Church in Dunnville, down in Casey Coun-

Anything for an Easter Sermon

The summer after my sophomore year at Cincinnati Bible College and Seminary, I was fortunate to do my internship with Wayne and Southland's youth minister, Brewster McLeod. What a summer. Between practical jokes and laughter, I saw up close Wayne's humility, his servant's heart and his generosity.

During my internship, I broke my ankle. Unbeknownst to me, he came to the doctor's office and paid my bill. The first day of the 1981 North American Christian Convention, he gave me $100 of his own money to buy books.

On one occasion, Brewster and I got into Wayne's house when we knew he and Marge were coming home in a matter of minutes. We hid in the bedroom closet, and when he opened it, we scared the man to death.

Our laughter subsided the next day — Sunday — when he told the story to the entire congregation and concluded by saying, "I am so glad Brewster and Dave have finally *come out of the closet.*"

After I joined the staff at Southeast Christian Church in

Louisville, our friendship continued to grow as we worked on sermons together. Wayne would humbly say that he was driving over to "pick up his sermon for Sunday."

He was so good-natured in agreeing to be a part of humorous videos that I would script for our Leadership Conference. My favorite was one I talked him into doing called <u>Wayne's Workout</u>. It had Wayne in shorts and an undershirt doing aerobics with a group of young ladies. I'll never forget what he mumbled to me on his way to the bathroom to change back into his dress clothes. He said, "The things I do for an Easter sermon."

I dedicated my book on leadership, *Keeping Your Head Above Water*, as follows: "This book is dedicated to Wayne B. Smith. Your willingness to mentor a 20-year-old Bible college student was pivotal to my future service. Thanks for loving Christ, giving generously and serving others. In 50 years of ministry *you've kept your head above water* and inspired me to lead."

— Dave Stone, Preaching Associate,
Southeast Christian Church, Louisville, Kentucky

ty. Her husband had retired because he'd had a stroke, and he wasn't that old. Every Sunday he watched us on television. When we took Communion, he took Communion. When we prayed, he prayed. Sometimes at Southland I'd have visiting preachers stand, because there were usually several in the audience. This woman said that when I asked all the preachers to stand, he couldn't stand up, but he raised his hand. I cried when I read her letter."

Wayne remembered one Sunday in particular when he asked a visiting preacher to stand. Wayne had recommended Bruce Templeton to First Christian at Huntington Beach, California. Templeton had served on Southland's staff several years earlier.

"I understood the church had a big debt," said Wayne. "I told them, 'He will smile right through it. He's got a great personality, and he's a good preacher.' So they took him."

Templeton's in-laws lived close to Lexington, and one Sunday he and his family were in the audience at Southland.

During announcement time, Wayne told the crowd, "I understand Bruce Templeton is here. I don't see him, but if he is, I want him to come up front."

Bruce came to the platform wearing a California-style short-sleeved shirt and casual slacks.

"He looked like someone out of Hawaii," said Wayne. "I said, 'We're happy to have you, but I would like to suggest that here in the heartland of the Gospel, we get dressed before we go to the Lord's house."

The audience loved it and loved Templeton's reply even more: "It's good to be with you today," Bruce said, "but you've insulted me, and I won't be back."

Fortunately, Templeton has since relented and returned often to Southland.

Encouraging other preachers

A young preacher from Alabama called Wayne. "I graduated a couple of years ago from Bible college, and I'm having a difficult time getting sermons."

"What can I do for you?" Wayne asked.

The voice continued: "I heard that you said, 'God gives some the talent to write and some the talent to preach.' "

"I don't know if I said that," Wayne answered, "but I agree with it anyway, although most can do both."

The caller kept on: "The people here don't like it when I get material from others," he said. "They want it all to be mine."

Wayne thought for a moment, and was serious as he responded. "If your people really mean that, then I might suggest you look for another

Words From Wayne

Methods are many, doctrines are few;
methods change, but doctrines never do.

church."

Some time later Smith received a second call from the man in Alabama, saying that he had relocated and was doing well in a new ministry. "He asked me to preach a revival," Wayne said, "and I did."

Smith has a special concern for other ministers. "I love preachers," he said. "Many of them need to be recognized. Sometimes they don't get much appreciation."

Wayne's door is always open to preachers. Professor Bruce Smith of Cincinnati Bible College and Seminary told how Wayne influenced his life.

"I was a senior student at Kentucky Christian College," Bruce said. "I was considering going on to seminary, wondering where to go, and at that stage just looking at the validity of graduate study.

"I had heard Wayne speak, but I didn't know him. I called him on the phone. He graciously set a time, and I drove to Lexington. He took time with me and was really patient. He said to me, 'You've got to call. To see the people. And you have to study. Your ministry can die in your office.'"

Bruce went on to Emmanuel School of Religion, Vanderbilt University, and has his Ph.D. from Ohio University. Bruce recently completed his 25th year teaching preachers.

Wayne Smith's office was a magnet for discouraged preachers, not only from Christian Churches but from nearly every denomination in town. Ann, his secretary, said, "He was always there for them. He would listen and lighten their load. That happened time after time."

Invited to lecture to Bob Russell's class at Kentucky Christian College for the school's Master of Ministry program, Smith knew that his task was to encourage, to lift and to motivate.

He started, but broke into tears, telling the students, "I gotta tell you, I just had somebody from my church ream me out, and the criticism has got me down."

The instructor thought, "Here's the best-known preacher in the brotherhood and he's discouraged. What's that going to do to these guys?"

At the end of the session, however, when the evaluation forms were gathered up, almost every student said that the high point of the class was when Wayne Smith came and opened his heart to them.

KCC's Tom Lawson said of Wayne, "Most people know him for his laugh, but he's got plenty of tears." Smith's transparency and humility are genuine.

Wayne is no stranger to tragedy. One hot afternoon, Keith Honaker, 38 years old, Vice President of Commonwealth Technology, father of five children, and an elder at Southland, climbed into his attic to fix the exhaust fan. Something went wrong.

The hospital called Wayne, telling him, "Better get over here quick."

"They lived in the Stonewall subdivision," Wayne said. "A very close-knit community. The police brought me. I got out of the police car to tell the family, with neighbors standing around. I still remember how the children and their mother screamed when I said he was gone. It breaks your heart."

Wayne's first cousin, Jack Metts, was an elder. Jack worked for a company that built bridges, and he decided to fabricate a new cross for the coming Easter program. Co-workers found him lying beside the cross, and rushed him to the hospital, but it was too late. A heart attack.

"I had to go and tell the family," Wayne said. "They don't teach that in Bible college."

Wayne listens to a fine young preacher tell about a problem he is having with some of his leaders. How will Smith handle this?

"Tears," Wayne began. "Tears are a part of the ministry. Jesus wept. Jesus sweat blood in the Garden. Paul was mistreated. God told Paul how he must suffer. That's part of the ministry."

Hanging on Smith's office wall where he could see it every day was a quotation from Theodore Roosevelt, which said in part, ... "(the credit belongs to the man) who knows the great enthusiasms, the great devotions; who spends himself in a worthy cause; who at the best knows in the end a triumph of high achievement, and who at the worst, if he fails, at least fails while daring greatly, so that his place shall never be with those cold and timid souls who know neither victory or defeat!" (From a plaque given to Wayne by Judge Ray Corns.)

"The up-and-outers need help, too."

Though he is one of the most successful ministers in America, Wayne B. Smith discounts his ability. He downplays his own role in Southland's growth, referring instead to the quality of the nucleus that Broadway provided, the coming of IBM to Lexington, his staff, and so on.

Roger Wellman offered his explanation for the growth of Southland. "When Wayne started our class, which he called the Keystone Class, we were all just coming out of college. We hadn't been married very long; maybe our first child or a couple of children.

"Wayne hung around with us. He took us with him to places to speak. I remember one time two or three of us were in the back of the room, and we made a sign and held it up: Your fly is open. He got all flustered, and you could see him trying to check and see if anything was wrong. Finally, he realized we were putting him on.

"But look at the church today. A lot of our men who are now elders or deacons started out in that class."

Roger continued: "He probably neglected Marge and the girls to spend that time with us. When one of my parents was in the hospital, he brought us a bucket of chicken. Half the people in central Kentucky tell time by clocks Wayne Smith has given us.

"Nearly all of us are still married. We're all still in the church, even those who have moved away. Wayne made a point of being in our lives.

"It was always when you least expected it. I remember one Derby Day, when everybody is at the track or glued to the TV, and here he comes. 'I just dropped by to make sure you were all right.' He built the class, and the class built the church."

According to Wellman, members of Smith's class developed not only spiritually but also professionally: Larry Wells, Ph.D., associate dean of the College of Engineering at the University of Kentucky; Guy Colson, managing partner in a Lexington law firm; Bill Doggett, now an executive at Kentucky Utilities; Tony Wash, successful entrepreneur in the entertainment business, including the arcade concession for the World's Fair at Knoxville; Gino Guarnieri, owner of Geno's Formal Affair; and others.

"My brother, Wayne Wellman, is a successful businessman and has been tremendous help to Wayne financially with some of his projects. He continues to drive Wayne to preaching engagements," Wellman said.

There's a doctoral thesis here for some enterprising grad student interested in pursuing the phenomenal linkage between the growth of Southland Christian Church and the growth of these men: Wayne's optimism, his example of hard work, his way of bringing out the best in others.

Goal-directed leadership

Southland's development was not accidental; it was intentional, and it extended beyond the Keystone Class.

Wayne sought young families for his church, and once they began coming, he worked to keep them coming.

Buddy and Martha Mossbarger started going to Southland in 1959. Buddy received his B.S. from the University of Kentucky in 1961 and his master's degree in 1964. He and two friends were determined to go into business together. "Two of us quit our jobs and started the business," Buddy said. "The third stayed with his current employment and split his salary so we could have a guaranteed income. This was 1966."

Mossbarger was elected a deacon as a young man; he later became an elder and then chairman of the church board.

Buddy's company, Fuller, Mossbarger, Scott, and May, is one of Lexington's premier engineering firms with 250 employees. Mossbarger served as president and chairman of the board for 35 years, retiring in 2002. Craig Avery, his Methodist friend whom he asked Smith to call in the '70s, another of Southland's elders, is now company president.

John Burk was Southland's first board chairman, and Burk's sister,

Words From Wayne

If you want to catch a big fish, go where the big fish are.

Louise, was a teller at First National. She approached John Everton, then a new hire in the loan department of First National: "There's a young preacher starting a church out in Southland. His name is Wayne Smith. I think you'd like him."

John and Estelle visited, then came back the following Sunday and transferred their membership. John became a deacon and has served a number of terms over the years.

John worked his way up at the bank, then bought part interest in Kentucky Account Service, a loan collection agency. Two years later, he owned the company. Over the following quarter century, he acquired a number of other collection agencies. At the age of 55, John sold his business and retired. There are few places in the world he and Estelle have not seen. "The Lord has been good to us," John testified.

"John is one of the finest businessmen in town," said Smith. "He is sharp and a good man. He said to me, 'Wayne, they're building a chapel at your alma mater. I'll give $500, if you will.' How was I to answer that? Of course, I said yes. So the school got $1,000."

Leading the leaders

"Smith is like a good politician," said Everton. "He would lobby for what he wanted, and nine times out of 10 he got it. I voted against his Living Christmas Tree idea and that turned out to be one of the best things the church ever did."

Though Everton was opposed to the Christmas tree project, he was assigned a major role. "I was in charge of the live animals. Charles Cassity and I — he has a farm across from the church — would round up sheep and goats for the pageant, and we'd keep them at Cassity's place. We did that for several years."

At Wayne's insistence, Southland rotates leadership positions. During the period when John was serving as church treasurer, he advised Wayne, "You spend all your time with the down-and-outers. The up-and-outers need help, too."

John said of Wayne, "I've always considered him not just my minister but my friend. I have driven the car when he was speaking different places.

On the way there or the way back, he knows the greasiest, dirtiest, orneriest-looking places on the outside but with the best chili or burgers and fries. I remember one Chinese restaurant where Wayne said, 'Let's stop here; but for goodness sake, don't tell Marge.' "

Looking at the membership of Southland, Wayne speaks of the members' loyalty. "Some of them are millionaires now. I knew them when they were dirt poor. When you've been with them in their dark hour, that's when you get close. A preacher can't do that when he moves to a different church every other year."

Reaching the movers and shakers

Another factor in Southland's growth was Wayne's leadership in the Bluegrass Breakfast Lions Club. "I joined Lions because I wanted a doctor and a lawyer in my church," said Wayne.

When the club began in 1963, John Everton was one of the first to join and served as secretary-treasurer. Before long the membership roster of the Lions Club began to resemble the membership roll of Southland Christian Church.

One Lion who remained at large was Tom Bloemer, whose father had played football for Notre Dame. Bloemer began his career with Time Finance, then moved to Preferred Thrift, which grew in the 1950s to become Bank of the Bluegrass, with Tom as president.

Bloemer, Everton and Smith eat lunch together frequently.

Though Bloemer remains a Roman Catholic, he has contributed to a number of Smith's benevolent causes and may have kept Wayne and Marge out of the poorhouse.

Tom Bloemer knows that Wayne Smith is a soft touch, so the two men devised the following plan: When someone asked Wayne to co-sign a note on a car or a loan, he would tell the applicant, "I'll sign if my banker will go along."

Wayne is emphatic: "How am I going to tell somebody no when they're standing in front of me and they need help? I can't do it. I can't."

When Smith and the applicant reached the bank, if Tom deemed the proposition a risky one for Wayne, he would refuse the loan.

Through the Lions Club, Wayne found his first lawyer in Paul Ross, who is still a deacon at Southland. Paul's brother, Jim, is a surgeon. Jim started coming, and one day Smith dropped by his office.

"Jim," Wayne asked, "do you feel it's about time?" Jim had hesitated, because he was afraid he would show emotion, so Smith baptized him privately.

"I got my tie wet," Wayne said. "He wanted that tie. He gave me one back. Not being current with quality merchandise, I was wearing it and was in the drugstore when someone asked me, 'Isn't that a Countess Mara tie you have on?' That was better than the one he got from me."

"Truck drivers know truck drivers," Wayne said. "Bankers know

I Feel Honored to Call Him My Friend

Wayne Smith is a truly unique person. He has always shown a very broad interest in his community by not only tending to his own "flock," but also being very supportive of other congregations.

Wayne is a well-rounded individual (in more ways than one). For example, he worked tirelessly to help his church grow and still found time to keep up with the affairs of the state of Kentucky.

I always enjoyed accompanying him to retirement services for his colleagues. He loved to surprise them and had the best time conducting a friendly "roast." Of course, Wayne (and I) also made time to indulge in the wonderful food prepared by the ladies of the church.

On a more serious note, I admire Wayne for his courage and his strength. He had to overcome injuries sustained in a terrible car accident, and his determination and sense of humor never wavered. I feel very honored and fortunate to be able to call Wayne Smith a friend.

— *Martha Layne Collins, Governor of the*
Commonwealth of Kentucky, 1983-1987

bankers." Southland's membership roll contains a cross section of central Kentucky, ranging all the way up to the governor's mansion.

In the 1980s, Wayne received a phone call from former Gov. Julian M. Carroll: "I have a friend who's a great singer. Can you use him at Southland?"

Southland Christian Church is the second-largest Christian Church in the state, with another 50,000 watching on television. "He came and did a good job," Wayne said, "and I saw to it that he got some money." Said, Wayne, "I paid him out of my own pocket and waited until someone gave me money and repaid myself."

John Y. Brown Jr., who followed Carroll in the governor's office, asked Carroll to be a spokesman against drugs. Smith wanted Carroll to speak at Southland, but several elders were opposed, citing instances of corruption in Carroll's administration.

Elder Joe McKinney settled the matter: "Men, it's my understanding Julian Carroll is a Christian. If we fail to ask him to come, we'll be questioning the work of the Holy Spirit." Carroll came and was well received.

When word came to Wayne that Carroll might be changing churches, Smith made an appointment and drove to Frankfort. "Wayne," said the governor, "you may not know it, but I'm charismatic."

"The longer I talked to him," Wayne said later, "I told him, 'You'll probably not enjoy our church.' " Carroll found another church, but he was a frequent visitor to Southland's Easter and Christmas programs.

Brown, governor of Kentucky from 1979 to 1983, said, "We went to our church in Louisville before we moved. In 1979, when we came to Lexington, everybody said that Wayne Smith was the best minister in town, so Phyllis and I started going to Southland.

"I've always tried to search out a church that had a message," Brown said. "I felt like I would hear something special every Sunday. What you like to get out of church is a lesson that you can use in everyday life. Every Sunday he was on target."

It is not only Smith's preaching that reaches men like Brown. "He is such a good motivator," said the former governor. "So warm, so engaging, and so giving. The community loves him."

Brown flew Wayne to meetings with him in Owensboro, Paducah and Maysville and arranged for Smith to meet Norman Vincent Peale when Peale was in Louisville. The governor was so impressed by a sermon Wayne delivered during the Gulf War that he arranged for Smith to speak to the House and then to the Senate in Frankfort. The date was February 14, 1991. The legislators gave Wayne a standing ovation, an honor seldom given to any speaker and rarer still for a minister.

"I think a lot of preachers lack appreciation," Wayne said. "A lot of people don't even recognize when others are being good to them. The very fact that I have felt inadequate, woefully inadequate, has made me so much more grateful for things that have come my way."

Wayne downplays his own ability. "I'm not that great a speaker, and I certainly couldn't run the church by myself. I'm glad I've always had good men."

Wayne says that "faith and good business go hand in hand. If most of your elders have arthritis, you're not going very far. And if a man has never made a decision over a matter costing $300,000 or half a million dollars, he will not take much of a risk. You want people who will take a challenge."

Attorney Jim Ishmael was a faithful attendee and a man of ability, and his name surfaced again and again as a nominee for deacon. The football stadium at Lafayette High School is named for his father.

Jim was a lifelong Democrat, a member of the American Civil Liberties Union, and a firm advocate of individual rights.

"Everybody knew my feelings about the ACLU," Wayne said. "It's an organization with noble goals that has been kidnapped by the left."

Finally, near the end of a long discussion at an elders meeting, Dr. George Park, an elder and a cardiologist whose father was a professor at Eastern Kentucky University, spoke in favor of Jim. "Men," he said, "if we're going to hold back Jim Ishmael because he's a member of the ACLU, then we can't put any Democrats on the board, either. In some areas, their views are similar."

That ended the discussion. Ishmael was nominated and elected, and he resigned from the ACLU the following week. He served as a deacon and elder with distinction.

Friendship with the legal profession is no shield from Smith's humor. "Did you hear about the woman who was dying and sent for two lawyers?" he asked. "They came to her bedside and just stood there, one on each side of the bed. Finally, one of them asked, 'What do you want us to do?' 'Nothing,' she replied. 'I just wanted to die like Jesus, between two thieves.' "

Mention the name Jim Host to anyone in Lexington and they know who you're talking about. Raised in Ashland, W. James Host came to UK on a full baseball scholarship — the first in history to do so — and was moving up in the White Sox organization when an injury ended his athletic career.

He sold soap for Procter and Gamble — very successfully — then moved back to Lexington and started an insurance and real-estate business. Crain, Hardwick and Host quickly became one of the largest insurance agencies in the city.

When Louie Nunn ran for governor in 1967, he recruited Host, and after the election Governor Nunn appointed him commissioner of the Department of Public Information. At 30, Jim Host was the youngest member of Nunn's cabinet. Appointed Kentucky's commissioner of parks, Host developed the Kentucky Horse Park, one of the commonwealth's most popular attractions.

Defeated in a race for lieutenant governor, Host returned to Lexington with $107 in the bank, campaign debts of $77,887, no job, two car payments, a wife and two children.

"I didn't tell anybody, not even my wife, how bad off we were," he said.

The next day Jim went to Ray Tuttle, his barber, negotiated the use of an apartment above the barbershop as an office, and started over. Jim Shropshire, former cabinet member in Nunn's administration and a fraternity brother, contacted Host and offered him $1,000 to help

Words From Wayne

*We can provide the vehicles for involvement,
but you've got to get onboard.*

him get under way. Rather than accept the gift, Host said, "Jim, I will make you my first shareholder in a company I'm going to call Jim Host and Associates."

That was January 1972.

Today, Host Communications Inc. ranks among the top affinity and sports marketing companies in the world, managing CrossSphere (formerly the National Tour Association), producing more than 150 NCAA publications, marketing collegiate and high-school athletics, and offering clients top-of-the-line multimedia services through offices in Lexington, New York City, and across the country.

In 2001 Jim was named "Kentuckian of the Year," an award presented by the A.B. "Happy" Chandler Foundation.

On October 31, 2003, the University of Kentucky School of Journalism and Telecommunications Alumni Association honored Host with the Lifetime Achievement Award.

When Dr. Ernie L. Fletcher was elected governor on November 4, 2003, one of his first appointments was to name Host secretary of commerce for the commonwealth of Kentucky.

Years earlier, Jim and his family were members at Second Presbyterian, where he was chairman of the trustees, chairman of the elders, and chairman of a capital campaign that raised $3 million for the church. He had seen Smith in action at UK athletic events and had heard Wayne preach. He even called on Wayne in the hospital after Wayne's 1985 automobile accident.

Host's first marriage had ended in divorce, and when Jim and Pat were married in 1990, Jim said, "One of the first people we reached out to was Wayne Smith."

Before long Wayne had baptized Jim and Pat and Pat's daughter, Tiffany. On Sundays when Jim and Pat are in Lexington, they are in their places at Southland Christian Church.

Host believes that one of the keys to Wayne's success is Wayne's passion for UK athletics. "He understands the people here," Host said. "He knows what they are thinking about."

Host, himself a well-known speaker, said of Smith, "He had the ability from the pulpit to communicate to the public things they understood and weave it together with a story about what he wanted to get across, whether it was abortion or underage drinking or whatever."

Host told Smith, "I went to Southland for the music. The preaching was secondary."

Wayne gave it right back: "You're too kind."

Athletes and athletics

Not all has been smooth for Wayne Smith. In his "Parson to Person" column in *The Voice of Southland,* March 27, 1964, he wrote,

> Normally there is no preacher in Lexington happier than Wayne Smith, however, I have surely had my share of blue days of late. If our folks don't quit moving out of town I'm going to be out of tears. The news of the moving of Coach Matt Lair and his wife, Helen, to Texas Tech at Lubbock, Tex. is received with sincere remorse. This is a couple we have all grown to know and love. Their attendance in the first service each Sunday was characterized by marked regularity. Matt had a "concern list" of football players at the University and thus, it was his custom to attend first service with his wife and then go to the University and "round up" players and bring them to the 10:30 service. Not many folk would gladly sit through two services in order to recruit people for Christ and His Church. Matt will be remembered by the youth for his sermons in Junior Church. The leaving of the Lairs will not only be a loss to our church but to the football program of the University. Any time a school loses a coach of deep conviction, high principle and sterling character, the best they can do is bring in a substitute. I certainly doubt if he can be replaced.

The following month Wayne was feeling a bit better. The April 24, 1964, *Voice* carried the headline "Bowling Team Tied" with this paragraph:

"Everybody loves a winner, but we are proud of our losers especially since they are our own people. A bowling team made up of Abe Lowry, Alvin Lowry, Harry Brockmeier, Lawrence Souder and Gerald Carman tied for last place in the league with 44 losses and 22 wins. They bowled faithfully each Thursday night for 26 weeks at the Wildcat Lanes. We congratulate this team for their zeal and enthusiasm. We wish them better luck next year."

Smith's memory for sports statistics is phenomenal. His mind registers the little known as well as the more celebrated: for example, that Corinth won the Sweet Sixteen in 1930, that Kentucky "won everything" in 1978.

Incidentally, the Sunday following Kentucky's 1978 triumph was

Preacher Smith Meets Muhammed Ali

Muhammed Ali and I are good friends. I helped him start his museum in Louisville. I helped him write some of his contracts, to be sure he received the kind of money he should be getting. I would go to his dressing room before his fights. I consider him a dear friend.

We had some trouble in Lexington. An officer shot a young black man, and there was unrest. At the request of a friend who worked at the university, I brought Ali in. He walked the streets, visited schools, talked to people, sat on the bench with Rick Pitino. Everything cooled down.

Sunday morning I called and told Wayne I was bringing Ali to church. When Wayne came out on the platform, there was Ali right in front of him. Wayne couldn't say anything; he just kept looking at Ali. Finally, Wayne said, "I can't believe I'm speaking to one of the most famous men in the world."

I love Wayne's enthusiasm. I think I influenced his sermons. When I first started going to Southland, I said to him, "People don't want to hear what's wrong with everything. They want to hear how to live day by day; they want to hear a message that is positive."

I know the kind of work he must have put into his sermons, because every message was special. We were very fortunate at Southland to have him.

— *John Y. Brown Jr., Governor of Kentucky, 1979-1983*

Easter, and when the folks came to church, Smith had the pulpit festooned in UK's blue and white.

"Some churches would have fired the preacher over that," Wayne said laughing.

After Adolph Rupp retired as the legendary head coach of the UK Wildcats, Joe B. Hall (1972-1985) quickly built a legend of his own. Hall had an extraordinary record, averaging 22.8 wins per year, with a winning percentage of 74.8. His teams played in three Final Fours and won an NCAA title, and 23 of his players were drafted by the National Basketball Association.

Hall's winning formula included two banquets each year, both sellouts, one at the beginning of the season to create momentum and motivate and the other an awards banquet at season's end. Hall asked Wayne to emcee one of his early banquets, and for the remainder of Hall's career with the University of Kentucky, Wayne Smith emceed both banquets.

UK's 101 Club commissioned a regulation jersey for Wayne with "UK" on the front, "REV SMITH" and the number 3 on the back. "God first, others second, me last," Wayne explained. Smith's uniform hangs with the other All-American memorabilia in the University of Kentucky Basketball Museum in the Civic Center, adjacent to Rupp Arena in downtown Lexington.

Eddie Sutton followed Hall as head coach of the Wildcats and bought a farm out near the church. Sutton came regularly to Southland during his last year at UK. One Sunday, on his way out of church, he asked Wayne, "Could I talk to you this afternoon?" Wayne drove to Sutton's office in Memorial Coliseum, where the two men talked at length.

"Sometimes when people call you," Wayne said, "what they need is somebody to listen. I was glad Eddie called me." Sutton is now coaching at Oklahoma State, his alma mater.

The preacher makes a match
Wayne has been known to play matchmaker. On one occasion he received a letter from Janey Greene, with a substantial check enclosed. He called her to meet him for lunch.

She turned out to be the daughter of Dr. George G. Greene a highly respected ob-gyn specialist in Lexington. Janey told how during her father's last days, she would sit with him on Sunday mornings while the two of them, lifelong Baptists, tuned in to The Southland Hour.

"I've watched you on television," she said. "I want to be a member of your church."

Janey was divorced and told Wayne about her 17-year-old son. "He's interested in radio and television. Is there anything he can do along that line?"

Wayne introduced her to Pat Moores, the attorney who managed Southland's TV program. Pat had married his high-school sweetheart, but the marriage ended in divorce, and he was now approaching 40.

Janey finished Georgetown College in three years, graduating magna cum laude with a triple major: English, French, and history, yet she could not get a job, because she lacked training in business. Undaunted, Janey started working in an employment agency for $2.10 an hour and, within a year, owned the business.

Guy Colson, Moores' law partner, advised him, "Marry that girl and she will cure every problem you'll ever have." Moores had already made that decision.

Today Janey owns agencies in Frankfort and Georgetown as well as Lexington and is one of the top female executives in the United States. Janey teaches business courses as an adjunct and conducts training seminars across the country.

The *Herald-Leader* did a story on Janey, in which she gave testimony to her faith and to prayer. "Other than saving a soul," she said, "or saving someone medically, the most important way you can help another person is to get him or her a job so that he can support himself and his family."

Pat Moores said, "There have been times I have seen Wayne down at the courthouse, where he would be testifying as a character witness for someone. After his time was over, he would go into every courtroom and listen for a few minutes. This was fascinating to him. I think he's a frustrated lawyer."

Pat's association with Southland began early. "I started going there in

1978 after I came back from Alabama, where I'd been in law school," he said. "I liked to hear Wayne preach, so I'd go to the 9:00 service at Southland, then across town to my church at 11:00. In 1982 I became a part of Southland."

Today Pat has his own law firm, E. Patrick Moores, Attorney-at-Law. Janey and Pat return to Charleston, South Carolina, every year to remember their honeymoon there and always send Smith a card or a note that reads, "Lightning has struck again."

Ministry on many levels

Wayne and Marge share the date of their wedding anniversary, August 28, with Dr. and Mrs. Jack Geren. The Gerens moved from Ohio, where Marilyn played the organ in a Catholic church. She heard Wayne speak at the Kentucky Horse Park for a banquet celebrating Realtors' Week and suggested to her husband that he might like Wayne Smith. Neither Jack nor Marilyn were attending church at the time.

They began coming to Southland and, in the course of time, were baptized. Dr. Geren was on duty at St. Joseph Hospital April 12, 1985, when Wayne was brought in following an automobile accident. Dr. Geren was shocked at the severity of Wayne's injuries, and he followed Smith's recovery during Smith's 29 days in the hospital.

The Gerens now teach a class on marriage. Jack and Marilyn, and Wayne and Marge, regularly celebrate their anniversaries together.

Wayne described his first visit to Dr. Tom Daniel, an oral surgeon. "His home was out on Lakewood Drive, and it looked like a state park," Wayne said. "The maid came to the door. I wasn't accustomed to that, but I sure enjoyed being in that company."

When Smith needed dental care recently, Dr. Daniel provided Wayne with 15 implants. One of the photos taken of Smith at the dedication of the Wayne B. Smith Oratorium at CBS shows Wayne laughing and presents a good view of Smith's now perfect teeth. Wayne sent the photo to Tom with a note complimenting his friend on his fine work.

Reading through the above examples, one could suppose that Smith spent most of his time with the wealthy and prominent. However, the opposite is true. "It's the Cadillacs that get attention," he said, "but there's more Chevrolets."

Who could possibly count the thousands who were touched by his generosity, given time and counsel and money — usually out of his own pocket? Who can tabulate the hours and energy invested in people who were hurting, many with no connection to Southland Christian Church?

"Other people talk about love," said Gino Guarinieri. "With Wayne it is natural." A roomful of people is like a tonic to Smith. Buddy Mossbarger said, "He can walk into a funeral home and liven it up. He's got that laugh. He doesn't mind laughing at himself. He's never met a stranger. He would do anything he could for anyone he thought was in need. He's got a big heart, and that draws people to him."

When Earl Sims was vice president and registrar at Cincinnati Bible College and Seminary, he received a letter from Wayne dated November 30, 1989, which said, "The main purpose of this letter is to ask your blessing on reinstating (name). He was president of the freshman class last year, but then he fell into difficulty with his grades.

"He wants to try again, and I hope you will give your blessing. His father is a bartender, and not able to help much financially, although his parents are excited about his thoughts of becoming a minister."

The boy was given a second chance and went on to achieve his goal. "He became a minister," Wayne said, "and he's a good one."

Bob Russell said of Wayne, "He has a tremendous gift. I was in Frankfort, and Governor Martha Layne Collins was there and several other people, and Wayne wasn't there yet. The governor was talking about Wayne. He was the center of their attention. He's such a colorful personality, yet he is not intimidated in those settings."

Considering Russell's words, Wayne commented, "There've been times I've been a good actor."

"It isn't always that I do what I want to do; I do what I feel I ought to do."

Smith's blood pressure soars when the talk turns to weddings. "Funerals, that's a ministry," he said. "Weddings are something else."

Wayne's first wedding was at Robinson Christian Church, his first ministry. The bride was Bess Landrum, Marge's best friend. This was even before his own wedding, so Wayne was nervous. Two railroad tracks run past the church building, and just as Mr. Landrum was to give Bessie away, a train went by. Landrum was so deaf that he probably did not hear the train, let alone the preacher.

"I took my hand and pushed him back toward his seat," Wayne said grimly, then added, "It was a nice wedding."

That may have been Wayne's last to be so described. Weddings were on Saturday night, when he prepared his sermon. Weddings required time, lots of it. Weddings were unpredictable, which threatened Smith's perfectionism.

"I've had less than five rehearsals in 54 years that started on time," he snorted. "Someone's not there, and you can't start till the last one straggles in. There's two mothers, both of them fussing over the bride, and they know how they want it done.

"Then you go out to eat. Some preachers don't do this, but you can't fellowship unless you go eat with them."

There's more.

"Many are divorced. Father of the bride can't sit on the second row. He's not married to the mother anymore.

"The ceremony never starts when it's supposed to. They're all out in the vestibule talking. I had one bride — 31 years old and should have known better. I asked, 'Where is she?' They said, 'Out on Harrodsburg Road picking more greenery for her bouquet.'

"Wedding photographers — some are fine. Others? I don't think they'll be saved. They take 150 pictures, and here's all the guests waiting to cut the cake. I had one photographer climb on the Communion table to get a picture.

"The worst are the little kids. Crying. Or afraid. But the grandparents want them in the wedding. It really is a distraction. I've had three weddings where the people didn't show. They forgot to call me and say it was canceled. I had one where they wouldn't kiss. The marriage lasted a month."

A wedding to remember

Gino Guarnieri's first contact with Southland was at a Keystone Class meeting at one member's apartment. The couple had tried another church in town, but a staff minister there had informed Gino that he and his family were going to hell because they were Roman Catholics.

Gino contrasted that with his experience at Southland. "Wayne is such a good example. He draws rather than pushes people," he said.

Gino's father was a tailor and had come from Italy to Cincinnati, then to Lexington, where he felt there was less competition. In Lexington, Mr. Guarnieri bought a few tuxedos and began renting them for formal occasions. The old man, a devout Catholic, would tell Wayne, "You're a gooda priesta."

Gino had no interest in becoming a tailor, so he asked his father if he could take over the rental part of the business. Today, Geno's Formal Affair is the largest supplier of formal wear in the United States.

So it was natural for Gino to supply the garb for the biggest wedding Wayne ever had, the marriage of Gordon Walls and Karen Rogers. "There were 27 people on the platform," said Wayne, "600 in the audience. Cars up and down Hill 'N Dale and the side streets."

Gordon and his groomsmen were downstairs a few minutes before the ceremony and Walls said to Smith, "Wayne, you're more nervous than I am." What Gordon did not know was that Wayne had just hung up the phone and that the caller had told the preacher that a bomb was set to go off at 8:00 p.m. The ceremony began at 7:30.

Wayne passed the word to a staff member, with instructions to say nothing to the wedding party, though he did tell Duane, Karen's father. Duane Rogers was a highly successful automobile dealer. He said to Wayne, "Let's go on with it, but get us out of here by eight o'clock."

Wayne's ceremony set a record for brevity. The minute the formalities were completed, Smith stopped the proceedings, cutting off a guitarist in the middle of his solo: "Folks, we've had an unfortunate phone call and need to evacuate the building immediately."

"He didn't even let us kiss," Gordon complained.

Once outside, the wedding party and guests were astonished to see police cars and fire trucks — they had kept their sirens turned off — and uniforms everywhere.

Walls said, "We have wedding pictures of Karen and me on fire trucks, and our picture still hangs in the fire station."

Standing there looking at his church building, empty except for the bomb squad, Wayne turned to Gino. "Gino," said Smith, "if you don't mind, go back inside and look for that bomb. One less Italian Catholic is no detriment to our community."

Gino loved it. Soon after that, Guarnieri was baptized, and today he is one of Wayne B. Smith's closest friends. Wayne often stops by Gino's business on the way home and leaves Guarnieri a bag of pecan M & M's, which are his favorite.

Wayne has been known to also leave chocolate-covered peanuts in Gino's care: "Here, keep these till tomorrow. Don't tell Marge I'm eating them again."

Comforting those in crisis

When Wayne has a funeral, the occasion is memorable. He spends time with those who knew the deceased and finds out as much as he can, then personalizes his message, including interesting aspects of the person's life some of the family may not know.

His most difficult and possibly most memorable funeral was the service he conducted for his close friend and brother-in-law, Larry Johnson. Sue Johnson and Marge are sisters. After Wayne's opening remarks, he shared several remembrances of his brother-in-law, including the following:

Wayne Does Not Realize the Influence He Has

Wayne B. Smith is one of those unique individuals who touches lives, impacts decisions, provides support and simply leaves a lasting impression without ever knowing he has done so.

I have known Wayne since I was a junior high school student and even then his subtle influence changed my life. So much of what he said has remained with me throughout my life and continues to resonate with me as I sit on the Fayette County Circuit Court bench.

I learned from him that taking the right position is more important than taking the popular one.

Wayne's influence extends far beyond the generations that were privileged to have him as their pastor. Hundreds of those families still are worshipping with their children and grandchildren at Southland Christian Church because of the pastoral care he provided for so many years.

Wayne has a gift for knowing just when and where God needs him to minister. I can recall numerous occasions that he was present in our lives in times that no one else could have made such a difference. He has shared in times of illness as well as in the celebration of marriages and births.

He has been a pillar of strength during professional times of trial and provided comic relief at every opportunity!

His unselfish spirit and seemingly unending energy creates an enthusiasm for life wherever he goes.

I will be forever grateful for the way he has touched my life as a pastor, a mentor and friend.

— Rebecca M. Overstreet, Circuit Judge,
Commonwealth of Kentucky Fayette Circuit Court

"Larry drove fast, I mean fast," Wayne said. "If he were not such a good driver, we'd have been here sooner. Larry drove Sue, Marge, and me to the National Quartet Convention in Louisville. I sat in the front seat. I was scared to death. I started praying in Versailles. I rededicated my life as we passed Frankfort. I felt a second work of grace as we passed Shelbyville, and when we arrived at Freedom Hall in Louisville, I was speaking in tongues."

Wayne spoke of Larry's generosity, then of his impact on Southland.

"Sue and Larry were married in 1959 and gave birth to The Messengers Quartet one year later," Wayne said. "They have been singing 42 years. They sang most Sundays for the remaining 35 years of my ministry at Southland. They inspired me, moved me, and helped us to clap, cry and rejoice. Nothing moved me like The Messengers . . . Whatever I accomplished at this church, I owe a great deal to Larry Johnson, Sue and The Messengers."

Near the close of his message, Wayne quoted Will Rogers, who said, "You can judge the greatness of a man by how much he will be missed." Then Wayne added, "Larry took a big bite out of life. His works were many and will be long remembered. We need not embellish, for he was always larger than life to those who loved him.

"Not much more can be said. We shall huddle by the fire, dry our tears and carry on."

In Larry's funeral, as so often in his sermons, Wayne blended humor, Scripture, tears, Christian assurance and deep faith.

Pat Moores told what Wayne did for his father. "Wayne had an incredible way of reaching people," Pat said. "On the Monday after the Fourth of July in 1994, my dad found out that he had an inoperable brain tumor. I got a call from my mother about 8 in the morning; they had taken Dad to the hospital in the middle of the night. When my mother called, they had just told my dad that he had a tumor and that they could not operate.

"I got to the hospital at 9, and Dad was sitting on the edge of the bed

Words From Wayne

When the horse is dead, get off. Some methods need put to rest.

staring at the wall. He wouldn't talk; he didn't move; he just sat there.

"I'd been there about 30 minutes when my nephew, whom my father had raised, showed up. He was taking it pretty hard. I took him down to the coffee shop to help him get his composure, because I didn't want Dad to be any more upset.

"On the way to the hospital, I had called Ann Nelson, Wayne's secretary, at the church. My nephew and I were out of the room only about 20 minutes, but in that time Wayne had come and gone. I don't know what he said to my dad. I've asked Wayne and he doesn't know. But my dad was sitting up in bed, smiling and talking. He didn't quit till they nailed the lid on him. He died on Labor Day, and he was ready to go. It was amazing the effect Wayne had on him."

Was Smith ever tempted to give up? He often inserted motivational quotations in *The Voice of Southland:* "Henry Ford went bankrupt five times before he found success. We all fail. We all experience depression to some degree. Get up off that couch and say, 'With God's help I'm going to try.' "

Wayne's schedule would exhaust most men. "Sometimes I made a decision on the basis of how I will feel if I don't go. Man alive, late at night to get out of bed and make a hospital call? I didn't want to go, but how will I feel if I don't go?"

He reflected, then added, "The ministry is not a cafeteria where you can take what you want and leave the rest. Some will say, 'That's not in my job description.' What we ought to be saying is 'Nevertheless; not what I want but what you want.' "

Referring to the commitment he made at the campfire at Northward Christian Assembly: "There's never been any doubt. It has kept me going to this day. Psalm 15 talks about the man who 'keeps his oath even when it hurts.' You've got to stick with it. It isn't always that I do what I want to do; I do what I feel I ought to do. Nevertheless."

Preparing for the pulpit and the podium

Wayne constantly had to dig for good material for his sermons at Southland. He disliked writing sermons almost as much as he disliked the routines of administration. The actual preaching? That was different. "I enjoyed it," he said, "but I was nervous. I can't count how many times I got up before dawn on Sunday morning to get the rest of my sermon."

Speaking dates were not much easier. "After 40 years, I had material I could use," he said. "But I had to work it into the message I wanted to give wherever I was speaking. It usually takes me about two or three hours to prepare a talk for a civic club. A Sunday sermon takes nine to 15 hours. A convention sermon — months."

Finding jokes to fit his varied audiences took work of the hardest kind. Speaking to a room filled with engineers at the Hyatt Regency, Smith told them, "Four thousand architects at the bottom of the ocean is a good start." The engineers had their turn when he told a group of architects, "An engineer died and the minister was eulogizing at his funeral: 'We are burying an engineer, a good man.' An architect was heard to say, 'Apparently, they're burying two people in one grave now.' "

For physicians, Smith might use this: "The basement drain in a doctor's house stopped up, and he called a plumber. The plumber was there 20 minutes, then handed the doctor a bill for $600. The doctor said, 'I don't make that kind of money, and I'm a doctor.' The plumber said, 'Neither did I when I was a doctor.' "

"You have to get the feel of an audience," Wayne said. "Banquets are good, because you can eat first and get a feel of the situation. I always make them turn the lights up; I'm not speaking unless the lights are on bright. They've got to see your eyes."

Occasions memorable and otherwise

The Lions Club in Corbin, Kentucky, gave Smith a cool reception. "Usually, the Rotarians own the town, the Kiwanians run the town, and the Lions enjoy the town," Wayne said. "But not this bunch. I opened with some of my best jokes, but they just sat there dead. So I tried a line from Johnny Carson: 'I know you're there; I can hear you breathing.' "

Wayne held a meeting at Minersville Christian Church, Scott County, Kentucky. Some time later, Demory Murphy, an elder, telephoned Wayne. "The Limosin Club is having their annual meeting at the Campbell House. Would you come and speak?"

The Campbell House is one of Lexington's oldest and finest inns. Wayne accepted, unaware that "limosin" is an exotic cross-cattle breed introduced from abroad. "I didn't know until I got there that it wasn't cars."

Not a week went by without a call or calls to come somewhere and speak. Wayne never asked how big the place was or how much he might receive for speaking.

After one engagement in Manhattan, Kansas, Wayne and his companion, Billy Kerr, were eating breakfast in the little airport coffee shop when the pilot came, leaned over their table, and said, "I'm ready when you are."

Wayne flew to Washington state for a conference at Overlake Christian Church in Kirkland.

David Paul Jeremiah spoke Wednesday, Smith spoke Thursday, and David Hocking spoke Friday. "They wanted me to talk an hour," Wayne said. "I was out of my league." He felt better about his class the following day, however.

Worship during the conference was Wayne's first experience with the raising of hands and dancing in the aisles. "I told them, 'I've never been to a church where you had to have a physical before you could join.'"

The other speakers emphasized their journaling and quiet times and spiritual disciplines. Smith confessed that he needed to grow in these areas.

Afterward, those present spoke of Wayne's transparency and warmth and of his evident love for people, in contrast to the more elaborate presentations of the scholars.

Wayne said his biggest laugh came at the Kiamichi Clinic in southeastern Oklahoma in 1977, the year he was president of the North American Christian Convention. In those days, the Kiamichi Clinic drew 5,000 men for several days of rustic accommodations and rousing preaching.

"We drove up this dirt road," Wayne said, "and I explained to McReynolds that I had trouble sleeping. He said he'd take care of me."

A. B. McReynolds was the director of the clinic. He put Smith in the hallway. "It was like trying to sleep in the street. I was tired before I got started," Wayne said.

"The previous speaker had not used notes," said Smith, "so I made a crack about being tied to my notes. About 15 minutes into the message, a gust of wind came through and my notes flew up into the air, the pages separating, some of them over my head, and fluttering down across the front of the big warehouse where we were meeting. I stopped and, like everyone else, watched my sermon until the last page was on the ground. Finally, the laughter ceased, and I said, 'And in conclusion,' and sat down."

Several minutes passed before the presider managed to get the crowd under control.

Wayne and the North American Christian Convention

Aside from that experience, Wayne enjoyed the excitement and inspiration of large gatherings.

"My first North American was Louisville in the old Armory," he said, "1956. I slept in the basement of the Highland Park Christian Church with two other preachers. We each had a cot. It was not a Sunday-school room. It was near the coal furnace. That's the only time I ever heard P.H. Welshimer."

Welshimer was pastor of First Christian Church in Canton, Ohio, at that time the largest Christian Church in the United States.

"That was his last speech," Wayne said, "and his Timothys gave him a plaque. I don't remember his speech, but I remember the plaque." Years later, at his own retirement, the Timothys of Wayne B. Smith would honor him in a similar way.

Wayne had one more observation about Louisville: "That was also the first time I ever ate pizza. I'd never heard of it before."

The convention came to Lexington in 1962. Harold Hockley, minister of Westwood-Cheviot Church of Christ in Cincinnati, was president; Ard

Words From Wayne

*It's not how high you jump; it's how straight you walk
after you hit the ground.*

Hoven, minister at Broadway in Lexington, was in charge of local arrangements. In one of his wisest acts as NACC president, Hockley asked Wayne
to be publicity chairman.

"I really put my heart into it," said Wayne. "It was a tiring, very tiring
job."

Wayne put up signs welcoming attendees, put a banner across North
Broadway near the Christian Church, enlisted the help of all and sundry,
including Kentucky Governor Bert Combs, and the newspapers.

When he approached the city about stretching the banner across
Broadway, he was told he would need a policeman to stop the traffic.

"So I got the police," Wayne said. "While the police were there, someone hit the telephone truck that was putting up the banner. The man who
drove the telephone truck was a faithful member of the church. The company suspended him for 30 days without pay. I felt bad about that."

Wayne had already established a friendship with the editor of *The Lexington Leader*. "I met him because I was a member of the Quarterback
Club," Smith explained.

During their discussions of the coming convention, Smith mentioned
that the main venue would be the Coliseum on the UK campus.

The editor shook his head. "I'm so tempted to write something about
the lions and the Christians in the coliseum. The last time I wrote something like that was when Mordecai Hamm held a temperance meeting
here."

Hamm was the preacher when Billy Graham went forward to commit
his life to Christ.

"I ran an article, 'Hamm on rye,' " the editor said. "The Baptists never
forgave me. So I'm not going to touch the idea of the Christians in the
Coliseum."

Smith advises young preachers, "Make friends with editors. You don't
want to make enemies of people who buy ink by the barrel. You can't
win."

The NACC became a regular part of Smith's ministry. He had just
completed a revival in Ashland, Kentucky, with Royce Robey when he
published this note in his church paper about the upcoming convention

the following year, 1963:

> My return to the labors of Southland Church were made quite enjoyable by the news that our General Board had voted unanimously to send "ye ole preacher" to the North American Christian Convention in Long Beach, California, all expenses paid, and by jet! Honestly folks, words just cannot express my appreciation for this gesture, because deeds like this say something to a preacher more than simply, "We want you to attend the convention." Rest assured I will do all in my power to return to you a better and more informed minister. It goes without saying I shall strive to express my appreciation in terms of service. I have been asked to speak on the convention program Friday afternoon, June 28, on the subject, "Conserving New Members." I am honored by the request and humbled by the decision of our Church Board. Needless to say, a happy preacher will greet you this Sunday.

Following the convention, Smith wanted to go to church in Riverside, where Paul Neal was preaching. Omar "Pokie" Miller, minister at Russell, Kentucky, and his wife, Nina, were also attending the NACC and planned to go to Riverside as well. They had driven to Long Beach. They offered Smith a ride.

This was Wayne's first experience on the California freeways. "They have five lanes going one direction, five lanes going the other direction; 10 lanes in all. Nina was driving and was in the left lane when Pokie said, 'I believe that's our exit.' Nina drove right across all five lanes. I rededicated my life three times before we got to the exit ramp."

Smith was appointed national registration chairman for the Detroit NACC in 1969. Not content with doing only the advance promotion, Wayne enlisted a crew from Southland to accompany him to Detroit for on-site work: Bev Williams, Barb Turner, Betty McKinney and Bobbye Soard. "It was a big undertaking," he said. When the totals were added up, 37,526 people registered, 2,386 of them from Southland Christian Church.

Wayne described his commitment to the NACC: "I really enjoyed the NACC. I love preachers. I always felt like the North American was an oasis in the desert for many preachers. Most don't have choirs like the North American. When you get with 10,000 people at one time, you feel as though there's a lot of us going the same direction."

President of the NACC

Wayne served on the 100 Man Committee, which planned each convention, and was elected president for the 1977 NACC in Cincinnati. His theme was "The Word of God — Forever."

Convention director Leonard G. Wymore said, "Each convention becomes an extension of the personality and commitment of that year's president. His convention took on the personality of Wayne: his humor, yet his ability to be very forthright and serious as well."

W. F. Lown, president of Manhattan (Kansas) Bible College and himself a past president of the NACC, offered this evaluation in the August 28, 1977, *Christian Standard*: "In his keynote presidential message he harkened back to the Biblical record and its divine injunction: 'preach the word,' that sacred sacrament by which Almighty God called (and calls) His church into existence and by which he sustains her."

Wayne's sermon was a bit more pointed than Lown's ecclesiastical encomium.

"Whatever happened to preaching?" Wayne asked. He quoted Billy Sunday, the famous ballplayer who became an evangelist and who had died 42 years earlier: "A group of men went to Chicago to consult with Billy Sunday. They went to the seventh floor of his hotel. They knocked on the door. He asked why they came. They said, 'We want to know about your preaching. What gives power to your preaching?'

Thankful for Wayne's Encouragement

Wayne Smith has been and continues to be an inspiration to me. I shall always be thankful for his encouragement, advice and friendship. I respect and love him for what he is.

— Mark Jones, former Senior Minister,
First Christian Church, Columbus, Indiana, now
planting a new church in Bluffton, South Carolina

"He said little before he walked over to the window, looked down seven floors, called the men over to look. They looked down and saw the people walking to and fro on the sidewalk, and all that Billy Sunday said were these words: 'They are going to hell. They are going to hell.' "

Wayne used illustration after illustration, piling on evidence of the importance of preaching, challenging his audience to renewed energy and dedication to this God-given task.

He told of his years at Western Hills High School, of failing algebra and geometry and Latin, and of going to summer school to pass the first two.

Then, "Let me tell you, my brother, I do not glory in my poor academic record. But I'll tell you this — I wanted to preach. I had a weakness and the Lord had a strength, and we teamed up. How much do you want to preach?"

He spoke of Marian Anderson, the singer, who practiced eight hours a day. He referred to John Pierce, who was in the audience, "who broke every field goal record at the University of Kentucky. When he broke the last one, he was in our pulpit the following Sunday, and I said, 'How did you do it, John?' And he said, 'That week I kicked 3,000 balls.' "

Wayne spoke of Olympic star Bill Bradley, "one of the greatest basketball players that ever put on a uniform. Someone said to him, 'I wish I could shoot a basket like you,' and Bradley said, 'Would you stay in one place until you hit 24 consecutive baskets?' "

Challenging our colleges to provide practice rooms for preaching just as they provide practice rooms for voice and piano, Wayne told of his own early days.

"In the Delhi Church of Christ — my home church — every week of my life I preached my sermon to those empty pews over and over and over."

He reminded his hearers of church history: "Notice the place of preach-

Words From Wayne

A cross is "I" crossed out; it's no longer me,
but it's Christ living in me.

ing in the early church — its history began with a sermon; the New Testament church moved across the pagan Roman Empire on the wings of preaching. The first martyr was a preacher. Gentiles were ushered into the Kingdom through preaching."

But more than method, it was the content that stirred Wayne: "I lay no claim to scholarship, but I'll tell you this — that the bedrock bottom foundation, the heart and the soul and the substance of the message of the apostles was the Son of God: crucified, buried, resurrected, ascended on high, reigning, returning, rewarding Redeemer."

Here, as elsewhere, his message was often interrupted by applause.

He closed with this verse:

Preach the Gospel, brother, preach it;
Put it high, where men can teach it;
Put it low, where men can reach it;
But preach the Gospel, brother, preach it.

The convention reflected Wayne's generosity as well as his conviction. On Tuesday evening, gifts were presented to missionaries; on Wednesday to those serving in our colleges; on Thursday, to officers and committee members of the convention itself; and on Friday, to those leading in the Christian service camp movement.

What was it like to be president? "Well, it was certainly a great honor," Wayne said. "I spoke in 22 states. It could have been more; you go where you want to go. I was pleasantly surprised that when you went to a place, they respected you, but it wasn't like, 'Here's the bishop,' and I appreciated that.

"I thought the convention went well," Wayne said. "I threatened the fellows if they spoke over 30 minutes. Only one went over. I had a different emcee every night; Dr. Hoven was emcee closing night. He said, 'Let us stand for prayer,' and Baltimore Taylor had the prayer. He prayed 11 minutes."

After the convention ended, Smith took the NACC office staff to the Wigwam Restaurant, one of Cincinnati's best. "The convention staff treated me good," he said. "I wanted to show them I was appreciative."

The convention has a personal meaning for Smith. For years, during every convention, he, by himself, climbs to the top tier of seats in the convention arena during a time when the huge room is empty. There he gets down on the concrete on his hands and knees and expresses his gratitude to God.

"Thank you, God, for another year in the ministry. Thank you for preserving my life. Thank you for preserving my church. Thank you for preserving my family. Thank you most of all for giving me one more year to serve you in the ministry."

Wiping away the tears, Smith gets up, goes back down to the main level, and mingles again with the unsuspecting crowds.

"I never said I was the smartest, but I figured I could outwork about anybody."

I n 1945 Wayne's Latin teacher at Hughes High School, Miss Gladys H. Busch, sent this note to Lillie B. Smith: "That nice boy of yours is at last really getting to work. Only during this week has he begun to understand what we are trying to do, and so I am hoping that this next report will be passing and that it, together with his exam grade, will pull him through. Wayne is not dull but he is certainly my 'youngest.' He is trying awfully hard right now to stop the fooling around and to begin really to think. I am beginning to have hopes."

Though Wayne was failing the class, Miss Busch promised that if he passed the final, she would give him credit for the whole year. "I got 67," he said. "Passing was 70. I told her I wasn't going to be a priest and didn't need Latin anyway."

Though her hopes were not realized, Gladys Busch's words give a preview of the man: outgoing personality, indifferent student, capable of intense effort.

Determined to compensate by hard work

"I tried to make up in work for what I lacked mentally," Wayne said. "I like the story of the man explaining to a friend about his days in college. He said, 'I may not have been in the top half of my class, but I was in the half that made the top half possible.' "

Early in life, Wayne showed the drive that contributed to his success, whether selling tickets to church dinners or gathering scrap iron for the war effort. As a college student, while taking a full load of classes, delivering dry cleaning after school and preaching every weekend, he became business manager for the *Nautilus*, the school annual.

Wayne is a natural salesman, and his job was selling ads in the *Nautilus* to churches and businesses. Smith's record still stands. That year's *Nautilus* nearly became all ads. Wayne sold so many pages of advertising that he had to return some of his clients' money and cancel their contracts.

Woodrow W. Perry was president of Cincinnati Bible Seminary at the time, and Wayne said, "My best one was from Cincinnati's largest Oldsmobile dealer. I found out where President Perry bought his car — Columbia Oldsmobile — and gently suggested that the purchase of a full-page ad might curry favor with the head man when he needed future transportation."

Since boyhood, Wayne has felt that he lacked the talents others had, and he worked to compensate.

"We're not equal," he said "Some have five talents. Some have two. I always felt some intimidation about my academic qualities. But if the Moonies and the cults can do it, as little as they know about the Word, I certainly could do it. I learned that God keeps his promise: If we plant and if we water, he will give the increase."

His secretary described her boss

Ann Nelson, Wayne's secretary for his last 17 years at Southland, described his work habits this way:

"He was always here. I never could beat him.

"By the time I would get here at nine, he would have a list of things for me to do. He would write letters by hand, then give them to me to type.

"He opened his own mail, set his own schedule. His door was, for the most part, always open.

"But he liked for me to make phone calls for him," Ann said. "One morning he had a list of 25 names — he usually gave me the numbers, too. He started dictating letters and got through three or four when he asked me, 'Did you get Buddy Mossbarger yet?' 'Wayne,' I told him, 'I have never moved from this chair.' "

Wayne expected excellence. "I learned the hard way," Ann said. "He came in one day — I had just started; this was 1979 — he brought a half-

Words From Wayne

*Your attitude determines your altitude, and
your outlook determines your outcome.*

sheet of paper with a note written on it, and he said to send this to so and so. I looked up the address, put it in an envelope, and sent it out.

"A few days later he asked me, 'Did you send my note on that half-piece of paper?' 'Well,' I said, 'you just handed it to me.'

"He was emphatic," Ann said. "He told me, 'I always want my things typed; nobody can read my writing.' I remember one letter he revised 12 times. In between taking his calls, he wrote the *Voice*, all of it. Monday was a terrible day. As we added staff, we'd have the staff do their columns, and it was better. He would go to the printer and lay it out himself.

"Every day he made calls; always two or three he needed to see during the day; probably that many coming to the office to see him, some he initiated, some who'd drop by.

"If he'd get involved in a cause — Sunday closing, liquor sales, the building at CBC&S — he would have a lot of things for me to do. 'I need you to call these 50 people and tell them to be at a certain place next week.'

"It was amazing. He would always come back at the end of the day and check and see what I had accomplished. I would really hustle to make all that happen for him.

"He would say, 'Order flowers for so and so's funeral.' I found out about a year into my job that he was calling the florist to see if I'd ordered the flowers. I talked to him about it, and he stopped doing that. Sometimes he'd give three people the same project, counting on one of them to see it through."

Wayne always made a morning inspection on Sundays. Coat closets and bathrooms had to be spotless, flowers had to be fresh, pew pencils sharpened. Wayne apologized: "I was too much of a hands-on guy. I'd give someone a job and then keep at him and see that he did it, and if he didn't, then I'd do it myself."

Wayne asks more of himself than he does of others. September 1, 1988, was a typical day. Midmorning, Ann asked him, "How do you do it? How can you keep this pace?"

"I don't know," Wayne replied, catching his breath. "But I have an idea that one of these days it will all end abruptly." He continued: "It's hard to slow down. Where do you stop? Where do you say no? We only go through here once."

With that he was out the door to speak at a luncheon, then to the funeral home, then to Louisville for a meeting, then to Salem, Indiana, to speak that evening.

Tomorrow there would be two funerals, a staff luncheon, a dinner meeting, plus the calls that would be sandwiched between.

The preacher designed his office for efficiency

Working in his tiny office in that first building at Southland, Wayne developed a system that he used for the next 40 years. He divided his office: an outer section with desk, chair, a few books and knick-knacks where he met people for counseling and other appointments; a smaller section behind a room divider with his "working desk," papers, notes, the blue sheets with appointments, books piled on the desk and across the floor — and woe to the custodian who moved one scrap of paper.

"He was so full of energy," Ann said. "It was always 20 projects at the same time: community projects, the college, other things. I would have a file on this one and a file on that one; it was hard to keep them straight. He went to so many of their meetings, too."

Southland's new building gave Smith the opportunity to design better accommodations. Ann's office was just outside his door. His outer office was larger than the old place on Hill 'N Dale: a desk, comfortable chairs, a table and several books.

Wayne would take visitors into Roy's office with its books wall to wall, then show them the six or seven books on his side table. "See," Wayne would say, "it doesn't take all those books to preach."

Smith's outer office matched what visitors might expect of the senior minister's office in a church the size of Southland. His inner sanctum was another world. Somewhere under the pile lay Wayne's work desk. Three

Words From Wayne

I've always thought that some people have two speeds:
here he comes and there he goes.

wide shelves protruded from the wall behind it, laden with a dozen or so blue plastic tote tubs squatting side by side, giving the place a Wal-Mart look.

"He sent me to Gold Circle to get plastic storage containers," Ann said. "Then I made labels: one for weddings, one for funerals, one for the NACC and so on. After he was finished with a project, I made a new label. Sometimes he would pick up a tub and take it home with him, or if he were going someplace."

Ann continued: "A preacher called one day and said he heard Brother Smith mention his filing system and wanted to know where to buy one. I told him to go to Gold Circle or Kmart and get these Rubbermaid storage boxes and put a label on each one. He asked me, 'Are you sure that's all there is to it?' "

One wall of Wayne's inner office was plastered with notes taped or tacked haphazardly in place, to be removed when the matter was finished. Every day, new ones appeared, Smith's two- or three-word scrawl serving as a reminder of the task to be done.

Expecting much of himself and others

Roy Mays III said of Wayne, "He never asked anyone to do anything he had not already done himself or was going to do by next week. He led; he always led."

"Three words make the difference," Wayne said. "James Byrnes, FDR's secretary of state said them. Employees that do what is required — *and then some*. People who can be counted on in an emergency — *and then some*. I don't think people were impressed by my preaching, but I tried to go that extra mile to cover up what I lacked."

Those close to Smith were intensely loyal. His secretaries stayed with him; his leaders stayed with him; his staff stayed with him. Even so, the occasional problem arose.

"Ask my daughter about the maddest she ever saw me," Wayne said. "We had an intern, and he had agreed to go calling with me on Monday night. He called and said he was going to play tennis with the youth minister. I went berserk. Berserk. 'You came here to work. If I call, you're going to call.' I jumped on the youth minister: 'If I were to tell the elders, you'd both be gone.' "

Maurice Howard was on staff in the 1970s. Wayne was out of town when a death occurred, and Maurice went to call. Finding nobody home, Maurice wrote a note on his business card saying he would return later. When Smith learned of it, he was indignant. "Maurice," he said firmly, "when someone dies and you're calling on the family, you don't leave a note. You *find* them."

Wayne recalled another situation. "One time I was having trouble with two of my staff at the same time. They were popular — the people liked them — but they weren't putting out. I talked to Jim Whalen about it. Jim was an elder and CEO of General Telephone. Jim told me, 'The cure could be worse than the curse.'

"So I went to Myrtle Beach alone. Kicked the sand. Prayed about it. Thought about what he said: 'The cure could be worse than the curse.' So I kept them. Eventually, they left, and all was well."

Smith's humor was always close to the surface. Referring to Scripture, he said, "When the apostle Paul said rejoice in all things, he never had a church bus or tried to run a church camp."

Standing for the truth with uncommon wisdom

Whit Criswell said of Wayne, "He has the most common sense, the most wisdom. I have watched how he created unity, what wars he picked to try to win, what ones he just let go.

"Wayne has always been intimidated by those he considers above him," Criswell said. "He told me about his first lawyer, about his first doctor. But he wanted them. He told me, 'We'd get the first one, and the others would come.'

"I've heard him say to people, 'You don't really want to come to our church. We don't let women lead as much as your wife gets to do in that church. Your preacher preaches good sermons.' I think it's this transparency," Whit said, "which moves people, which makes them want to connect with him."

Criswell described his early days with Wayne. "It was like <u>Driving</u>

<u>Miss</u> <u>Daisy</u>. He took me with him when he went to speak. He knew all the eating places on the country roads. We hardly ever took the interstate. He took me to visit people in the hospitals, in jails. I enjoy doing that now because of the way he showed me then. We went to so many small churches. Being faithful in little things — I picked that up from him."

Smith the Motivator

I first became aware of Wayne when he took over a small church in Harrison County. Wayne was a human dynamo, and his dedication to serve gained him statewide recognition. He had a personality and a sense of commitment that would have led him to greatness in many fields of endeavor. His sincerity and religious convictions were never questioned.

In my mind, he is the finest public speaker ever to stand in a pulpit. He is the only person I know who can make you laugh and cry within the same story.

I have called on him many times to give a charge to the Kentucky basketball team. His message was always well directed and most helpful, but always with an entertaining style. That style sets him apart — all alone in first place.

He was always willing to contribute his time as a Wildcat banquet speaker or to serve as emcee. His contributions were perfect for the occasion.

Wayne is a friend when you need companionship, a counselor when you need advice, a listener when you need support and the provider of just the right joke or anecdote when you need a good laugh.

As a minister, he is the best.

— *Joe B. Hall, legendary coach of the*
Kentucky Wildcats, 1972-1985

"I'm not really a very good caller," Wayne said. "But I enjoy it. I go the first time, and if they want to get very deep, I'd send Earl Swank or somebody else. But the initial call, to go and view the spiritual landscape, that's me."

He said, "When people ask me about baptism, I tell them, 'Jesus walked 70 miles to be baptized, and he was perfect. He did it for an example for us.' "

Wayne reflected a moment, then added, "We ask the wrong question. Instead of asking, 'Have you been baptized?' we ought to ask, 'Have you accepted Christ?' and take it from there."

Few people came forward at Southland Christian Church whom Wayne did not already know. He had already been in their homes and had already talked to them about Christ and about the church.

"I just don't know how you can do it outside the home," Wayne said. "Jesus said go out to the highways and hedges and compel them to come in. I quit buying medicine at CVS, even though I saved money. I'd rather go into a place called the Pharmacy Shop. When I walk in they say, 'Good to see you, Brother Smith.' That's why when Southland was running 4,000, I went out in the audience and shook hands. People are honored if you know their name."

Bad weather was no deterrent. "I always liked to go when it was rough," said Smith. "I remember one night I called on the Summers family on Barkley Drive; the snow was deep. He said to me, 'We were not planning to change churches, but if you'd come out on a night like this, next Sunday we're going to place our membership.' "

Wayne's unflinching stand on doctrine and on social issues turned some away. "I had a man who was in the House of Representatives, and he wanted to come to Southland. I went to see them, and his wife persisted on the subject of baptism. When I said that we practice immersion, the visit soon ended.

Words From Wayne

If it doesn't cost, it doesn't count.
The service that counts is the service that costs.

"If you get people coming to your church, and they love it, then they'll do what they need to do. It's like falling in love. Get them to love the Lord and love the church. Then you can get to the other issues," Wayne said.

Dr. George Park and his wife went to another variety of the Christian Church before they started coming to Southland. Park told Smith, "Peggy and I love Southland. We didn't realize we were in the wrong church until it was too late."

People first, not numbers

Wayne is a competitor, competing most of all against himself. He remembers attendance figures and numbers of baptisms from years back. That may explain the sign in his office: "If you're not the lead dog, the scenery never changes."

He said, "I wasn't going to be embarrassed by this year's attendance being less than last year's."

Most of all he remembers people.

"He remembers names," Ann said. "Where they lived, when they joined the church, how he met them. Twenty years later, he can recall how he married them, buried their mother, saw them in the hospital."

Because he spends so much time in the car, Wayne listens to tapes, replaying some passages over and over, absorbing the content, hearing the phrasing, dissecting the style, the message.

As a young preacher, he always practiced his sermons, and even today, he will sit at his desk rehearsing and practicing, correcting his manuscript, working to get the words and timing just right.

He can watch Shelby Foote on cable, and the next day, quote entire sections from the program. "I would rather listen to something like that, oral history, than the regular channels."

For his 35th anniversary with the church, Southland's elders, led by chairmen Dick Veinot and Butch Locklar, sent Wayne and Marge on a cruise to Alaska with Charles Stanley. The elders were thinking "*reward*," but they were also thinking "*rest*." One of the board's perennial problems was how to keep Smith from doing too much.

What kind of man is Wayne B. Smith? Jim Warren, *Herald-Leader* staff writer, described Smith in a 1989 article entitled "Pastor of Ceremonies." "He is a warm and friendly man who preaches love, disarms his critics with a smile, specializes in building up people and always seems to be there when his parishioners need him."

Warren went on to say, "He's a traditionalist and a modernist, a builder and a battler. He laughs much but also is easily moved to tears. Somehow all the parts work."

The article featured four color photos, including a large picture of Wayne singing, prompting Brewster McLeod to tell his boss, "You're a hypocrite. They show you holding a songbook, and you can't sing a lick. They show you hugging a kid, and you never spend time with the youth."

Smith likes the joke even better than the article and has retold McLeod's words again and again.

Brewster also described going into the church building one Saturday night after 11:00 and finding Smith, armed with Diet Coke and chocolate-covered peanuts, working on his sermon.

"I know it will be fresh," Wayne said. "I want it to be good."

"I forgot a funeral."

One of Wayne's first funerals was held at Smith and Rees' Funeral Home in Cynthiana, but the burial was to be in Berry. In those days, the minister preceded the cortege. After the service, Wayne saw the body safely into the hearse, then got into his car and headed toward the burial plot.

Wayne in the lead, his mind on his graveside remarks, came to Cynthiana's main intersection. Immediately, a traffic cop stopped him.

"Are you in this funeral?" the officer asked.

"Sir, I'm leading it," Wayne responded.

"Then you're leading it the wrong way."

This wasn't the last time over the past 50 years that Smith has had to reverse himself.

The trustees of Wayne's alma mater made a decision Smith disliked, and Wayne called H. David Hale, president and CEO of First Capital Bank in Louisville and the chairman of the board of trustees of Cincinnati Bible College and Seminary.

"David, I want to register my disagreement with the decision you men made in regard to. . ."

When Smith finally ran down, Hale explained the course of action taken by the trustees and the steps leading up to that decision.

"Then I was wrong," Wayne admitted and promptly apologized.

Open to his own weaknesses

Bob Russell said of Wayne, "He is so totally human. There's no pretense with him. That's why people love him."

Wayne described a meal at one home: country ham, turkey and dressing, seven-layer salad, noodles, green beans, mashed potatoes, broccoli casserole, macaroni and cheese, sweet potatoes, baked pineapple with pears, peas, homemade rolls, tea, banana pudding and birthday cake.

Left: "Billy Kerr is one of the dearest friends I've ever had. Billy was a partner with Kerr Brothers Funeral Home. He and Wilma gave new meaning to generosity. I just love the sign he's holding."

Above: "One acre of Holy ground. . . purchased by Broadway Christian Church in 1955."

Right: "Not everything has worked as planned. A couple of broken pot belly stoves at a church in Grant County — where I was for two years while also preaching at Unity — were a real headache for Deacon Eugene Ogden and the rest of us."

Above: "Mike Breaux brings a word of greeting to the crowd and thanks to Marge and me at my final service. Mike was called from the Canyon Ridge Christian Church in Las Vegas to follow me as Senior Minister. He served 7 1/2 years and was followed by Jon Weece."

Left: "Andy Carter of the Lexington Police, First Security Bank's Jim Powell and Larry Long of the FBI offer some help during a major fund drive."

"I spoke at the Capital City Christian Church in Frankfort for an Easter sunrise service in 1974. . . just days after a tornado destroyed the church."

Left: "When an aborted baby was found at a sewage plant, the coroner called me to conduct a funeral. There were only three present, but the coroner, undertaker and I believed that God knew this little one before she was born."

Right: "To celebrate my 20th year at Southland, I was given this 1976 Cadillac. Marge and the girls got a refrigerator, bicycles and jewelry."

Left: "President Keith Keeran of the Kentucky Christian College, and Bob Russell, Senior Minister of Southeast Christian Church in Louisville, in May of 2000 at the dedication of the building named the Wayne B. Smith Center for Christian Leadership. Bob noted it says Leadership not Scholarship."

"A view from above... of Southland Christian Church in Lexington, Ky."

Above left: "Wayne Spangler and Jack Ballard are two of my best *older* minister friends."
Above right: "UK Dental School Graduation. They asked me to speak for 14 minutes. . . and I did.
Me finishing in 14 minutes, now that's quite the accomplishment."

Left: "The Messenger's Quartet
performs in 1995 on the last
Sunday of my ministry.
Members of the group are:
(left to right) Wally Schmidt,
Larry Johnson, Roger Wellman
and Ron Beckett. Larry and
Ron have since graduated to
the heavenly chorus."

Right: "More than
8,000 attended
our Easter service
at Rupp Arena
in 1995."

Above: "A crowd of 7,000 gathered for my last service. It was pretty overwhelming and I have not forgotten the wonderful Southland people and our Lord that made a dream become a reality."

Left: "No company has been closer to me than KFC and great store owners Carol and John Rasmussen."

Right: "Barry Cameron and I standing in front of the new 12 Million Crossroads Church in Grand Prairie, Texas, on Grand Dedication Day (July 18, 2004). Barry is Senior Minister and I was the dedication speaker."

Below: "Actor Macaulay Culkin came to Lexington to visit then-Kentucky coach Rick Pitino's sons. All the gyms on campus were occupied. They called Southland Church and we were glad for them to use our facilities."

Above: "My good friends at Donut Days are (right to left) Neill and Cathy Day (the owners) plus Katie and Trish."

Left: "Jon Weece became Senior Minister at Southland in 2003. The good work continues."
Below: "Good friends at the Blue Room at UK (left to right) are Tommy Bell, me, Dr. Otis Singletary and Roy Mays III."

"Two couples that have certainly gone the extra mile for my family and me
are Len and Ann Aldridge (left) and Claudette and Roy Switzer."

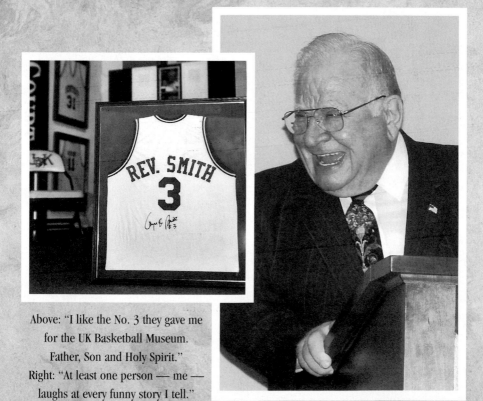

Above: "I like the No. 3 they gave me
for the UK Basketball Museum.
Father, Son and Holy Spirit."
Right: "At least one person — me —
laughs at every funny story I tell."

Left: "Legendary basketball coach John Wooden and I had a chance to be speakers for an event in Louisville in 1995."
Below: "Frank Anderson took many photos for Southland and the *Herald-Leader* during my Southland years."

Above: "Governor Ernie Fletcher asked me to have prayer at midnight of his inauguration and the next day in 2004."
Right: "I guess you could say this guy (Muhammad Ali) added a little punch to a service at Southland in 1995."

Then he added, "That's why I'm fat. It's an occupational hazard."

Chuck McNeely described a time when Smith was speaking at St. Louis Christian College and Chuck's daughter, Shannon, was a student there. McNeely also was on the program, and he had brought his wife, Jane, with him so they could spend time with their daughter.

As a part of a college assignment, Shannon had to do an interview. She asked her dad, "Do you think there's any way I could interview Mr. Smith?"

Shannon had seen Wayne on the platform at the North American Christian Convention and had read about the big church in Lexington where he preached, but she had never met the man.

"Sure," Chuck said. "Ask him."

After speaking twice, after meeting and talking with students and faculty all day, Wayne invited Shannon and her parents to his room that night and spent two hours answering her questions, at times serious, at times laughing and making her laugh.

She had her interview.

"Because of Wayne," said Chuck, "her opinion of notable preachers is high."

Years later, McNeely resigned as president of Lincoln Christian College. Wayne was one of the first to phone condolences, telling Chuck, "Some time ago I was involved in asking a college president to step down, and I'm still not convinced we did the right thing. I feel for you."

When he's wrong, he admits it

During his Palm Sunday sermon, preaching on the crucifixion, Smith talked about Jesus' bones being broken. Roger and Wayne Wellman's parents were visiting from Ashland. On the way home, Mr. Wellman said to his wife, Doris, "I don't believe Christ's bones were broken." She responded, "If Wayne Smith said they were broken, they were broken."

Hearing about this, Wayne laughed. "Every preacher needs a Mrs.

Words From Wayne

There are some things in life you can't change.

Wellman. She always sides with her minister."

During the following week, Leonard Delautre, retired Methodist preacher, called Wayne. "You probably know by now you made a mistake," he said. "Tell them next Sunday you knew it was a mistake but wanted to see if they were paying any attention."

Easter Sunday, to a full house, Wayne apologized for his mistake.

Probably the best-known and most often quoted statement from Smith is his line "When better sermons are written, I will preach them."

Well into his sermon during Southland's first service one Sunday morning, following his manuscript as he usually did, Wayne stopped abruptly. "I don't believe that," he said to the audience, then repeated the offending sentence: "If it flows, it's of the Spirit. If it doesn't, it's not God's will."

His voice grew firm. "That looks good on paper, but it's not true. Have you ever been to a zoning meeting? A zoning meeting doesn't flow. Satan will dog you every step of the way."

Recovering, he went on and finished the sermon, resolving to be more careful about his material next time. The troublesome sentence was deleted during the second service that morning.

"One reason preachers get into trouble," he said, "and I don't mean moral trouble — just ordinary trouble — we just have so many opportunities."

Wayne was particularly pained when he overlooked a deserving person in a list of others who were recognized for Christian service, as in the following from the March 27, 1964, issue of the *Voice*:

"In last week's *Voice*, I mentioned the names of 22 calling teams and mistakenly left out the name of the man who makes as many calls as anyone in our church. I am speaking of Ray Acke. As humble and mature as he is, he would never have called my attention to this oversight. I gladly insert his name now. You know it's people like Ray that make a church great!"

An elder came to Wayne after a minor incident and asked, "Wayne, do you think you ought to apologize?"

Wayne agreed: "I said, 'Of course I ought to apologize.' And I did. When I've said something I shouldn't have said, I need to make it right."

When All Else Fails . . .

Our law firm, McBrayer, McGinnis, Leslie & Kirkland, does considerable health care work.

I was an active member of Tates Creek Christian Church here in Lexington and served on the Sayre Christian Village Board.

We did a great deal of pro bono work for them and were in the process of attempting to convert a number of personal-care beds to intermediate-care beds so that when a patient's level of care increased, the patient would not be shipped to a nursing home in other places. We argued that the patient needed continuity of care, and being moved from family, minister, physician and other support persons would be detrimental.

We filed a Certificate of Need application in Frankfort to convert 12 personal-care beds to intermediate-care beds.

Such certificates are difficult to obtain. Applicants are required to appear before the three-person Certificate of Need Board to plead their cases.

In preparation for our hearing, I asked Wayne Smith to be one of our lay witnesses. I carefully laid out for him 'continuity of care, spiritual and medical and family relationships, and so on.'

I explained to Wayne that the board often asked witnesses if they had read the application. Wayne leafed through the 80 to 100 page application and said, "I've seen it and I'm ready to go."

When the day of the hearing came, we gathered our witnesses and discussed our game plan before appearing before the board.

He was sworn in, introduced himself and said he'd been senior minister at Southland for 35 years, had helped found Sayre Christian Village and now served on its board. He spoke of the need for continuity of care. He described the problem caused by moving a loved one outside the reach of family, physician and church.

One of the board members asked if he had seen the application. He said, "Yes." They asked if he had read it, and he said, "Absolutely."

Then they asked him to turn to page 87, paragraph 1, parenthesis 2, which Wayne did.

They asked him to note that in the application it said if they transferred these 12 beds from personal to intermediate care, the ratio of difference in reimbursement would be .54782, which Wayne acknowledged.

Then they asked him to turn to page 26 of the application, paragraph 3, parenthesis 2, subsection A, where the same language was used but the projections were to be .34716, and he so noted.

Then they asked him to explain the two conclusions, which were different, though drawn from the same facts.

Wayne looked at them and said nothing for a moment; then he said, "I'll answer the same way I do when one of my board members in a meeting asks me something I neither understand nor have the answer for," and he stood and said, "I believe we ought to have a word of prayer."

Right there, in front of those three board members and the audience, he prayed, prayed for the board members, asking for wisdom, for guidance and for strength to approve the application.

The three board members didn't know whether to stand, stay seated, bow their heads or what. Neither did the audience.

Wayne ended his prayer and sat down. I said, "No further questions, and I conclude the hearing."

The board members got together quickly and gave us everything we wanted, though technically they probably should not have. We walked out of the auditorium, Wayne waving good-bye to the board members and being congratulated by the audience.

— *W. Terry McBrayer, Attorney at Law, Lexington*

NOTE: Sayre Christian Village, built and operated by Christian Churches and Churches of Christ of Central Kentucky, consists of 200 apartments and a nursing home of 109 beds situated in southeast Lexington.

If the discussion during a board meeting became hot, Wayne often went to the home of a member with whom he had disagreed to mend the relationship. "I always went to the person right after the meeting," he said. "There's no sense in letting a situation fester."

The apology might be something as simple as two lines in the church paper: "I made two mistakes in recent issues. I left out the name of Zedtta Wellman, and I will be gone the Sunday of November 29th."

Or, an admission of a human foible, with gratitude toward those who came to his aid, as in *The Voice of Southland Christian Church*, January 25, 1995:

"Three Sundays ago I preached a sermon on the subject of 'Using God's Money Carelessly.'

I admitted in that message using several illustrations that I have not always been a good steward of my income. Years ago I found a poem that describes a part of my life. I misplaced it, but now it is found. Before I share it with you, permit me to thank three people who went out of their way to go to the library, etc., to find this writing for me."

Then followed the poem, "*The Man Who Couldn't Save*," printed in its entirety.

An anonymous caller gets an apology

Wayne can't stand to let a phone ring; he has to pick it up. "It might be someone in trouble or someone hurting," he says. "Or an accident."

One Sunday between services, Wayne had gone into his office to get something when the phone rang.

"Southland Christian Church."

"Who is this?" a man's voice asked.

"Wayne Smith."

"You mean the preacher?"

"Yes."

Words From Wayne

I personally cannot foresee Southland ever maintaining an average in excess of 1,000. — February 6, 1975

"I'm surprised you answered the phone."

Wayne laughed, and the voice on the other end kept going. "I don't agree with what you said in your sermon. I just got through watching it."

Southland's services are edited and telecast one week later. The viewer had been watching last Sunday's message.

The man continued: "What verse was that you used?"

Wayne didn't remember. "Oh, gosh, I don't know."

"Are you sure you're Wayne Smith?"

"Yes, sir."

"Well, I'd be ashamed to say I didn't remember what I preached last week."

Wayne answered, "I am, quite frankly."

Smith and a series on sin

In the summer of 1994, Smith preached a series on the topic "The Seven Deadly Sins." Asbury Seminary's Dr. Maxie D. Dunnam, described two of these sermons:

"I moved to Wilmore, Kentucky, in July 1994 to become president of Asbury Theological Seminary. I had heard of Southland Christian Church and their senior minister, Wayne B. Smith. I wanted to attend their church and hear Wayne preach before I settled into the local United Methodist congregation.

"The Sunday I attended was the last Sunday in August. Wayne was preaching on lust. It was an outstanding sermon. I was intrigued by Wayne's announcement that he would preach the last sermon in the series the next Sunday. He had saved it for that weekend, since it was Labor Day weekend and attendance would be down.

"The people of the congregation, who knew and loved their preacher, began to laugh as he completed his announcement by saying he would preach on gluttony.

"Wayne weighed 265 pounds, and his people knew that weight was a constant battle. I didn't get to hear his sermon in person, but I requested an audiotape and listened to it. He could not say with Paul, 'Imitate me. Follow my example,' and he confessed that. He demonstrated a very healthy sense of humor."

Wayne had included in the sermon one of his best-known stories, which Dunnam quoted:

" 'My secretary,' Wayne said, 'received a phone call. The caller said, "I would like to speak with the head hog." She said, "I know Wayne is overweight but no one has ever been that disrespectful." "Well," he said, "let me apologize. I'm a hog farmer over in Scott County. I raise hogs and I just sold some of them for $5,000. I watch Wayne on television, and I really like him. I don't go to church anywhere. I thought I might send $500 to Southland Christian Church." She said, "Just a minute — I think the big pig just walked in."

Dunnam continued: "But he did not hide behind that sense of humor," then resumed quoting from Wayne's message:

" 'Does being 120 pounds overweight bother me? Yes, mentally and spiritually. Does it hurt my witness? Of course it does! It's hard to sell a product you do not use and a religion that you do not live. Am I a hypocrite? Yes. How can I preach if I am a hypocrite? If only perfect birds sang, the forest would be quiet. If only perfect preachers stood in the pulpit, we would not have a message. All have sinned and fallen short of the glory of God. Is that an excuse? No, it is a statement of guilt and also why I'm preaching.'

"That's the honesty we need," Dunnam said, "for we are all guilty in one way or another."

Willingness to re-examine his views

His openness has permitted Smith to examine his positions on issues and sometimes to change. For years, no divorced person could serve as an elder or deacon at Southland. "God said he hates divorce," Smith said, "and I hated it, too."

However, at his last elders meeting at Southland, in December 1995, Wayne asked the elders to re-examine this issue. After much study, he decided that his position was wrong.

He invited Gene Appel, a Christian minister from Las Vegas, to preach at Southland on Sunday morning. Gene's first marriage had ended in divorce.

"The two greatest hurts are losing a child and divorce," Wayne said, introducing Gene. "Many within our church body have experienced divorce, and you will be blessed as he speaks to us on 'The Hidden Hurt of a Broken Heart.' "

A turning point for Southland came during a baby-sitting session at the church when a member of the elders board talked to several single parents trying to juggle family, work and church. Maureene McCoy held the area's first Children of Divorced Parents workshop at Southland, and today the church hosts a regular divorce-recovery support group.

"Those who have a lot of truth sometimes don't have a lot of grace," Wayne said. "When you have a lot of truth, you feel grace is a compromise." Then he added, "Those who have a lot of grace sometimes don't have a lot of truth, either."

The preacher misses a funeral

Every preacher dreads the possibility of missing a wedding or a funeral. "I missed a funeral," Wayne admitted.

He told what happened. "I've always had trouble sleeping. We had three pharmacists in the church, and I told each one, 'If you get something new, let me know.'

"I never took anything on Saturday night, but one Friday I took a pill. Ten o'clock the next morning the phone rang. It was the funeral director in Winchester, 25 miles away. The people were there for the service, which was supposed to start, and I was still at home. Had it been close, I could have gone, but not 25 miles away.

"The funeral director said that Frank Curtis, a Church of God minister, was there, so I asked if I could talk to him. He agreed to do the service. He was a friend of the family. I said, 'Tell the family I'll get in touch with them.'

"There were seven children in the family, and I went out and bought seven boxes of candy — big boxes — $12.95 a box. That day I visited all seven homes."

Wayne and Frank are still close friends.

Wayne's worst embarrassment

In Wayne's mind, nothing equals what happened soon after he and Marge were married.

"My most embarrassing moment in the ministry," Wayne said, "was at a revival at Mulberry Church of Christ on the east side of Cincinnati. This was in 1952."

Smith had come by himself for the two-week meeting in November of that year, leaving Marge in Cynthiana, because she was teaching school.

"I told Marge, 'If you won't vote the Democratic ticket, I won't have to come back and vote for Ike.' She promised."

Mulberry's revival was for every night, including two Sundays. John Kinner was the host preacher.

"I don't like to eat before I speak," Wayne said, "and I had forgotten to tell him."

The preachers had the noon meal in someone's home, then dinner in another home, day after day, for two weeks. Unspoken rivalry among the cooks ensured that the clergy would be adequately nourished.

"I can eat now," Wayne said, "but I could really eat then, being younger."

On Thursday of the second week, the host preacher and the guest evangelist had just sat down and said the blessing when the tragedy began to unfold.

"It's not polite to eat until the food is passed to everyone," Wayne said, "but a person can eat his salad. There was this dish pushed up against my plate, and I took a couple of bites of my slaw. I really like cole slaw.

"Then I looked around. Nobody else had cole slaw. I thought it was my salad. I'd eaten half the dish, and it was for everybody."

When Wayne apologized, the lady of the house tried to minimize the damage. "That's all right," she said. "We don't like cole slaw anyway."

"Man! I was embarrassed," Wayne said. "Besides, it was at the end of the second week, and Brother Kinner and I tried to take only small amounts. She said, 'I don't believe Brother Smith likes my cooking.' So I just shoveled it in. I had to."

The evening service was less than an hour away, and Wayne knew he was in trouble. "It's very rare that I've ever thrown up," he said. "I didn't get this size by giving it away."

He managed to get through the song service, but halfway into the sermon he stopped, stepped back from the pulpit, and decorated the platform.

Smith looked around to find the back door, but there was none to be seen.

"I had to walk out the center aisle facing everyone," he said. "I went outside and leaned against a tree and completely threw up what was left. Probably the greatest feeling I ever had."

Marge was supposed to come up over the weekend, but when Wayne told her what happened — they had been married less than a year — she responded, "Anybody who stuffs himself and then pukes in church — I'm not coming."

"She didn't come," Wayne said. "So I lost my wife for the weekend and my vote for four years."

Years later, when Don Miller was minister at Mulberry, the church added an educational wing and invited Wayne for the dedication service. After telling the story of the revival to the crowd, he said to the preacher, "You may be responsible for the Sunday-school rooms, but I — ," pointing to the door behind him — "I'm the reason for this escape route."

"Here he comes with a bucket of chicken."

Seven thousand people gathered in the University of Kentucky's Memorial Coliseum December 21, 1995, in a special service of worship and celebration for Wayne's retirement. During the service, Garrett Stevens, Southland's senior-adults minister, asked, "How many of you have had Wayne bring you a plaque or candy or a bucket of chicken?"

Hundreds got to their feet, in every part of the arena.

Andy Rasmussen's Starlite Restaurant was the second restaurant to sell the famed Kentucky Fried Chicken. The first was in Corbin, where Harlan Sanders introduced his "finger lickin' good" recipe.

Wayne was at the Starlite about as much as the Rasmussens.

"He came in all the time," said Carol, Andy's daughter. "He'd come in one end of the kitchen and pick up a piece of chicken and be through with it by the time he got to the other end of the kitchen. Then he and Marge would sit down in the dining room and eat supper. Then he'd go out through the kitchen and talk to everybody and pick up another piece on his way out."

Andy's father-in-law had started the restaurant, which had both curb service and two dining rooms for inside eating. The Starlite had a full menu, and at first, the new Kentucky Fried Chicken was merely one more item on the list.

"If we had dessert or something like that left over, he would take it," Carol said. "He was always stopping by to get something to take to somebody."

Wayne performed a wedding here in 1976 for Cindy Portwood, who worked on the curb. The ceremony was conducted outside in Cindy's "workplace."

And the reception? Where else?

Naomi Rasmussen, Andy's wife, was the first member of the family to join Southland. The others followed. Almost immediately Wayne noticed a characteristic of Naomi: "She was very generous with money."

Mr. Rasmussen, too, would give Smith money.

"Here," Andy would say. "Do some good with it."

"One time he gave me $200," Wayne said. "He wanted to know what I intended to do with it. I told him, 'I have a missionary friend in India, and it'll go to him.' 'Oh no, it won't,' Andy said. 'People are dying here in America.' And he took the money back."

Wayne said, "That was the end of my foreign-missions effort with Andy."

Smith makes a discovery

When the dinner hour was over, Andy closed the rear dining room, keeping the front dining room and the curb service in operation until 11 p.m. More than once, Wayne slipped into that empty back room, sometimes pacing the floor, sometimes sitting in the dark alone if he was worried about something. "A person needs time to think and pray," he said.

Plus, he learned something interesting.

"They had to keep chicken on hand right up to closing time," Wayne said, "because if someone came in, they had to have it ready. Or maybe someone ordered and didn't pick it up. But after they closed, they had to do something with it."

That discovery changed Smith's life and the lives of hundreds of others as well.

"Dad would go by at closing time and pick up leftover chicken and take buckets to needy families," said Judy. "Of course, there might be a few pieces missing. He had to make sure it was tasty enough to give away."

About 9 p.m., Wayne would call Carol: "Got any chicken left over?"

A bucket or two of Kentucky Fried in Smith's hand became a pat on the shoulder, a token of compassion, a means of encouragement.

He said, "Some weeks I'd go there three or four nights and pick up chicken and take it to somebody."

Healing hurts with a bucket of chicken

Divorce, death, loss of job, illness, family emergencies — the needs might vary, but the pattern was the same: a call from Wayne and soon the preacher was on the front porch; the breaking of bread — uh, chicken — and hearts mended and burdens lightened.

As Kentucky Fried Chicken became more widely known, the corporation decreed that every franchisee could sell only KFC: no more "extra item on the menu" situations. So the Starlite was torn down, and Carol and her brother John, who by now were owners, put up the familiar structure associated with the brand.

Smith managed to find other nourishment during construction; but when the new place opened, he made up for lost time.

Pat Moores told about what happened when his aunt died: "My dad's sister died during surgery. She lived down in the lower part of Jessamine County, near the river. You had to turn off the main road, take another road off that, and another road off that one — really down in the boonies.

"On the night after the visitation, the family had gathered in the house, and about 9:15, here comes Wayne Smith with two buckets of chicken. My aunt wasn't a member of Southland. Wayne didn't know her or my uncle, but he knew me and knew it was my aunt. By the time he left, everybody there felt like he was a member of the family. It was just natural for him."

Clara Fields told about her experience.

"My mother and my father died 10 months apart," she said. "I don't remember which funeral it was. In between the death and the funeral, it's about noon, and here he comes with a bucket of chicken. He sat down and ate with us. I'll never forget that."

As noted earlier, when Wally and Barb Rendel's daughter was killed in a car accident, they asked Wayne to conduct Jill's funeral. Jill was a student at Cincinnati Bible College and lost her life during a midwinter trip for CBC when the school's van skidded off an icy road and rolled over.

Two weeks earlier, she had been crowned queen at CBC's Valentine Banquet. The theme of Wayne's funeral message was "The Queen Has Met the King." Through his own tears, Wayne gave a powerful sermon on the life to come. Afterward, those present stood in small groups talking about the sermon and how Smith had taken a tragedy and turned it into an affirmation of salvation through Jesus Christ.

Wayne's service did not end with the benediction.

"For a couple of weeks after she died," Wally said, "Wayne would come by, just drop in. He'd have a bucket or two of chicken with him. We would sit down and dive into that chicken and he would dive in with us. It might be 9:30 or 10:00 at night. We'd talk, laugh, cry sometimes. He really helped us get through."

J.L. Lynn, a prominent businessman in Lexington and a Southland member, suggested that the title of this book should be *He Delivered the Gospel; Also the Chicken.* At the mention of Lynn's name, Smith commented, "The reason I've been able to give away so many copies of my sermons over the years is that J.L. has never charged me for printing them. He's been extremely generous."

The preacher sets up a blind date

"When we lost our first baby," Joyce Moore said. "Wayne was a great help to Harold and me."

Joyce has known Smith since his days in Harrison County, when he first came to Unity Christian at age 20.

"Mother took us to the Methodist church," Joyce said, "but she was very happy when Wayne made his appearance and was trying to get everybody in the neighborhood into his church. He baptized me, my brother and my sister." Later, as an adult, Joyce moved to Lexington and started going to Southland.

One day Wayne stopped at Begley's Drug Store in the Southland Shopping Center for a snack. Turning to the man sitting at the lunch counter with him, Smith asked, "Where you from?"

"I'm Harold Moore," the man said. "I'm from Harrison County. I came to Lexington to work for the phone company."

Surprised, Wayne said, "I preached in Harrison County." He told about Unity Christian and how he started at Robinson and had preached at String Town as well.

"Is your family from there? Your wife's people? I might know some of them."

"I'm not married," Harold answered.

"Why not?"

"I haven't met the right girl."

"I've got just the one," Wayne told his friend.

Joyce laughed as she remembered. "He introduced us on a blind date," she said. "I blame him. That was in February 1957, and we married in 1958."

She started working at Southland in 1977 as bookkeeper, a task she continued for the next 22 years.

"His memory still amazes me," said Joyce. "Addresses. Phone numbers. He is better with numbers than with names. He would say to the secretaries, 'I can't remember their name' but he could always tell where they lived or their phone number. We had to guess who he was talking about."

Harold sometimes drives for Wayne, taking Smith to speaking dates or out-of-town meetings.

"Wayne has brought us chicken many times," said Joyce. "And pies."

She described one midnight visit. "Mother was very ill and was having her eye removed at St. Joseph's Hospital. I was spending the night with her. We heard steps coming down the hall — it must have been 11:30 or later — and I knew who it was. When he came into the room, I could smell him."

Wayne found a place still open that sold chili dogs and brought a supply with him. "I guess he thought everybody ate at that time of night," Joyce said.

When Joyce's mother lay on her deathbed, she made Joyce promise to have Wayne conduct the funeral. "My mother was very fond of him."

Smith's generosity takes many forms

"I don't know too many people who run a tab at a candy store," said Jana Thore, Wayne's younger daughter. "He's kept Old Kentucky Candies in business for years."

Words From Wayne

You make a living by what you get;
you make a life by what you give.

Marge agreed. "I told Wayne, 'I hope nothing happens to you. I'll have to go down there and pay a huge bill.' " Laughing, she added, "I'm going to be upset."

The same with plaques. One year at the personnel dinner at the North American Christian Convention, Meredith Williams suggested to the more than 500 notables present, "If there is anyone here who did not receive a plaque from Wayne Smith the year he was convention president, please raise your hand, and we'll see that you get one." The roar of laughter proved that no one in the room had been left out.

The text of a plaque awarded to members of Southland's planning committee July 31, 1976, quotes from John F. Kennedy's inaugural address: "Some men see things as they are and say, 'Why?' I dream things that never were and say 'Why not?' "

The words on the back of that plaque are as significant as those on the front:

> You are a member of the Planning Committee charged with suggesting a charted course for the future of Southland Christian Church. No committee in the 20 year history of our church has met more often or invested more time than this committee during the years of 1974, 1975 and 1976. When I saw this plaque in a store at Myrtle Beach, I thought of the Planning Committee. Please accept this as an expression of love from a preacher and a congregation who are extremely grateful. Since we pass this way but once, it is satisfying to know men who give their best, willingly. John Ruskin said,
>
> *"Therefore, when we build, let us think that we build forever. Let it not be for present delight, nor for present use alone, let it be such work as descendants will thank us for, and let us think, as we lay stone on stone, that a time is to come when those stones will be held sacred because our hands have touched them, and that men will say as they look upon the labor and the wrought substance of them, 'See! this our fathers did for us.' "*
>
> I remain — In His Service, (followed by the signature, WAYNE B. SMITH).

Dr. Clark Standiford is an elder at Southland. When Jana stopped at his office for a minor ear problem, the girls at the desk told her, "We just love it when your dad comes, because he always brings us candy or pies.

The trunk of Smith's car ought to have a gift rack alongside the spare tire.

Judy described how Wayne managed to be so generous. "Dad gave so many gifts he could not afford to pay too much for each one. What's the solution? He was always looking for a good buy, such as 100 saucers, at a flea market or someplace else. Put a small plaque on each one, get a few friends to wrap them, and he was set. All he needed to do was pop the trunk."

One evening Wayne drove past the home of one of his members and, noticing the cars and people, stopped to see if something was wrong. "It was a wedding reception," Smith said. "I wasn't aware of it."

He went out to his car, opened the trunk, selected a gift and headed back into the house, his treasure wrapped in newspaper.

"You can always wrap it in newspaper," Wayne tells. "I say, 'This gift was so expensive I couldn't afford wrapping paper.' That always starts things off on a good note."

"I have a relationship with the owners of Lexington Trophy Company," Wayne says. "Judy worked there for a while. These people don't go to Southland; they are Italian Catholics. But they love me and I love them." One of Wayne's best friends is their head engraver, Roy Staggs.

Wayne found a bakery that sold him pies for $8.95 each, and he gave these away at Christmas. Smith is known to be generous, but few people realize the extent of his gift-giving.

"I've never been honest with my wife about finances," he admitted. "When we first got married, the tips I left caused trouble. She is fairly conservative."

Tuxedos and candy bars

Geno's Formal Affair, owned by Gino Guarnieri, has clients across the country. On any given week, he will ship garments to 42 states. Prom time is the worst — or best — depending upon one's point of view.

"Nobody's on vacation then," Gino said. "My people, plus temps that we hire, work from dawn until late, really late, sometimes 2:00 or 3:00 in the morning, sorting, cleaning and pressing, packaging and shipping orders. We might have 80 people in this building.

"Wayne will come in about midnight," Gino said. "He will have 100 of these giant candy bars — they cost $1.50 apiece — and take them to every worker and talk to them and tell them how great they are. Now, every year they ask, 'When is Reverend Smith coming?' "

When Wayne was asked how he started this, and he told of Gino's help with special programs at the church: "We had at least 30 nights a year when Gino provided free tuxes to the orchestra and some of the cast. We're talking in the hundreds," Wayne said. "This is big money, and he does it for free. Taking candy is the least I could do."

The night before Easter in 1984, Wayne called Gino's home. His son answered the phone, and when it rang, Dad told the boy, "I'm not here. I don't care who it is, I'm not here."

Gino's company had supplied formal attire — again, free of charge — for

No Budget for His Gifts

Wayne has everything it takes not only to lead people to Christ but to lead a church to greater things.

He combines strong principles, a direct message and incredible vision with disarming humor and boundless compassion.

His generosity with gifts may have caused Marge to put him on a budget, but no one could ever convince him to budget his gifts of time and spirit to the church, to families and to people who needed both.

Thanks, Wayne, for all you've done for the church, for the community and, especially, for my family.

— *Hunter Daugherty, Circuit Judge,*
Commonwealth of Kentucky, 13th District

every person in Southland's Easter Pageant, and Gino was exhausted. The boy told his dad, "This is Wayne Smith, the preacher. I'm not lying to him."

The next morning Preacher Smith began his Easter message: "I called a home in our church last night. It is against my policy to embarrass anyone, but may I say that he lives in the Hartland subdivision, he is Italian, and he rents tuxes."

Wayne paused until the laughter died, then told what happened, emphasizing the words "I'm not lying to him."

Wayne went on: "I believe in the Resurrection. And I am not lying to you today."

Friendship with Wayne generally costs money

Most churches have a discretionary fund from which the minister or staff can give money to people who drop by asking for help. Were this his decision, Smith would have bankrupt Southland long ago. Southland provided such a fund, and it was generous, but the church set a limit: all requests above a certain amount had to go to the benevolence committee.

"I sometimes went beyond what the church allowed," Wayne confessed. "I had a drawer that I would keep bills in that I had paid or that weren't approved. People would hand me $200 or $500, and then I would take care of what was in the drawer."

Ann, Wayne's secretary, said, "When he would leave for a trip, he'd give me a list: 'Here's what I owe to different people. And don't tell Marge.' "

Ann continued: "These would be loans from the bank or personal loans from those on his list."

Over time Smith developed a group of friends to whom he could go for money.

"No bank would loan me a dollar to give to somebody that was broke," Wayne explained. "So I'd call a friend. Then I would go by and pick up the money. Maybe $400, maybe $1,000, $1,500. I'd pay them back in a month or two."

How was Smith able to manage this?

When he is telling jokes, Wayne enjoys portraying Marge as stingy, but, in actuality, Marge is the one who makes his generosity possible.

"Marge pays the bills," he said. "She does that from my salary. She believes a person should live within their harvest. That's why we have a house that's paid for. But she's allowed me to keep all the wedding and funeral and speaking-engagement money I receive. Marge never asked me, 'What did you get?' or 'What did you do with that money?' "

Wayne, too, maintains strict integrity in finances. If he charges something, he pays it on time. Wayne B. Smith has no bills outstanding in Lexington.

When a need arose that Wayne could not meet immediately, he would pick up the phone.

Roger Wellman, elder at Southland, said, "Wayne gave money to Bible college students — hundreds of dollars. If the student had no money at all, then Wayne would sign a note, hoping to lay money aside to meet the obligation. When the note came due and there was no money, he would call several of us and get maybe $100 or $200 or, in some cases, $500."

Was this a hardship?

Roger continued: "I was honored to know I was helping a kid in Bible college or someone else who needed help. I think all of us felt that way."

A tragedy and a discovery

At 5:30 Friday afternoon, April 12, 1985, Wayne was on his way to church to prepare for a wedding when an oncoming car smashed into him head-on. Fortunately, he was alone. The driver of a car behind Wayne had received medical training, and this driver and another man were first on the scene.

Wayne's body lay on the floor of the passenger side, crushed between the dashboard and the seat. "He's dead," the men said to each other and went to see if they could help the occupants of the other car. The driver and passenger in the offending car were so high on marijuana they hardly knew what had happened. One was unhurt; the other had a cut on his head.

The two Samaritans turned away in disgust and came back to Wayne. "Let's pray," one of them said. So they reached into the wrecked car and laid their hands on the still figure and prayed. Wayne gasped — "Like a baby spitting out his tongue," one of them said later — and began to breathe regularly.

It took some time to get Smith out of the wreckage, and he was taken by ambulance to St. Joseph Hospital. Word of the accident spread quickly. Some went to St. Joseph; some went to the church, where many were gathered in prayer. Traffic at the hospital became such a problem that the television stations asked people to go to the church instead.

Attendants at the hospital refused to permit anyone but the immediate family to see Smith. Gov. John Y. Brown was allowed into the ICU, but attorney Tommy Bell was refused. Bell pounded the table: "I'm a trustee of this hospital!" At that, they let him in. Hundreds were turned away. Smith's chances were less than 50-50.

The elders' regular meeting was approaching.

Brewster McLeod, like everybody else, was worried about whether his boss would live or die. He and Wayne "always covered for each other," to use Wayne's term, and now Brewster had an additional concern. Breaking precedent, he slipped into Wayne's office, opened the lower right-hand drawer and took inventory.

McLeod swallowed hard as he added up the figures.

At the elders meeting, he presented his findings. The response was instant. Guy Colson, head of the finance committee, spoke first: "I make a motion we pay them all."

Wayne spent 29 days in the hospital and faced months of rehab at home, some of it on crutches. Ann Nelson, Wayne's secretary, kept track of the mail: 2,304 cards containing 2,651 signatures from 22 states and seven foreign countries.

It was three months before Smith could return to the church and longer still before he could preach. Some months later, Brewster came to Wayne: "We've got some bills. We need another wreck."

"I said OK," Wayne said, "but I told Brewster, 'This time you have the wreck.' "

Words From Wayne

Sometimes the thought would hit me, and I'd take something by; you might not get another chance.

The preacher is audited

In the early days, Southland provided no remuneration for ministerial expenses. "The harder you worked, the less you made," as one staff member expressed it. But as the church grew, Southland's leaders set up expense accounts that provided not only reimbursement but accountability and adequate records of money received and money given. "It was a good thing," Roy, Wayne's senior assistant, said later, "because Wayne was audited."

When Smith received the letter from the Internal Revenue Service, he thought it was his death certificate. He called Glenn Norvell, his accountant, again and again. Finally, Norvell said, "Bring everything over here."

Wayne saves everything: bulletins from speaking dates, mileage records, mementos. He carted two suitcases, full of papers, receipts, bills and notes, to Glenn's office. Norvell took one look at the pile in front of him and said, "They deserve you." Considerable work, but no problems; Smith was pronounced clean by the Feds.

During late November and early December, while Southland was toiling night and day on the Christmas program, Santa Smith's elves were toiling night and day, also.

"Christmas is my favorite time of the year," Wayne explained. "I put my presents in Carol Rasmussen's garage. These were for people who had gone the extra mile for me during the year."

On average, Carol and her friend, Barbara McClain, wrapped 200 to 250 gifts.

"I've started sending cards now," Wayne said. "The issue is not finances. I can't stand the pressure any more."

When the girls were small, he enlisted their help. "We would start out Christmas Day. The back seat was full. Trunk was full. Judy and Jana loved it. We'd go to many homes. Then they got too old for that, and it got to the place I just couldn't deliver all of them, so I paid a friend, Bill Hennessee, to do it for me."

J- O- Y: Jesus first; others next; yourself last

Dr. David Ditto says, "I've never met anybody who went out of his way like Wayne. I have stuff hanging on my wall that Wayne has given me: a coin from India with a poem on it he wrote, a rock from the Czech Republic, a clock in my office. He's given me Kentucky Fried Chicken, Old Kentucky Candy. He loves giving gifts to people."

Smith helped with the 1989 merger of The Academy and the Lexington Christian School. At the time, their combined enrollment was 300. Today, Lexington Christian Academy is the fourth-largest Christian school in the United States, with an enrollment of 1,734.

Ditto said, "Without someone who had the trust and respect of all parties, I don't know whether we could have done it or not. He's been such an encourager and supporter to me. I wish I could give him a 10th of it back."

Ditto's father is a Methodist preacher, so when David and his wife — herself the daughter of a Methodist preacher — and three of their four daughters were to be immersed, Wayne asked David's father if he would like to immerse his family. He accepted at once, telling Wayne that he had baptized many in a similar manner.

"Anytime my father visited Southland," David said, "Wayne always made them feel welcome. Wayne made a person want to be better, because he would give you more credit than you deserved. He made you want to live up to the person he described you as being."

As people learn of Wayne's generosity, they in turn are generous with him. While driving past Donut Days Bakery on Southland Drive, he will tell his passenger, "They've never been to my church, but they won't let me pay for anything."

The owners, Neil and Cathy Day, have a house on the lake where they spend most weekends to recover from their labors during the week.

One weekend, the Days learned that Wayne would be speaking in Harrodsburg and came to hear him. They were aghast when he introduced them from the pulpit. "We'll have a good offering today," Smith told the crowd. "These people have money."

But there was more: "If you take your church bulletin to Days Donuts the next time you are in Lexington, Neil or Cathy will give you half off the price."

Wayne said later, "I embarrassed them, and everybody knew I was joking. But if anyone in the congregation had accepted the offer, they would have done it."

Several years ago, Wayne had to have a root canal. His case was complicated, and he needed the services of an endodontist. "He's never been in our building," Smith said, "yet he did it without sending me a bill. He loves football, so I got him a football autographed by Guy Morriss, UK's football coach."

Recently, Wayne and Marge took his three dentists and their spouses out to eat: Dr. and Mrs. Herman Blair, Dr. and Mrs. Tom Daniel and Dr. Pam Revel and her husband, Byron. "I shall continue giving them some gift," Wayne said. "Why? Because gratitude is only as good as the effort I make to express it."

A member at Southland said, "I came to Wayne when I was about as low as a person could get. I needed money. He had just received a check for $500. Never hesitating a moment, he endorsed that check and gave it to me."

A friend said to Smith, "You'd just as soon help a derelict as you would a governor."

Wayne's response was instant: "In fact, I would rather, because I felt more at home. It was more in agreement with my background. Growing up, I never knew anyone that was really affluent."

A homeless person approached Wayne on the street, asking, "Could you help me?"

"Sure," he answered and gave her a $20 bill. She nearly passed out, but to Smith it was nothing.

"I do it selfishly," he said. "I'm the one that gets a charge out of it — and the blessing. I have received so much; why wouldn't I want to share?"

"We're not running a Sunday school here, Reverend."

Lexington soon learned that Southland's preacher would stand up for what he believed. Early in his ministry, he wrote to E. William Henry, chairman of the Federal Communications Commission in Washington, D.C., regarding profanity on television. Smith's approach quickly moved beyond letter writing.

"In the 1960s," Wayne said, "Kentucky had a day of rest." What Wayne meant was that the commonwealth's blue laws were enforced; few people worked on Sundays, and stores were closed.

Abe Levine, manager of Mr. Wiggs, decided to change matters. With one store on Nicholasville Road and another on New Circle Road, Mr. Wiggs was one of Lexington's biggest retail outlets.

"We're going to open," Levine told his employees. "Somebody may get arrested. If that happens, don't worry about it."

Managers came from the home office and met with department heads, then with all the employees. One name surfaced repeatedly: the Rev. Wayne B. Smith.

"If you see Reverend Smith coming," they were told, "warn everybody. Announce it over the P.A."

Wayne had made arrangements at Southland to be away so he could attend the opening of both stores. Gino Guarnieri, then a young man, worked at Mr. Wiggs on New Circle Road. "I'd never heard of Reverend Smith, but this worried us employees. We needed our $1.20 an hour."

No sooner had they turned the key at New Circle Road when someone saw the preacher coming across the parking lot. As Wayne came in the front door, Gino went out the back.

Wayne headed next for the Nicholasville Road store. One girl there hesitated too long. The newspaper ran Ethel Taylor's picture under the headline, "Arrested for working on Sunday."

Ethel bears no grudge for her sudden fame. Wayne and Gino stopped recently for lunch at the Tea Room in the Meadowthorpe Shopping Center on Leestown Road. Ethel owns the business. She recognized Smith and showed him the clipping she had saved from the *Herald*.

"We were adversaries and didn't know each other," Wayne said laughing. She and Gino and Wayne talked about the incident and the changes that have come over the last four decades.

Mr. Wiggs survived, but Smith's action finished *The Christian Hour*, a program on Channel 18 shared by several Christian Churches in Lexington. The Mr. Wiggs stores were one of Channel 18's biggest advertisers.

The Christian Hour moved to Channel 27, and the other Christian Church preachers in Lexington reminded Wayne that this was their last chance, because Lexington, at the time, had only two television stations.

Wayne was invited to speak at the Governor's Prayer Breakfast in the 1970s, and he described what it was like: "Those things are hard," he said. "There would be a thousand present. Persons of different religious persuasions are at the head table so no one is overlooked. You'll have conservatives, and you'll have liberals. It is difficult to say anything without offending someone, yet it's important to say the right thing."

A sensational crime and a sensational sermon

Two men escaped from the Federal Building in downtown Lexington while being held during their trial. They stole a car and ran out of gas on a rural Fayette County road. The nearest house happened to be the home of an Episcopal minister.

The escapees murdered him, his teen-age son and daughter, and the dog. Driving through Falmouth, Kentucky, they shot randomly into several rooms at Fisher's Motel, killing three people.

The two men were caught and sentenced to the penitentiary. Both men died in prison, killed in anger by other prisoners who were angry because of the senseless murder of six innocent victims, including a minister and his two children. "That's known as sidewalk justice," said Wayne.

On October 7, 1973, Smith preached a sermon entitled "Restore Capital Punishment." Southland's general board, which consisted of 66 elders and deacons, and Southland's three assistant ministers voted their unanimous approval of the sermon. Dr. James R. Ross and Len Aldridge, C.P.A., had the entire sermon published in the Sunday *Herald-Leader on* February 3, 1974, at a cost of $4,000.

Thirty years later, Smith continues to get requests for this sermon, the cost of printing covered by Lynn Imaging through the courtesy of a former elder of Southland, J.L. Lynn.

Some preachers enjoy controversy. Not Wayne Smith. "Every time I get involved in a controversial issue, I hate every moment of it. Especially now; it was easier when I was younger."

In 1979 he, along with several other ministers, carried signs in front of City Hall stating their position on a matter of public morals.

"Was it fun?" Smith asked. "No! As a matter of fact, I went to my car and wept in silence, because I felt like a donkey. No one likes embarrassment. I do a lot of things in the ministry I do not enjoy doing, but it's my duty. You ought to take a stand, because it's your duty."

Winning over a determined opponent

During the 1984 North American Christian Convention in Atlanta, Smith was a guest on a live call-in television show. The hostess was a transplanted New Yorker, hard as flint, and out to make a name for herself.

During the opening minutes, she threw question after question intending to portray her guest as a superconservative hick. Whatever Smith was for, she was against. Within minutes the phones began ringing, and the pressure on Smith was intense.

Cameras, bright lights, hostile questions — Smith held court in complete control, sometimes laughing, sometimes serious, responding honestly to every caller and to his hostess as well. Both she and her guest were sorry when the half-hour program ended.

Once the lights were turned off, she asked, "Are you speaking over there at the convention?"

"Yes," Smith answered. "Friday night."

"What time?" she asked. "I want to come hear you."

Words From Wayne

I've never had a problem with my position; it's my disposition.

Advising an Attorney

I've known Wayne since I was a child, as he is a long-time friend of my father and mother. It was always a happy reunion for me and certainly a big deal when Wayne came to Grayson to preach, either at First Church of Christ or Kentucky Christian College. When I later began my college years at Transylvania University, I often attended Southland Christian Church to hear his preaching, and I continued to do so while in law school at U.K.

After I met Wes Phelps, we attended Southland together. Thus, it was a mutual and natural choice that Wes and I asked Wayne to perform our wedding ceremony. I have always remembered his advice that day to never forget Romans 8:28.

Wes and I live in Versailles now with our children, and Wayne has continued to be there for us and has also mentored me during my legal career. When I was an assistant commonwealth's attorney, he provided me with biblical references on the death penalty when I was prosecuting such a case.

His willingness to counsel me continued after I was elected, in 1998, a district judge for the 14th Judicial District, which includes Woodford, Scott and Bourbon counties. One of my first surprises as a district judge was when a young couple walked into my office and asked me to marry them. My minister, Randy Nation, preacher at Woodford Community Christian Church, solved my immediate problem by faxing me a ceremony. However, Wayne also came through by mailing me several wedding ceremonies that I continue to use today.

— *Judge Mary Jane Wilhoit Phelps,*
14th Judicial District, Commonwealth of Kentucky

Wayne and Marge and the girls were on vacation when he received a call from Ron Burden, pastor of Southern Heights Baptist Church on Clays Mill Road. "Smith," Ron said, "They put an X-rated movie in South Park. You are the only preacher who can get to Lawson King."

Lawson King was the county attorney. Wayne went to his office. "What do you want me to do?" King asked.

"I want you to close that movie."

"I can't do anything until you've seen it," King said.

So Wayne called and asked for a private showing for him and King. Two weeks earlier, Southland had hired Brewster McLeod as youth minister, and Brewster went along, plus Andy Carter, a police officer and member of Southland.

"We saw about 20 minutes," Wayne said later. "It started with a couple making love in a casket and went downhill from there."

When the owner of South Park Shopping Center learned that Smith and the county attorney might take action affecting not only the theater but all the stores in the shopping center, the owner himself closed down the movie house.

Wayne takes on the University of Kentucky

When the newspaper carried a story about UK's permitting co-ed dorms, Smith reached for the telephone. After being connected to the university, he asked to speak to the president.

"I was shocked when they put me through directly to him," Wayne said. "He invited me to come over and talk about it. I didn't want to talk about it; I just didn't want him to say not one preacher had objected."

Before leaving his office, Smith asked for help. "This can't be me, Lord; it has to be you. I can't do this by myself."

UK's 670-acre campus is on the southeast edge of Lexington's downtown. Wayne had come this way countless times before, but today he hardly noticed the traffic as he neared his destination, trying to think of what to say. Turning onto the campus, he swallowed again. Under other circumstances, the magnificent buildings were impressive; today they seemed intimidating.

He could not help but contrast the intellectual environment with his own academic shortcomings. This was a long way from Western Hills High School.

Smith had never met Dr. Otis Singletary, president of the University of Kentucky. As he mounted the steps to Singletary's office, Wayne wished he had never started this.

Smith approached the secretary and gave her his name. Moments later, Singletary emerged and shook his visitor's hand, then motioned him toward a hallway. "We'll go down to the boardroom."

The paneled room smelled faintly of furniture polish and tradition. There, Wayne was introduced to his welcoming committee: Tommy Bell, prominent Lexington attorney and possibly the best-known referee in the NFL, representing the university trustees; Jack Hall, the dean of men; Jack Blanton, university vice president; and Singletary.

"I was scared to death," says Wayne.

Singletary opened the conversation: "Reverend, I want to tell you something. We're not running a Sunday-school over here."

Wayne threw his head back and laughed, which immediately broke the tension. Everybody relaxed as Singletary continued: "I'll tell you why we're doing this. Our students are renting apartments off campus so they can live together. We have dorm rooms unused. This way we can monitor the students and have at least some control."

Wayne left feeling that at least the two sides understood each other. He had taken his stand; they had explained their position.

Not long after the meeting, Tommy Bell began attending Southland Christian Church, and soon after that, Wayne baptized him, his wife and son Bruce.

Sometime later, the Kiwanians roasted Singletary for charity and enlisted Wayne as master of ceremonies.

"He really did me in good," Wayne said laughing. "Singletary said, 'Wayne Smith really is a helpful person. I dreamed the other night I was trying to get to heaven. It was a pretty steep climb. Wayne Smith saw me and said, "Otis, get on my back, and I'll ride you to glory." "You mean, like a horse?" And Smith said, "Yes." I tried it,' Singletary said, 'but since

Smith is so short, my feet dragged the ground, and it was embarrassing. There I was, sitting on top of Wayne, and St. Peter said, "Come in, Otis, but leave your jackass over there."

Channel 18 ran a clip of this, including the story, on the eleven o'clock news. "From then on," Wayne said, "he and I were friends." Feigning offense, Smith added, "But he could have said 'donkey.' "

After that, Smith and Singletary appeared together at several events in Lexington, including the sumptuous festivities when Cawood Ledford, play-by-play announcer for UK, stepped down after 39 years. Jim Host was in charge of Cawood's retirement party, which was held on the floor of Rupp Arena. "Mr. Host spared no cost," Wayne said. "It was first-class and memorable."

Smith and Singletary were behind the curtain waiting to go on, and Smith approached Singletary: "Dr. Singletary, it seems to me that this program is better than the one for you when you retired."

Singletary laughed, then said, "Wayne, it may surprise you, but my reward is up there," and he pointed skyward.

When Wayne's turn came to speak, he repeated this conversation to the audience, then added, "And I am surprised," which brought a response from the crowd.

At Wayne's retirement, Singletary was one of those who spoke. During Singletary's last illness, Smith visited him in his home. Wayne said, "I was honored to be counted as one of his friends."

Looking back, Wayne observed, "I guess one surprise of my ministry is that a person could take a strong position on issues and still attract influential people, affluent people."

Throwing his weight into a good cause

The annual fund-raising telethon for Cardinal Hill Rehabilitation Hospital is one of Lexington's most prominent social events. As one person

Words From Wayne

It's hard to conduct a war when you don't know who your friends are.

put it, "Anyone who was anyone was there."

Outstanding UK athletes from past and present went on television to encourage viewers to make pledges. The phone banks were tended by celebrities, CEOs, attorneys and so on. Tommy Bell, mentioned earlier; Joe Hall, coach of the UK Wildcats; and Gov. John Y. Brown and his wife, Phyllis George, the former Miss America, would appear.

Wayne was an emcee for 15 years. His spontaneity kept the audience glued to their seats.

Smith remembers working with Judy Rose, who, with her husband, owned 10 banks, and with Mary Lou Whitney, whose first husband owned TWA and other holdings. The cameras were rolling when Smith turned to Mary Lou and whispered, "Is it true your new husband is 31 years old?"

Unfazed, she responded, "Reverend, it takes a good man to keep up with me."

Fran Curci was UK's football coach from 1973 to 1981. "He was always a hit," Wayne said.

"He was a fine-looking man. The girls counting the pledges had saliva running out of their mouths. He sure could raise money."

Smith observed, "There are some wealthy people in Lexington, yes; but Lexington is a generous city. Our telethon raised more than similar events in cities like Detroit and Philadelphia."

Smith's efforts for Cardinal Hill were especially effective during the campaigns that followed his near-fatal car wreck. Wayne was seriously injured, and he spent months in rehab, some of it at Cardinal Hill.

A close call indeed

Wayne's 1985 car accident nearly caused his death and could have caused ruin of another kind. Before the collision, he had met with a lawyer friend who was running for city council. The candidate's central issue was pornographic literature. Soon after the attorney had announced that he would run, the man's wife came to Smith's office with three magazines.

"You preachers should look at these and see how bad it is in Lexington," she told Smith.

With that she handed him a brown paper bag. "The first two were bad enough," Smith said. "The third was awful."

Where should he keep them, he wondered. He knew of a minister who was fired because someone found pornography in his desk.

Under the seat of his car? Not there. He lifted the trunk lid and tossed the sack with the magazines inside, then brought the lid back down.

The magazines were still in Wayne's trunk when an oncoming car smashed into his. It took a long time for the fire department to cut Wayne free of the wreck. Unconscious, he was rushed to the hospital and immediately taken into surgery.

As Wayne was coming out of the anesthetic, the nurses in the ICU heard him trying to say something, but then he would lapse into unconsciousness.

Finally, someone understood the whispered words: "Go get Gordon Walls — Gordon Walls."

"I was on the golf course," said Gordon. "Two men came up on a cart and said, 'Your minister is in intensive care and keeps asking for you.' I'm a deacon. I'm blown away that he wants me. When I get to the clubhouse, I'm shaking; and I call my wife and she says Garrett and Brewster had been to my house, and all he does is keep asking for you.' "

Gordon owned Cockrell's Collision Repair, which operated out of two locations. Minutes after getting the call, he was at Smith's bedside, leaning close to hear Wayne's request.

"Magazines — in my trunk — get them out."

Gordon went to the police compound; he located the car and retrieved the magazines. "Imagine a reporter finding those magazines in the back of Wayne's car," he said.

When Smith recovered, he insisted that Walls' business was not the reason he'd been summoned. "He was one of the youngest board members. I told him he was the least spiritual and the magazines wouldn't hurt him," Wayne said, laughing.

Gordon Walls would later become senior executive minister of Southland Christian Church.

Using humor to disarm the other side

Smith found himself opposite a Louisville attorney who was an administrator in Kentucky's Department of Alcoholic Beverage Control. The "wets" wanted to extend liquor sales to 4 a.m., and the issue was hot.

"Someone suggested we have a debate," Wayne said. "It was on the radio, a Lexington station. We were going at it. Then I thought of what Will Rogers said: 'If a man can't get drunk by 1 a.m., he ain't really tryin'.' He started laughing, and that was that."

Wayne frequently took on the newspaper, as in this question he asked while delivering an after-dinner speech at the annual basketball banquet: "Suppose you see a skunk and an editor of the *Lexington Herald* in the middle of the road. Can you tell the difference between them? The skunk has skid marks nearby." This was in response to the newspaper's investigation of the University of Kentucky athletic department in regard to cheating.

Frank Anderson, photographer for the *Herald-Leader*, was not happy over Smith's criticism of the paper, yet they have remained friends. "The history of Southland Christian Church can be traced through his many photographs," Smith said. When Frank married, Wayne performed the ceremony. At Wayne's retirement ceremony at Memorial Coliseum, Frank Anderson was the one taking the pictures.

Wayne said, "It is not what you say; it's how you say it. There are times I have to back up and apologize. At times I paint with too broad a brush. 'He that hath not the spirit of Christ is none of his.' That means you can be dead right, yet wrong. Frank Anderson is my good friend."

The preacher and the political arena

Smith makes no apology for his involvement in politics. "The easiest way to correct an evil is to elect Christian officials," he said. He quotes John Jay, the first chief justice of the Supreme Court, who said, "Providence has given our people the choice of their rulers. And it is the duty as well as the privilege and interest of a Christian nation to select and prefer Christians for its rulers."

Wayne's patriotism is well-known. Dr. C. Barry McCarty, preaching minister of Valley View Christian Church in Dallas, Texas, and radio preacher for *The Christian's Hour*, cited an example.

"I was 20 years old at the time," Barry says. "I was traveling for the summer with Teen Mission USA, and living with Southland's youth minister, Bob Lieve. "When I wasn't on the road, many times I'd go with Wayne.

"I was sitting with Wayne in his kitchen when on TV came the scene of Nixon's resignation. Both of us stopped talking and watched. I looked over at Wayne, and he was weeping. He felt this was such a tragedy for our country.

"I thought to myself, 'This man loves his nation so much that he took that resignation personally.' That night made me a better citizen and a better patriot because of what I saw in him."

Years later McCarty dedicated his book, *Well Said and Worth Saying: A Public Speaking Guide for Church Leaders* (Broadman Press, 1991), to Wayne B. Smith, "a faithful preacher of the gospel and a great American patriot whose voice has called the lost to salvation, edified the Lord's church, and summoned his country to do what is right in the eyes of the King of Glory."

Smith wrote not only sermons, but also letters of encouragement, letters and notes of sympathy, and letters to the editor, such as these samples:

August 16, 1990; to the editor of the *Lexington Herald-Leader*: "The American Bar Association is now officially neutral on the subject of abortion. One word describes this action — sad. If any group should fight for those who cannot defend themselves, it should be attorneys. These professionals who deal with the law know you can leave one-half your estate to an unborn child. . . . I find it interesting that the ACLU who supposedly defend an individual's rights are strangely silent about the 4,000 babies who die daily. Hypocrisy of the highest order."

Or this:

October 31, 1990; to the editor of the *Herald-Leader*: "Your paper has had some poor editorials. However, 'A Burning Issue' (October 31, 1990)

Words From Wayne

When it's your football, you can make the rules.

is the worst…. In my opinion, Biafra, former lead singer for the Dead Kennedys punk rock band, is a traitor to his country. I think burning the flag is a crime. I believe the students who cheered the burning should be kicked out of the University. The Student Activities Board sponsoring Biafra has learned a valuable lesson. You invite a punk, you get a punk."

And letters to individuals, such as Smith's April 5, 1991, letter to an official at Lexington's world-famous Keeneland, opposing horse racing on Sunday. In that letter, Wayne wrote about the changes that have surrounded Sunday through the years: "It was once a Holy Day, a Sabbath Day, the Lord's Day, but now it is the Weekend. In my opinion this is called erosion. My purpose in writing is to ask that you not race on Easter Sunday."

Keeneland did not open on Easter Sunday.

"The Keeneland CEO came to my office, and we reached an agreement," said Wayne. "I agreed that they could race on Good Friday if they closed Easter Sunday. He and I are still friends. He wrote me a lovely letter when I retired."

Wayne's reasoning was that if the Lord was in the grave three days and arose on Sunday, he could not have been crucified on Friday.

"Did I have the authority to make this decision? Not really," he said. "However, no one else seemed to be moving in that direction, and when a large church speaks, it is easier to get a hearing."

Sometimes Wayne was on the winning side; sometimes on the losing.

In *The Voice* for October 7, 1992, he wrote, "Congratulations to Jim Ishmael. The Life Chain was a total success. Fifty-seven hundred persons (5,701) stood holding signs from Commonwealth Stadium to the Jessamine County line. There were 1150 from Southland."

There was sorrow, however, in the next item: "Most are aware by now about our state's High Court legalizing homosexual sex. This is a great setback morally for our Commonwealth. If you would care to have a copy of 8 reasons why this is a wrong decision, please call or write me."

Wayne's words resulted in a painful loss. The *Herald-Leader* carried Smith's comments, especially his criticism of the state's highest court. One of the judges on that court read the item in the paper and was so angry that he tracked down Wayne, though the latter was out of town.

"I was in Bob Russell's office at Southeast when the phone rang, and it was for me. The judge didn't like what I said." Then Smith added, "That was a sad day. We were good friends."

Speaking to a group of ministers in 1993, Smith said, "I encourage you to cooperate with other churches. Through the years I have teamed up with Methodists, Baptists, Catholics and even the Mormons on the Sunday closing law and abortion. The issue is not doctrine; the issue is defeating an evil in the community. Numbers are important — very important."

Brotherhood responsibilities, an increasing number of calls upon his time from civic organizations and, above all, the workload of being pastor to the thousands at Southland — after 23 years, Wayne gave up the Lions Club.

"It was hard," he said, "but 'Nevertheless.' "

Wally Rendel said of Smith, "Wayne was a voice in the community on blue laws, porn, liberalizing drinking laws, gay-rights issues — a strong, strong voice in the community over the years. He led the cause."

The issue might be as innocuous as Meals on Wheels. Or as incendiary as abortion. When Smith was behind it, he pulled out all the stops: "It's not the size of the dog in the fight; it's the size of the fight in the dog."

Advocate for issues big and small

The January 18, 1995, *Voice* carried the headline, "Sanctity of Life Celebration Set for January 22," and this article followed:

"We will be observing the 22nd anniversary of the Roe vs. Wade decision on Sunday, January 22. In Southland's morning services, Women for Life will honor their founders (Shirley Daniel, Patty Gilpin, Garnett Langley, and Susan Wiley). We will also celebrate the 10th anniversary of the AA Pregnancy Help Center in Lexington. Sunday afternoon the Southland family is encouraged to participate in a Rally at 2 p.m. on the Courthouse steps."

Words From Wayne

Character is what you do when you don't feel a tingle. The Christian life is not emotion, it's commitment.

Since opening in 1985, the AA Pregnancy Help Center has been a "full service pregnancy help center," providing positive alternatives to abortion. Their 24/7 hotline takes an estimated 4,000 calls yearly. The agency sees nearly 1,000 girls and women annually for pregnancy counseling and hundreds more for other needs. Since 1985, the center has saved 1,415 babies, 102 in 2003. Wayne added, "And saved the mothers abortion's heartache."

Bluegrass Christian Adoption Services (BCAS) opened in 1987, a separately incorporated, state-licensed child-placing agency, operating under the auspices and direction of Women for Life Inc. As of this writing, BCAS has placed 99 babies in loving Christian two-parent families at a reasonable cost.

There may be no moral issue more repugnant to Wayne B. Smith than abortion, and he has gone to considerable lengths to encourage and to support Women for Life and allied agencies.

Speaking on the issue, Smith minces no words: "Roe vs. Wade was the ruling where Harry Blackmun and a few of his friends on the Supreme Court of the United States decided that the baby, as long as it is in its mother's womb, is not a legal person; it is the mother's property to do with as she pleases. A woman may own the house; it's not her right to kill the tenant. With this decision, it became legal for mothers, during the entire nine months of their pregnancy, at any time and for any reason, to have their babies killed — as long as the killing was done by a licensed physician."

Wayne continued: "Justice Blackman said he would take this decision to his grave. True, Mr. Blackman, and a lot farther."

Smith went every year to the Capitol at Frankfort on the anniversary of Roe vs. Wade, often as one of the speakers. "When I spoke one time, it was cold, and they took it into the rotunda," Wayne said. "The governor, Wallace Wilkinson, saw me and came over and put his arm around me and said, 'Wayne, why are you here?' I said, 'Governor, I'm trying to take a stand.' "

Size and status mattered little to Wayne. Later that year, a representative from the Gideons asked to make a presentation at Southland, and Wayne told him, "You don't have to speak, but we'll see what we can do."

No speech, no big appeal, just a few words from Wayne, and $3,060 was collected.

His pro-life activism brought him several invitations to speak at events hosted by the Catholic Church.

He tried to revive Eastland Christian Church, enlisting manpower and raising money from Southland to do so. Eastland was dying. The two remaining elders offered the building to Southland Christian Church if Southland would pay the outstanding bills.

Southland paid the bills.

Southland invested around $150,000 and many hours of work, then gave the building to Northern Heights. For a time, the property was used by Northern Heights Christian Church. Northern Heights built a new building in Hamburg Place and sold the Eastland property for nearly half a million. The legacy continues: from Broadway to Southland to Northern Heights.

Northern Heights is now NorthEast Christian Church and growing rapidly under the leadership of Whit Criswell.

The new Jessamine Christian Church in Nicholasville, Kentucky, was meeting in an elementary school. Alvin Lowry, a former elder at Southland, had taken part in this effort. Lowry phoned Smith: "There's a church on the bypass for sale."

Immediately, Wayne was interested. The brick building, situated on three acres, had been erected in 1989 by the Lutherans; the asking price was $500,000. Wayne approached Len Aldridge and Ron Switzer and sought their counsel concerning the best way to proceed. Aldridge and Switzer suggested making an offer of $400,000. The offer was refused.

"I had a church to run," Wayne said. "So I asked them, 'Would you take $415,000, and they said yes. My friends each contributed $5,000, plus another $5,000 from Charles 'Junior' Johnson, also a Southland member. Len Aldridge then presented a plan to raise the $400,000."

Smith lent his influence to P-NUTS (Parents Needing Understanding and Teen Support), a ministry sponsored by Gene and Karen Doyle. Gene hosted *Page One*, a Christian talk show.

"I met Gene several years ago when we were fighting to keep liquor out of restaurants on the Lord's Day," Wayne said. "He and Karen are two of my favorite people at Southland."

Smith was a strong supporter of everything from the Boy Scouts to the police. While promoting a men's meeting for August 14, 1995, he said, "We are privileged to have one of our own speak to the Men's Fellowship Monday night. Jerry Lovett served 26 years as a state trooper and two years as commissioner of the state police."

He described Lovett's spectacular career in public service, then closed with a rousing invitation for every Southland man to be there with their preacher.

"There were times I was tired and didn't want to go," Smith admitted. "But I knew if I didn't go, many of the men wouldn't go either. We were running close to 4,000 at the time, and I had a lot of other places I could have been. But the senior minister can go to these events if he wants to. So I went. 'Nevertheless.' "

Wayne spoke of Lovett with admiration. "It was a dream come true to have the head of the state police in our church. As a matter of fact, we had two. Judge Ray Corns was also appointed to that position."

Bob Russell spoke of Smith's courage: "I saw him in action at Cincinnati Bible College and Seminary. We were going through a difficult time.

Smith's Political Views — The Short Version

Who do you vote for?
I try to vote for the right person. However, I could never vote for a candidate or platform that includes homosexuality or abortion.

What do you see as America's greatest threat?
Secular parents, liberal judges and the American Civil Liberties Union.

If you were not a conservative, what would you be?
Ashamed.

The school was in danger of folding financially. The pressure was awful. Somebody sent a very critical letter to the trustees, telling us how it ought to be done.

We get in this room, 20 trustees on one side, 30 administrators and faculty members on the other side. The tension is so thick you can cut it with a knife.

"Smith is chairman. He got that letter out, in front of these men, and stood up. I remember seeing his stubby finger. 'Who wrote this? I want to know first of all who wrote this.' The letter writer finally raised his hand. Wayne said, 'This is a symptom of what our problem is right here.' "

Russell concluded: "Wayne Smith is authentic. He's not afraid to put his neck on the line and say, 'I'll be the point man.' Here's a guy who barely got through school and the scholars with doctorates are quaking in their boots in his presence. That's courage. I want him on my team, and I want to be on his."

"I don't enjoy controversy," Wayne said. "There was a time when I did. But not now. Age does make a difference. Speaking for these events, civic things, other events — these things are hard. You prepare, then you over-prepare. You want it to be good, to make it great if you can."

Protesting the play *O Calcutta*, which featured nudity; serving alcohol at a public golf course; horse racing on Sunday: this is only a partial list.

"Some issues are more important than others," said Wayne. "You can't fight issues all the time. Our main task is the Great Commission. If you spend all your time weeding the garden, you won't have time for planting."

"Expect opposition," Wayne continued. "It will come. Jesus didn't hide his scars to win disciples. Be willing to take great risks for a great God. God and one man are a majority. Our Lord made it plain if you desire to be a follower of his: 'If any man would come after me, (1) let him deny himself, (2) take up his cross, and (3) follow me.' That doesn't sound seeker-friendly to me."

In a survey by the (*Lexington*) *Herald-Leader* taken June 26, 1994, Wayne B. Smith, pastor of Southland Christian Church, was named one of Lexington's most influential citizens.

"It's time to turn the page and move on."

Neighbor Ed McKinney, seeing Wayne B. Smith going down the street behind Fluff, the Smiths' little white shih tzu, said, "I never thought I'd see the day when Wayne Smith would be walking a dog."

Daughters Judy and Jana bought Fluff for their parents' golden wedding anniversary, August 28, 2001. Judy decided that because the kids were gone and Wayne was home more, the ultimate anniversary gift would be a dog.

"That dog has changed their lives," she said. "Dad told me that if he comes home and is down, once he plays with Fluff, he feels so much better. I thought I had picked a fairly even-tempered dog, but I must have picked the wildest in the litter. That dog is hyper, overly friendly and loves people. Fluff fits right in."

The girls arranged an afternoon reception for their parents' anniversary and were preparing announcements to be placed in three newspapers when Wayne learned of it. He put the brakes on. Smith is not opposed to festivities; his decision came from another direction.

"The girls had the place lined up," Wayne said. "Invite our friends and so on. I said to Marge, 'Unless you would be hurt, I want to call it off.'"

Then he explained: "I don't want people to stand in line. I don't want the staff to have to come and shake hands with us. We've said good-bye. These are the people that gave us cars and gifts and love for 40 years. I don't want them to feel they need to do anything more for Wayne and Marge."

So they called it off. When Wayne retired, he received more than 1,000 cards and notes, most saying basically the same thing: "You were there when we needed you." To Wayne, that was more than enough.

Changes, but no slowdown

Retirement may have brought changes but hardly a slowdown. Since he left Southland, Wayne averages 190 engagements a year, speaking more times than many preachers with full-time pulpits.

"I love to preach," Wayne said. "One thing that's nice is that I can use some of the same material, whether it's Bluefield, West Virginia, or Arlington, Texas. That way I can take the best. You don't throw medicine away after you use it one time."

McKinney Associates, a Louisville talent agency affiliated with the National Speakers Association, asked Wayne if it could represent him, but he chose not to pursue the offer.

He accepts invitations on a first-come, first-served basis, depending upon his schedule. Even so, there is the occasional invitation that he declines. In 1996, a Nebraska preacher asked Wayne to come and speak several times to help preacher and congregation in their transition to a more contemporary approach.

Smith declined.

In his reply, Wayne wrote: I don't think I'm the man for your needs. I'm traditional. I accomplished what I did because I stayed 40 years. I'm a meat and potatoes man. I preached as best I could and knocked on doors. I'm a pastor at heart. I was there when there was a surgery, crisis, etc.

"You want change. You want to begin a new service on Sunday morning. That's foreign to me. We had three services and they were all the same. No overhead words to hymns, etc. My last year at Southland 1995, we averaged 3,761. Mike Breaux came and changed everything and they are near 1,000 more each Sunday. Seventy-six decisions in three weeks. They will soon begin Saturday night services. I praise God for this unbelievable increase, but I've never done it (emphasis Wayne's).

He suggested the names of several others, then closed the letter: I've enclosed a tape of Mike Breaux's sermon from 2/11/96. It is a masterpiece on change. I'm suggesting you get someone else because I feel uncomfortable about what you want. You want change. You need someone who can speak with experience and authority. It's difficult to get that from a 67-year-old preacher.

At Wilmore Elementary School in Jessamine County, Wayne spoke to the nonteaching employees: maintenance workers, bus drivers, teacher's aides and administrative personnel. At the time, the superintendent of schools was Linda France, a member of Southland, and the head of the school board was Eugene Peel, an elder at Southland.

Wayne said, "I told the audience, 'You are what holds this place together. People think Tim Couch of the Cleveland Browns is a great quarterback. Take away the line and see what happens. You're the glue. You're the infrastructure.' "

Looking back on the evening, Wayne observed, "We were there to compliment these people, not to challenge them but to thank them. You've got to make them feel important, because they are. I sat across from one teacher, an assistant, who said, 'I teach the handicapped.' I told her, 'If I was here, I would be in your class.' "

Berea College in Berea, Kentucky, asked Smith to deliver the baccalaureate address at the college's 143rd anniversary, May 24, 1998. Wayne gladly accepted, saying, "I was surprised they asked me."

Does he miss being senior minister of Southland Christian Church?

"I don't miss it at all. That's a chapter in my life that is past. I'm preaching each weekend, and my plate is full, so I continue to do what I love the most."

Smith reflected a moment. "I do miss the fellowship I had with some wonderful people, and I miss our great choir, and the Messengers quartet."

Most weekends are similar to his trip to Fort Myers, Florida, to speak at Southside Christian Church for its finance campaign. Wayne spoke Sunday morning and again Sunday night at a banquet, after which the congregation was asked for pledges.

Consider his trip to Colleyville Christian Church, northwest of Dallas. Smith flew in on Friday; spoke Saturday morning to a prayer breakfast for men and boys; spoke Saturday night to a banquet for the elders, staff and their wives; then preached three times on Sunday morning.

Mike Breaux, his successor at Southland, asked Wayne to speak for Southland's financial drive. Smith spoke for the 5:00 and 6:30 Saturday-evening services, then Sunday morning for the 8:30 service.

"I didn't give the sermon," Wayne explained. "This was a brief speech to encourage the people to give. I was more nervous than if I'd been preaching."

A previous commitment to Christ the King Catholic Church kept him from the other two services at Southland. He spoke one hour to the 9:45 adult-education class and gave the sermon at the 11:00 Mass. He honored the length they requested — his homily was 14 minutes.

"I was nervous but very honored," Wayne said later. "This privilege is seldom extended to a non-Catholic."

Despite such a schedule, Smith still has time for preachers. In conversation recently with a younger man who was having difficulty with his leadership, Wayne counseled, "Let them win some of the time. Nobody likes a preacher who has to be right all the time."

Maintaining a cherished commitment

There are two homes Wayne never misses on Christmas Day.

He moved to Lexington in March 1956. Marge came three months later, having finished out the school year at Buena Vista Elementary School in Harrison County. Although he moved in 1956, Wayne made numerous prior trips to Lexington in preparation for planting the new congregation.

Broadway Christian Church hired one of its members, William C. Bryant, as architect. In December 1955, Smith visited the Bryant home.

"His wife, Nell, answered the door," Wayne said. "She told me to go upstairs where his office was. Bill heard me coming, greeted me and asked me what company I was with. I said, 'I'm the minister of the new church.' "

Before leaving, Smith told Bryant that if he ever needed someone to hold a tape measure or help on a building project, "just give me a call."

That was the beginning of a great friendship. "I was a stranger," Wayne said, "and Bill and Nell took me in. Little did I know that would be my home away from home until Marge arrived."

Sometime later, the Bryants moved into a more spacious home and built an office in the back yard, but the friendship continued. "They gave us a used car, which we desperately needed," Wayne said. "They gave us money for our vacation, gave money for others, taught Sunday school and so on. Bill was called home in 1977 to a place not made with hands, eternal in the heavens.

Who Is This Man?

Beyond his personal commitment to helping people, Wayne Smith has been the soul and conscience of Lexington. His influence reached well outside the church doors to Rotaries, Kiwanis Clubs, business roundtables and meetings of all types — all gratified and uplifted by the humorous spirit of Wayne.

Wayne said often that, intellectually, he's not a deep person. I disagree. His disarming way, his illustrations and self-effacing manner always touched the heart, not only with alacrity, but with deep insight into human nature. He'd uncover our sins and inconsistencies and cover them with the love of Christ in the balm of laughter. He made the complex simple, the profound understandable.

As with myself, I suspect the reassuring wit and wisdom of Wayne Smith has been an anchor to hundreds, if not thousands, helping bring them assurance through their life's troubled waters.

In the early part of our nation, pastors took a leadership role in communities. They were relevant and respected. They signed our founding documents. They even fought in our wars. Today, too many are afraid of offending their congregations.

Wayne was one of a few who did not shy away from the issues of the day. I'm sure he gave his elders fits speaking out about the local controversial issues. Donations may have gone down, but he still spoke the relevant truth from his heart. I believe it can be rightly asserted that south Lexington is the heart of a strong community of faith in large part because of Wayne's courage and outspoken leadership.

There is no doubt that when Wayne meets his Maker, he will hear the words "Well done, my good and faithful servant." Wayne will likely reply, "Have you heard this one? I heard it on the way up here." He'll tell a hilarious story and burst out in his usual uncontrollable laughter with such contagion that even the Maker will join in. Then all the angels will rush to see who this man is that can make even the King laugh so.

— *Dr. Ernie L. Fletcher, Governor of the Commonwealth of Kentucky*

"Every Christmas day I return with gifts to say thanks to Nell and their two sons and daughter for helping me when I needed it most. Gratitude is dateless. You don't stop saying thank you."

Wayne was able to help Bill in one instance. Harrison County, where Marge had taught, planned four new school buildings. Wayne had some influence in those parts as well. William C. Bryant designed three of the four schools.

The other home where Smith goes on Christmas Day is that of Len and Ann Aldridge. Len, a certified public accountant (CPA), is an entrepreneur par excellence. Len and his partner developed the Firebrook subdivision, near Southland, and he named one of the streets Wayne's Boulevard.

Smith came into the Aldridges' lives through a tragedy in Ann's family. "Wayne stayed right there," Ann said. "He didn't know me; we had never met. But he helped me through that awful time."

Looking back, Wayne said, "Maybe I helped them, but he sure has helped me. Through their generosity, the Aldridges have made a much smoother road for Wayne, Marge and the girls."

Len was an old-timer at Southland Christian Church, all the way back to 1963. When Wayne had the automobile accident in 1985, Len approached his friend Charles "Junior" Johnson and asked him to make arrangements for Smith to exercise at Ron Switzer's Lexington Athletic Club. Ron presented Wayne with a membership.

Mention has already been made of Aldridge's help with Jessamine Christian Church, an effort of the Bluegrass Christian Men's Fellowship. To quote Smith's column in the *Southland Voice*, "the dream of securing a permanent home for the infant congregation became a reality because of the commitment of one man, Len Aldridge, who spearheaded the effort."

In 1995, Aldridge, Switzer and Johnson formed a small group to help Smith with "his various projects," as Len put it.

Wayne's next project was Mount Zion Christian Church, in a rural area known as Becknerville, eight miles from Winchester, Kentucky. Wayne's son-in-law, Kenny Speakes, is minister of this church. Mount Zion needed a new house of worship, but difficulties during the building program necessitated hiring a new contractor and additional funding. Once again,

Wayne's "committee" came through, contributing considerable money and enlisting the help of others.

"The campaign was successful," Wayne said. "And the building is beautiful."

Most CPAs are not risk takers, but Aldridge says, "Wayne developed that side of me." Ann explained it this way: "Len has trouble saying no to Wayne."

Len responded, "I've been able to say no to him a couple of times, but not very often."

Wayne is the first to acknowledge the generosity of friends who have made his ministry possible. Over the years, he has had three Lincoln Town Cars supplied by friends: the first by Len Aldridge, Junior Johnson and Chris Carton. Aldridge provided the second car. The current Lincoln Wayne drives was paid for half by Johnson and half by Switzer and his wife, Claudette.

The church had previously given Smith a new Cadillac on his 20th anniversary and a new Lincoln on his 30th.

Ron and Len knew each other from working for the same CPA firm. Ron started going to Southland in the early 1990s. "Junior Johnson introduced him to me," said Ron. "Junior talked all the time about Wayne."

Ron's son, Clark, became involved with drugs, and Ron asked Wayne for help. "Let him go with me," suggested Wayne. "All it will cost you is a motel room, if I'm out of town, and a plane ticket."

So for a year, Clark accompanied Wayne to the latter's speaking engagements. Wayne had retired from Southland Christian Church at the beginning of 1996, so it was an ideal time to mentor Clark. During that year, Wayne B. Smith spoke three times a week, a total of 161 times. Nineteen of those trips were by air; Clark drove the car for the remainder. Together they visited 13 states.

Today, Clark Switzer is celebrating seven years drug-free. During those years he drove for Wayne, Clark married and earned two degrees from the University of Kentucky. "Wayne is so common, so down to earth," Ron said. "He's a person you can talk to, be buddies with."

Ron continued: "Wayne is very perceptive. He knows what buttons to push. He could have been successful in any field he chose. It takes a remarkable person to be minister of one church 40 years and hold the flock together."

The Winner's Circle

Tracy Farmer invited Wayne and Marge to go to lunch at Keeneland with him and his wife, Carol, and the Smiths accepted. Lexington's Keeneland is arguably the best track in the world for horse racing and is the world's largest seller of thoroughbreds. After lunch, Tracy said, "I've got a horse I'd like for you to see."

Wayne had never seen the back side of the racetrack, the barns and stables smelling of horses and hay, the colors and bustling preparation for the day's races.

"Let's go this way," said Tracy, and led Wayne and Marge into the stands to his personal box. The four watched several races; then the turn came for the Farmers' horse, and the horse won!

"We need to go down," Tracy said, inviting the Smiths to follow.

"He took us right into the Winner's Circle," Wayne said.

The following week, one of Southland's members asked Smith, "That wasn't you I saw on TV last Sunday, was it?"

"The first time I go to the track," Wayne said, "I make it to the Winner's Circle. I got several calls about that, all humorous."

A dozen or so heavy hitters in Lexington's economic life meet several times a year to discuss various subjects, usually politics, at the country club.

This unofficial gathering includes a U.S. federal judge, a former governor, owners of some of Lexington's finest horse farms, business leaders and two college presidents. Smith is the only preacher.

He described a recent meeting: "I was sitting across from former Governor Ned Breathitt. Next to him was Charles T. Wethington Jr., who had stepped down as president of the University of Kentucky. Next to me was Ben Chandler, grandson of Governor "Happy" Chandler. So easy to talk to.

"We were talking, and he asked me, 'Aren't you connected with Cincinnati Bible Seminary?' and I said 'Yes.' He said, 'My great-grandfather helped found that school.' I could have fainted."

Chandler went on to tell how his family started out in the Christian Church in Corydon, Kentucky, south of Henderson, and changed to the Episcopal church when his grandfather married. After the meeting, Wayne did his research, and though Cincinnati Bible Seminary opened in 1924, incorporation came in 1929. One of the incorporators was indeed Chandler's ancestor, Ira M. Boswell.

Wayne is often asked to endorse candidates, as in this February 20, 2001, example:

" *'The smiles of heaven can never be expected on a nation that disregards the eternal rules of order and right.'* (George Washington, 1789). I support Dr. A. Patrick Schneider II and ask you to vote for this fine physician because he will use his influence to uphold those core values that have made our nation great."

Smith actively supported Scott Crosbie's campaign for mayor in 2001-2002. John Roach, a Lexington attorney, was Crosbie's campaign manager. "John is chairman of the board at Broadway," Wayne said, then laughed: "He switched from the Democratic to the Republican Party. When you do that, you don't have to be baptized."

Crosbie held several fund-raisers in private homes — "These aren't starter homes, either," Wayne said — where many guests contributed $1,000 each. Wayne spoke at four of these meetings.

"I spoke a few minutes for each one," said Smith. "They felt that my name would help the cause."

Wayne's sentiments were widely known; his Lincoln displayed a "Crosbie for Mayor" bumper sticker for months.

Joy at Southland's continued growth

Smith was giving a Saturday-afternoon tour of the church grounds to a couple of friends and came to a pair of metal buildings out on the back lot, away from the main building. Several old cars were parked alongside one of the sheds, and dozens of people stood around waiting and talking, most with several children. Others were loading furniture and household items into their cars.

With pride in his voice, Smith told his guests, "I didn't have anything to do with this, but I think it's great."

The program is Helping Through Him, and the prime mover is Charlie Easterly. "God got my attention," Charlie said. "He did it through Roy Mays. My sister, Carol Reynolds, goes to Southland, and she set up this meeting between me and Roy at a church picnic in 1986. I had been in depression for eight months. I didn't care if I lived or died. The hour I spent with Roy was the first hope, the first daylight, for me.

"Roy baptized me in 1989, and he became my mentor, working with me, helping me. About 12 to 15 of us in Whit Criswell's Higher Ground class founded Helping Through Him on June 29, 1992. Whit was the encourager and go-between with all us rag-tag new Christians and the elders.

"I went on a mission trip in 1992 to Jamaica. My dad and I had a NAPA Auto Parts store in Danville, Kentucky, and when I came back, instead of spending time in my store, I wanted to be at Southland. I meant to do something for people, instead of seeing how much money I could make.

"We started out mowing yards and cleaning gutters and trimming hedges for single moms. One Saturday a month, we would do one or two yards. Our only assets were one drawer, a filing cabinet and a barn. I felt God was telling me to do more.

"I didn't know Wayne very well, but he knew me. Always called me by my name — 'Hey, Charlie, how ya doing?' — and all that.

"I did some driving for him. One night when he was speaking, he had me stand up. He told the entire crowd, 'This guy is single and needs a date. If you know any available women, or if any of you here are interested, see me after the service.'

"I kept pushing to do more in Helping Through Him, and he called me into his office one time and talked to me. 'Do you really want to mess around with all this clothing and stuff? I sure wouldn't want to, but if you do, that's great.'

"So the church hired me. I found out later that he was really a strong supporter for me in taking the program to the elders."

Helping Through Him serves an average of 93 families every week. People call in and describe what they need, and the staff — most of them volunteers — see if those items are on hand. "They call this 'Dillard's South,'" said Wayne. Dillard's is an upscale department store with outlets in Lexington and elsewhere.

Recipients are invited to a large room, given a loaf of bread and told about Jesus, the Bread of Life. Furniture, clothing, toys — last year Helping Through Him gave away 37 cars in addition to everything else. Each car was completely rebuilt to make it safe before it was given away.

Wayne helps select his successor

After announcing his retirement, Wayne had some influence in selecting his successor. Mike Breaux was involved in a dynamic ministry with Canyon Ridge Christian Church in Las Vegas. Breaux grew up in Lexington, and his ministries included a youth ministry at Broadway and senior ministry of Southside in Harrodsburg.

Gordon Walls was chairman of Southland's search committee. Wayne and Roy Mays III knew that Breaux was high on Walls' list, but they also knew that the committee had never heard him preach. Wayne was ill, and he asked Roy to telephone Mike and see if he could fill the pulpit. Once they had heard Breaux, the committee agreed to hire him.

Smith believes that God led Breaux to Southland. Southland's attendance has continued to climb. Under Breaux, the church is reaching out to a younger generation.

Wayne's last column in *The Voice of Southland Christian Church* encouraged the church to accept Mike and to release him. "It is time to turn the page and move on," Smith wrote. "Rearview mirrors have value, but they make terrible windshields."

Eight years later, Breaux accepted a call to become teaching pastor of Willow Creek Community Church in South Barrington, Illinois. Southland then named Jon Weese, its own minister of adult discipleship, as senior minister.

Working hard and loving it

Someone asked Wayne, "Now that you're retired, is it difficult to sit through church?"

"No," he responded. "I preach most Sundays, and I have an office in my basement, because I normally have several projects I'm working on."

However, Wayne doesn't spend much time in the basement. For example, he spoke for the 25th anniversary of Gateway Christian Church in Mount Sterling, and at an annual churchwide banquet at First Baptist in Cold Springs. For the Shelby County Cattlemen's Association, he gave a speech to more than 200 that, according to Smith, "went real well."

What made Wayne feel especially good was that the head of the association was from Mount Eden Christian Church, 10 miles south of Shelbyville. "It makes you feel great to see Christian people in high places," Smith said.

The brother from Mount Eden probably felt good, too, recalling Smith's last appearance at Mount Eden, when Wayne lost his false teeth during the sermon.

Smith was in the process of getting dental implants. "There's six months between the time they put in the implants and the time they put on the permanent teeth," Wayne explained. "If your body rejects an implant, that's serious money. They gave me a special set of false teeth to use until the time for the permanent teeth, and I hadn't used them in preaching before."

Wayne's topic was the second coming. "Toward the end they came," he said. His uppers landed on the pulpit, and Wayne calmly reached down and put them back in. After the laughter died down, Smith proceeded: "Now folks, I'm 72 years old. If I were younger, I'd be embarrassed, but at my age, I don't really care."

Wayne received a bonus. "My friend Len Aldridge heard about it and sent me this joke: There was a preacher who preached 10 minutes one Sunday, 20 the next, and an hour and one-half on the third Sunday. The

Words From Wayne

The Christian is the only one that has the right to be happy.

elders asked why the variation in length. The preacher said, 'I had my teeth extracted. The first Sunday, my gums were sore; the second Sunday, my gums were better.' The elders asked, 'What happened when you preached an hour and one-half?' 'I got my wife's teeth by mistake.' "

Smith's implants worked; he now has permanent teeth, thanks to Dr. Tom Daniel, oral surgeon, and Dr. Pam Revel.

While speaking at Whit Criswell's church, NorthEast Christian in Lexington, Wayne said, "Now folks, the only thing going for Whit is his looks. And someday he'll look like me." "Never," said Marge.

Wayne's engagement with the chamber-of-commerce annual dinner in Seymour, Indiana, "was first class," he says. Two hundred fifty people were present for the catered event, everyone properly attired, and Smith's message met the occasion. After several jokes, he outlined six signs of growth and six signs of stagnation.

"You say, 'I love Seymour, Indiana.' Love is a noun, but love is also a verb. Maybe you heard about the little girl invited down the street for dinner. Mother told her to be polite, to always be positive.

"The lady asked, 'Do you like broccoli?' 'Oh, yes, I love broccoli.' So the lady served the little girl a helping of broccoli, which she did not eat. 'I thought you loved broccoli.' 'Yes, I love broccoli,' the little girl said, 'but not enough to eat it.' You love Seymour, but not enough to join the chamber of commerce, not enough to do anything for your town. When somebody tells you he loves Seymour, ask him what he's doing for your town."

Because of his success in Seymour, Wayne received a call from another Indiana chamber of commerce. As the caller described the venue where he would speak, Smith knew he had a problem.

"We are expecting about 220 people," the caller said. "We only have two places in the county to hold a crowd like that: either the Shriners Temple, with 150 or the fairgrounds, which will hold 500."

Wayne turned down the invitation, taking care not to insult the person extending the invitation. "The setting is so important," he said later. "Trying to speak to 200 people in a room for 500 won't work for me. You need the people close; you need to see them. I can't do it in a big, empty room. A banquet is different from a convention sermon."

When he was asked to participate in a roast for Bob Russell, Wayne met with David Novak, a member of Southeast Christian and the head of the company that owns KFC, Pizza Hut, Taco Bell and other food outlets.

Wayne said, "It thrills you to see these young guys so successful and so dedicated to the Lord."

No regrets

While meeting with friends at the Dry Ridge exit just off I-75, Wayne suggested the Country Grill rather than the Cracker Barrel. "I hate to stand in line," he explained. "Besides, we can talk there." After lunch, he asked for a to-go cup for his diet cola. "Lots of ice," he told the waitress. She brought a lid, but Smith left it on the table. "I never use a lid," he said. "That's one of my peculiarities. I like to see what I'm drinking."

When Wayne learned of a preacher who wanted to change pastorates, he called three churches he knew of that were seeking ministers. "I put your name in at First Christian today," he told his friend. "That's a great church. You'd do a great job there."

Smith and another preacher were having lunch at another place when a woman and her husband approached their table.

"You don't remember me," she began. "We live in Indianapolis now, but I became a Christian because of you. When I was a girl, my family went to Southland, and I used to think you followed me around. It was as if you knew what I had done and then preached at me on Sunday."

Many people grieve over lost opportunities. Not Wayne B. Smith. Few people have made better use of what life has given them. "God is good," he said and meant it.

Does he regret leaving Southland? "No. Never one regret," he answered. "To preach to the same people 40 years is privilege enough. It was time to go. I left at the right time."

Smith referred to a quotation from Elton Trueblood: "A man has at least begun to understand the meaning of human life when he plants shade trees under which he knows full well he will never sit."

Words From Wayne

Two men looked through bars; one saw mud, the other saw stars.

Building dedications point to Smith's future influence

October 9, 2003, was a significant day for Wayne B. Smith. Cincinnati Bible College and Seminary was hosting the first annual Preaching Summit in its new $4 million Worship and Ministry Center. CBC&S president David Faust asked Smith to dedicate the Wayne B. Smith Oratorium with a message aimed at ministers and students who were attending the summit.

Years ago, during his sermon at the 1977 North American Christian Convention, Smith challenged colleges to set aside a practice room for preaching, just as they had done for students to practice piano or choir.

Now Wayne's dream had become reality, for a central feature of the new center was this special room. Here, students aspiring to become preachers would train in a churchlike setting.

Wayne surveyed the packed house and whispered, "I didn't realize there would be so many young people here."

A friend reminded him, "Wayne, they are the ones who will use this room. Here's where they'll learn how to preach."

The moment was particularly significant for Smith, because as he came to the platform, he stood behind the pulpit he stood behind when he first came to Lexington in 1956; it had been beautifully restored and presented to the school by Hill 'N Dale Christian Church.

In his message — a Wayne Smith mixture of humor, emotion and challenge — he told of the need for ministers to get out among the people as well as stand behind the pulpit. "It bothers me when preachers say, 'I'm not gifted at calling.' " Wayne stopped, looked the crowd over, then thundered, "Well, *he can learn.*"

He went on. "You can learn to call, much as I learned to prepare sermons, which is not my talent. But as Jesus said just before the cross, 'Nevertheless, not my will but thine,' then we can learn to do a lot of things we may not feel comfortable at first doing."

Continuing, he said, "The measure of a man's devotion to the Lord is how much he is willing to do that he doesn't like to do, because he knows this is what God wants him to do."

On May 4, 2000, Kentucky Christian College (KCC) dedicated the $3.2 million Wayne B. Smith Center for Christian Leadership. In his dedication message, Bob Russell, senior minister of Southeast Christian Church in Louisville, said, "You will notice that the building says 'Wayne B. Smith "Leadership," not "Scholarship," Center.' Politicians come to him for advice, and he's never been a politician. Athletes look to him as an example, and he's never been an athlete. Ministers come to him for sermon material, and he's never preached an original sermon in his life."

Smith laughed the loudest, and he still tells the story.

KCC president Keith Keeran said, "Wayne's ministry has touched the lives of thousands throughout America and the world. He has grown and shepherded one of the nation's largest congregations and is one of the most respected Christian ministers in the United States. Wayne has planted churches, mentored others for ministry and has been the leading spiritual and moral conscience in his community. Few, if any, have invested more of themselves in others or have been more generous and compassionate than Wayne Smith. It is fitting that this building should bear the name of this beloved Christian servant."

Big shoes to fill

Fifty-eight state troopers were graduating in Frankfort October 17, 2003. After 22 weeks of intensive training, Cadet Class # 81 was ready to serve the commonwealth. Many of the state's highest officials would be in attendance, as well as news media, other officers and families of the cadets.

Gov. Paul Patton was the announced speaker.

However, two days before the event, former Gov. Ned Breathitt died, and Breathitt's funeral was to be held the same morning as the ceremonies honoring the graduating troopers. The Kentucky State Police Headquarters called Wayne B. Smith. Could Pastor Smith take Governor Patton's place on the program?

On the morning of the ceremony, a Kentucky State Police car picked Smith up at his home, drove him to the capital city and back home after his message.

"I had to fill some mighty big shoes," Wayne said afterward. "Of course, it was an honor, and I was pleased to be asked. Besides, I need a healthy relationship with state troopers."

Recently a worker from India asked Wayne for help. The man needed additional money to support new churches and a training school for preachers. Wayne swung into action and enlisted 28 preachers from Lexington and the surrounding area to come to Springs Inn for lunch to hear the man's presentation. After the brother from India spoke, Wayne gave a vigorous endorsement, asking each man to do whatever he could on behalf of this worker from overseas. When everyone had gone, Wayne paid the bill — out of his own pocket.

When Ernie Fletcher was elected governor of Kentucky in 2003, he asked Wayne to offer the invocation at the private swearing-in ceremony at midnight, December 8, and the benediction at the public ceremony at 3 p.m., December 9.

Standing near the statue of Abraham Lincoln in the rotunda of the

Speaking Dates in Retirement for Wayne B. Smith

Wayne preached or spoke for an event nearly four times every week (3.7 average) the first eight years of his retirement. He continues to do so as opportunity and health permit.

Year	Number of Times Each Week	Total for the Year
1996	3.1	161
1997	5.4	282
1998	4.7	245
1999	2.9	155
2000	3.1	161
2001	3.7	193
2002	3.3	171
2003	2.9	154
Total		1,522

2004 continues this pace and his calendar is filling up for 2005 and into 2006. Thus far in his retirement Wayne has preached or spoken in 28 states, 401,000 of those miles by air.

Capitol in Frankfort during the private ceremony, Wayne thanked God "for Ernie L. Fletcher, a man who has chosen opportunity, not security, and who took the calculated risk to fail and has succeeded in attaining the highest office in the Commonwealth to share his giftedness and vision."

Smith quoted the prophet Jeremiah and asked that God would "give wisdom to these men that they will never become a slave to the urgent while ignoring the essential."

In his benediction at the public ceremony, Wayne referred to Fletcher's background, which "has made him uniquely qualified to meet the needs of Kentuckians physically and spiritually," then prayed, "Some questioned whether his efforts would lead to Frankfort. We now know that God will never lead you where his grace cannot sustain you."

Smith closed with the following:

"The Bible says, 'Think it not strange when fiery trials come upon you.' When this inevitably comes to pass, remember, 'Greater is He that is in you than He that is in the world.'

"The strife will not be long; this day the noise of battle, the next the victor's song. O God, give thy servants Governor Fletcher and Glenna, and Lieutenant Governor Pence and Ruth Ann, the wisdom to lead; and give the people of our Commonwealth the discernment to follow. In Jesus' name, Amen."

In 1956, when Wayne started Southland, John Burk was the first chairman of the board. John passed away several months ago, but his widow remembers. Marie's description still fits: "Wayne's great. He's done a lot for the Christian Churches. And he's still full of it."

Southland Christian Church has called a new preacher since Mike Breaux moved to Willow Creek Community Church, near Chicago, and over lunch, Wayne was talking about Breaux's successor, Jon Weece. Jon was on Southland's staff as minister of adult discipleship.

The elders interviewed Weece and decided to look no further. He has been enthusiastically received by the congregation.

Over lunch, Wayne was talking about the change. Smith's mind went

Words From Wayne

Tomorrow is a good word for optimism. It's also an excuse for delay.

back to a 13-year-old girl by the name of Kelly, and he told the following story:

"Kelly's parents are Tommy and Judy Weaver, faithful Southland members. Kelly invited her good friend, Allison, also 13, to spend the night and go to church with them. Soon Allison was a regular, thanks to an invitation from Kelly and transportation by Tommy. Allison accepted Christ and was baptized.

"Jon Weece was an intern at Southland, and he and Allison met each other, but only briefly. When he graduated from Ozark Christian College, Jon felt called to go to Haiti. Four years in a place with no electricity nor running water speaks volumes about commitment.

"Through Brewster, Allison took a short-term mission trip to Haiti. When she went back a second time, she stayed there for a year. While there, the love of two committed people bloomed. They were married, and the rest is history."

Wayne's voice quavered. "I said to Tommy the other day, 'Look at the contribution you and Judy and your daughter made for the Lord's work when you invited Allison.' "

Wiping the tears from his eyes, Wayne said, "Big doors swing on small hinges. Who knows what God can do with a life if we'll just let him do it?"

"Playing Hurt"

Calvary Christian Church, Winchester, Kentucky
January 28, 2001

Today is Super Bowl Sunday. It's cold outside, but warm in here. I'm thrilled to be here. Several dear friends are in the audience this morning. I appreciate that.

Where's Marge?

My daughter and granddaughter walked in awhile ago, and said, "Is Mother here?" She's here someplace.

(To his wife:) Marge? Marge, where are you?

We've been married 50 years in August. As a matter of fact, 51 years ago I was a sophomore at Cincinnati Bible Seminary and a fellow asked me to hold a two-week revival for him. Who would ever believe that the first revival I ever held was at Ruckerville here in your county, and I was dating Marge at the time.

Speaking of my wife, she looks at money a little different than I do. I feel as though you can't take it with you, and since Jesus may come at any time, you need to get rid of it and spend it. When I buy something I don't want Marge to know about, I have it delivered to my brother-in-law's office. But I forgot, and had 50 boxes of Girl Scout cookies delivered to my home.

Marge said, "What on earth is this?"

I said, "I couldn't help myself. Amanda is in a contest and there was somebody in her church who sold 48, so what was I going to do?"

I mean, you know ... nobody can make a fool out of you like a grandchild ... grandparents are people who have pictures where they used to have money.

Well, I'm very appreciative of my family, and I'm honored, I really am, to be here this morning.

My Super Bowl tradition

Eighteen years ago, 1983, I started a tradition at Southland Christian Church, preaching this sermon or a variation of it, every Super Bowl Sunday.

When I preached, I'd always have a couple of athletes in the pulpit with me to share a testimony and add emphasis to the sermon.

I don't need to explain what the Super Bowl is. The Super Bowl is played to determine who is the number one team in professional football. Tonight's game is the 35th Super Bowl; the New York Giants and Baltimore Ravens tonight at 6:25 played in Tampa, Florida. In excess of 150 million people will see it in 144 countries.

The greatest thrill, the greatest dream, and the greatest goal of a football player's career is to play in the Super Bowl, and then to wear the ring of a Super Bowl champion.

Play on, regardless

I'm told that running with a football in a National Football League game and being tackled is somewhat like running into a brick wall or into an automobile. In spite of their almost unbelievable conditioning, nearly all of these players play hurt. The question begs to be asked: Why do these fellows do this?

Some do it because of the money, but for most of them, it's just in their blood, and they love it.

They interviewed, this week on television, a fellow who is now in a wheelchair. He played 383 games; had 40 surgeries; 30 on his knees; three on his back; and he played with five rods in his back. No one retires from the NFL in one piece! And here is a man in a wheelchair, and he was asked, "Would you do it again?"

"Absolutely," he replied, without hesitation.

The Herald-Leader in August '96 said this about the Super Bowl: "Athletes are willing to sacrifice body parts and endure needles, biting their lips when the throbbing pain becomes unbearable. Their job is to play regardless." The bottom line is, they play hurt or they don't play.

The first time I preached this sermon, my first guest in the pulpit with me was a member of Southland Church, Tommy Bell. Tommy Bell was a

National Football League official for 15 years and one of the leading lawyers in Lexington.

He told how Joe Namath, when his team won the Super Bowl, shouldn't have even been on the field. His knees were wrapped, and he was in terrible shape.

Tommy Bell liked to tell about the time when he played football for Henry Clay High School and he came out of the game. The coach said, "Bell, why did you come out of the game?" Bell said, "I think my leg's broke." The coach said, "Get back in there until you're sure."

Tommy Bell's funeral was the largest I ever had in my 51 years of ministry. It was just unbelievable. I told this story, humorous story, on Tommy Bell because it's a true story and he loved to tell it.

Tommy Bell was an official in Super Bowl I and Super Bowl III. The Kansas City Chiefs were playing, and Fred Arbanas, an end, on a cross play hit another fellow head-on, and one of Fred's eyes fell out. Not until then did millions know that he had an artificial eye. And, for an end to have an artificial eye is almost unbelievable.

Well, there wasn't any problem to find the eye. They called the water boy and he came out. Arbanas rinsed off the eye, and put it back in!

Tommy Bell, who was rather short, looked up and said, "Fred, I just don't believe this. I mean, you know, you've got one eye. Your livelihood, your security, your profession, your future, everything depends on your eyesight. You already lost one of your eyes. What would you do if you lost your other eye?"

Arbanas said, "I guess I'd become a referee like you, Mr. Bell."

Medicine for where it hurts

I think this is my most well-known sermon because so many in the ministry are called to play hurt. I was asked once to deliver this message by the planning committee of the North American Christian Convention because they felt there was widespread discouragement among preachers.

It's easy to be discouraged in the ministry. Thirteen hundred ministers are fired every month in America. In the last 25 years, divorce has increased in the parsonage 65 percent. The average length of the ministry in a Christian Church is a little less than three years. For every 10 ministers who begin the ministry, only two retire in the ministry.

Folks, my sermon is this. It all boils down to this. Whether you're on a football field or in the kitchen or in the office, you're going to be hurt.

All of us have hurt in our lives. We've either had problems, are having them now, or will have them. The Bible tells us that suffering is inevitable.

Everyone has heartaches. Job 14:1 "Man that is born of a woman is of few days and full of trouble." The only way to avoid trouble is to die!

Have you ever been depressed, misunderstood, feelings were hurt, offended, raw deal, rumors about you, jealousy? You've had a lot of illness; you're lonely; discouraged? Children are not what you hoped they would be? Your marriage is not what you had hoped it would be?

What's the Bible say? It says stay in the game.

Will you stay in the game? "No man, having put his hand to the plow, and looking back, is fit for the kingdom of God." "He that endureth to the end shall be saved." "Be ye stedfast, unmoveable, always abounding in the work of the Lord, forasmuch as ye know that your labour is not in vain in the Lord."

The question is: Will you stay in the game? That's my proposition. Are you going to stay in the game?

God had one Son without sin, but no Son without sorrow. Let me read for you three verses of scripture. II Corinthians 4:1, 8, and 9.

> Therefore seeing we have this ministry, as we have received
> mercy, we faint not;

> We are troubled on every side, yet not distressed; we are
> perplexed, but not in despair;

> Persecuted, but not forsaken; cast down, but not destroyed.

What is Paul saying? "I'm down, but not out." I received a call the other night from a young preacher who was discouraged because of problems with his church board. He said, "Brother Smith, I'm so discouraged. I just came from a board meeting." (Wayne laughs) I don't have those anymore! I said to him, "Brother, what you're going through is the norm, that's not the exception. You may get to the place where you and your men have greater maturity, but this is the norm."

> My father's way may twist and turn;
> My heart may throb and ache,
> But in my soul I'm glad to know
> He maketh no mistake.

Romans 8 asks, "What's going to put you on the bench; what's going to take you out of this game? Tribulation, stress, persecution, nakedness, peril, or sword?" Someone said, "Christians are like teabags; you don't know how good they are until you put them in hot water." That's not in the Bible, but I thought it was pretty good.

What keeps me going

What's the one verse in the Bible that keeps me going? One verse. Oh, there's a lot of verses, but Romans 8:28. If I didn't believe that, I'd be gone.

I've had 10 operations. Sometimes it has been hard. But He said, "All things…" What did you say, Lord? All things, even bad things, work together for good to them that love the Lord.

Now, when you're in the middle of the forest, it's hard to see how all these trees are going to help you. When you're in the middle of that illness and you say, "I can't trace God, but I trust God."

That's when he says, "Well, put it on Me. Come unto Me all ye that labor and are heavy laden. I'll give you rest."

Play when you're hurt physically

I've got three points this morning. Number one: You must learn to play when you're hurt physically.

Paul did. "Five times, received 40 stripes less one. Thrice beaten with a rod. Once I was stoned, three times shipwrecked; I was in weariness and hunger and cold."

And then he said, "I was given a thorn. Therefore, I take pleasure in infirmities." Now can you believe that? I take pleasure in being hurt. "In reproaches, persecutions, and stress, for Christ's sake, for when I am weak, then I'm made strong."

Lou Gehrig played first base for the New York Yankees for 15 years. He was called the Iron Man of baseball. He hit 10 home runs in seven World Series, but that's not important. What's important is, he played 2,130 games without missing a game. Every time they had a game, he played. That's like a minister being in the pulpit 51 years; never being ill, never going to the hospital.

I mean, it's just unbelievable that you feel great every Sunday for the morning service.

When Lou Gehrig retired, they X-rayed his hands. Every finger had been broken once, some twice, and some three times! But he never missed a game. What did he do? He played when he was hurt.

What's the greatest football team ever to play? Sportswriters say it was 1899; Sewanee, Tennessee. They now call it The College of the South. I want you to know that in 1899 they didn't have airplanes to travel on. This team played five other teams in six days.

They didn't play on Sunday. They played Texas, Texas A & M, Tulane, LSU, Mississippi. They had only 14 players, and a barrel of Tennessee spring water. Whatever that was, we need to get some of it at UK! They played both offense and defense. No one does that anymore.

They scored 113 total points, and the opposition scored nothing. And they played five out of six days. They were broken and they were bruised and they were bloody, but they never missed a game!

The most lopsided score in the history of football was 1916 when Georgia Tech played Cumberland College in Cumberland, Tennessee. The score was 222 to nothing! I think if the coach had put a gun to his head, the Lord would have said, "I understand."

When reading about that unbelievable score, they said the Georgia Tech people were like animals, big, and the Cumberland players, small. One time the Cumberland quarterback fumbled the ball and it rolled toward one of his buddies. He yelled over and said, "Pick it up!" The other player yelled back, "You pick it up; you dropped it."

Play when you're hurt physically.

Play when you're hurt emotionally

The second thing I would like for you to remember is this: play when you're hurt emotionally. Our Lord must have been hurt. At the first Sunday School picnic our Lord fed 5,000 from a few loaves and fishes. Then he said, "I want someone to preach, and it dropped down to 500. I want someone to pray. It dropped down to 120. I want someone to witness. It dropped down to 70. I want some disciples, and it dropped down to 12. I want someone to pray with me all night, and it dropped down to three.

Jesus spent three years with his disciples. They saw every miracle. He stopped a funeral and raised a boy from the dead. He opened the eyes of the blind. Three long years. They ate with him and slept with him, and most of them left him! I'm sure He was hurt emotionally, but He "played on."

You mean, when I'm in the valley? Right. When I'm on the mountaintop? Right.

The greatest heartache of any parent is to bury a child. Let me tell you about Jackie. For eight years I went over every Thursday and worked on sermons with Bob Russell, minister in Louisville, along with seven other preachers. One of the employees at Bob's church was Jackie, a lovely divorcee in her 40s.

Jackie's from Pennsylvania. She went to Cincinnati Bible College and married a very promising young man, and not long into their marriage he decided he wanted somebody else.

Her father was a Christian minister in Pennsylvania, and he drowned at a Sunday School picnic at 38 years of age. Three years ago this past December, I drove to Louisville to the funeral of her 17-year old son, killed in an automobile accident.

She lost a husband; she lost her father; and lost her only son. I would call that, "playing hurt."

Today, Jackie is remarried and is serving alongside her husband as a missionary in Kosovo. She's happy, but she still plays hurt.

Jerry Yorks preaches at Hubbard, Ohio, near Youngstown. He and his wife, Judy, will never forget August 20, 1974. At that time Jerry ministered in Pennsylvania, and he and the family decided to go to the county fair. One of the attractions at the fair was race cars.

The Yorks were leaving a horse barn intent on going home when a race car crashed through the wall and struck both their little girls; one eight, one 10. One was killed immediately, and the other one died two days later.

Well, almost 30 years have passed and they're still in the ministry of the Lord. Are they playing hurt? Absolutely ... but they're still playing for Him.

Did they lose their happiness? Yes, but not their joy. They have joy because they believe to live is Christ, to die is gain. Joy says, "I know I will see them again some day."

How much do you love?

The third thing to remember about playing hurt is that your faithfulness will be measured by your depth of love. Why do people hang on? Because they're committed and surrendered to a cause they love.

How much do you love? That's how long you're going to stay in the game.

It's hard to be honest with yourself. I love that story of a preacher who walked down a street, and saw four boys standing around a dog.

"What are you all doing?"

"Well, we're standing here lying."

"What do you mean you're lying?"

"Whoever tells the biggest lie gets to keep this stray dog."

The preacher lambasted the boys, and said, "Oh, where are the young people going today?" Finally, he said, "Boys, I tell you, when I was your age, it never entered my mind to tell a lie."

One boy said, "It's your dog, preacher."

You see, we lie a lot. We don't know we're lying. "This won't hurt a bit." That's a lie. "One size fits all." That's a lie. "Easy to assemble." That's a lie. "I'm from the IRS and I'm here to help you." That's a BIG lie! I've got one more (Laughs). "Mother's only coming for a week. You'll hardly know she's here." I'll tell you what, when my mother came for a week, we knew she was there!

When your best friend hurts you or turns on you, you may be tempted to quit, but if you're really in love with the Lord, what will you do? You hang in there.

Several years ago *U.S. News and World Report* told about a little girl seven or eight years old, very thin, who somehow held up her father, 180 pounds, in a swimming pool and saved his life. When they asked her, "How did you do that?" she said, "Oh, it was easy. I love my daddy."

You see, when you love, I mean really depths of love, you'll do things that others won't do.

When a church has that kind of love for each other and for the Lord, your potential is unbelievable. God and one man equals a majority.

We live in horse country, but I've never seen a horse pull. I had a horse who won the Derby in 1966. I asked the jockey, Don Brumfield, "How did you win the Derby?" "Well," he said, "you've got to motivate the horse." I said, "How do you motivate a horse?" He said, "I whispered in his ear going down the closing stretch, 'Roses are red; violets are blue; horses that lose are turned into glue.' "

There are two motivators in life: one is love, the other fear. When people love each other, they can do remarkable things.

As I said, I've never seen a horse pull but a friend of mine told me about a horse pull in which one horse pulled 8,000 pounds and another horse pulled 9,000 pounds. Separately. What would they pull together? I would say 17,000.

Together they pulled 28,000.

It's a principle called "synergism." Two together are greater than their separate parts.

When you're in it for the long haul and your motive is love, your possibilities are amazing. The key is to not quit.

I don't care what people say. I don't care what people think. I don't want God to someday say to Wayne Smith, "You quit on me."

Folks, I've never been a good student. I love to preach. I love to call. But getting sermons together has always been a chore. To preach every Sunday for 40 years and "bring fresh bread" is hard. I mean, really hard. And so I put it off, always to the end of the week, Friday or Saturday.

My former secretary told me that the new preacher who replaced me sometimes starts on Monday morning.

I was shocked. "Mondays?" I said. "I didn't even pray 'til Thursday."

It always bothers me when people say, "You know, there's things I don't like about the ministry, or the Christian life, or being an elder or being a deacon." That has nothing to do with it. If you love Him, it's duty. I do a lot of things in life, not because I enjoy it, but it's my duty.

Salvation is free, but it's not cheap. We're not saved by works, but we're saved for works, and God wants you in that game, and it's only the love of God that will keep you in that game until you cross that finish line.

Go home and read I Peter 4:12. "Dear friends, do not be surprised about painful trials you're suffering, don't be surprised as though… (Reading from the Bible) …some strange thing is happening to you."

Don't act like, Oh, my, I didn't know this illness would come. I didn't know this offense would come. I didn't know someone in my church would disappoint me. (Reading again from the Bible) "But rejoice that you could participate in the sufferings of Christ."

He suffered, and the servant is no better than the Master.

There it is. Suffering is inevitable; misery is optional!

Suffering is inevitable; misery is optional! It will come to you one way or another, in some form, and you either play hurt or you don't play at all.

Wayne B. Smith presented a variation of this message to Southland Christian Church every Super Bowl Sunday since 1983. The above sermon was preached at Calvary Christian Church in Winchester, Kentucky — where Dale Adams is the senior minister — on Super Bowl Sunday, January 28, 2001, after Wayne's retirement.

Some Liked Him; Some Did Not

Dr. Sam E. Stone, editor of *Christian Standard*, in an editorial February 25, 1996 which announced Wayne's retirement, wrote, "A friend who knows the Restoration Movement as well as any other person commented, 'I think Wayne Smith is probably the best loved person in the brotherhood.' "

Yes, Smith had his admirers. He also had his detractors.

• I was pleased to learn the Kiwanis Club of Lexington could see fit to have a "Testimonial Dinner: for you. It is long overdue. My only regret is the program will not be long enough for all your friends to express their true feelings for you. I do imagine the speakers which have been chosen have sufficient information about you, as they include three judges, and an attorney...

(signed) Aaron
Aaron Smith Funeral Home
September 12, 1991

• I cannot stomach ayatollahs whether they live in Iran or Lexington. It frightens and angers me to think that Wayne Smith is also an ayatollah.

Smith is not content with freedom of religion and the right to hold worship services in his church.

Oh, no, he wants to dictate such mundane affairs as shopping hours and what kind of movies our minds can stand.

Several years ago Smith took out a whole page of advertising in the Sunday *Herald-Leader* advocating the need for capital punishment, citing several ancient Old Testament quotations as adequate proof. He forgot that his own savior had been a victim of capital punishment.

Like all ayatollahs, Smith cannot stand to be wrong. There are still X-rated movies in Lexington and the stores are going to open on Sunday because it makes sense, not to mention dollars. It has nothing to do with church or religion. Intelligent decisions usually don't. People are not going to be dragged backwards a thousand years because of the ranting of some ayatollah. Time goes forward.

I wonder if Smith would give up his church and run for the legislature. Since a lot of churches are open on Wednesday night, maybe in the legislature he could get them to close the stores on Wednesday, too.

Linda Williams, Lexington
Letter to the editor, *Lexington Leader*, Monday, September 10, 1979

• Thank you for your recent article on the Rev. Wayne B. Smith. May this testimony of his lifestyle be a challenge and an encouragement to us all, to be vessels of good in our community.

He has shown us that it is not the easy way to deny self and pride and to treat others as we wish to be treated…. The world has room for many disciples such as Smith. May each of us be willing to be called higher and make our stand for family, life and decency.

Lynn Harder, Nicholasville
Letter to the editor, *Lexington Herald-Leader*, Tuesday, September 19, 1989

• I found the Rev. Wayne Smith's remarks in Frankfort inflammatory, sensationalist, and unconscionable. Smith is supposed to be a spiritual leader, a man of God….

I am a woman who believes in freedom of choice, not a "femi-Nazi." I arrived at my decision through thoughtful consideration, and believe in the integrity of my position. I do not delight in counting the number of abortions performed. Abortion is never an easy choice. However, if an individual decides it is necessary, I would not presume to judge her action. She should have the right to a clean, safe, legal abortion.

Perhaps Smith should spend more time reviewing Scripture (especially Matthew 7:1) and ministering to the needs of those who face problem pregnancies, rather than spreading messages of intolerance and hate....

Colleen Decker, Versailles
Letter to the editor, *Lexington Herald-Leader*, Monday, February 17, 1992

• I am concerned over the political issues being expressed from the pulpit of Southland Christian Church. While the Rev. Wayne Smith is often quite comical in his remarks about those who have been elected, the separation of church and state means just that: They should be separate.

I go to church to hear about God's greatness and glory, not to hear of Ted Kennedy's sexual excursions or how the Democrats are ruining the country. I choose who I will vote for after careful consideration of the issues at hand, prayer and personal choice. When I come to church, I want spiritual guidance, not political.

Please, preach to the lost souls and those seeking guidance, and leave the political circus to the clowns....

James Lake, Lexington
Letter to the editor, *Lexington Herald-Leader*, Saturday, November 2, 1991

• A recent letter criticized the political nature of the Rev. Wayne Smith's sermons at Southland Christian Church. Smith is carrying on a tradition as old as our nation.

After battles at Lexington and Concord, the Rev. William Stearns urged his congregation to enlist. In Virginia, the Rev. Peter Muhlenberg preached that "for everything there is a season…a time to preach and a time to fight." He paused, then tore off his clerical robes to reveal the uniform of a colonel in the Continental Army….

The stories go on. Our history is full of them. The name of Wayne Smith and others like him can be added to a proud and distinguished list of American clergy who dared to go beyond cloistered walls of their churches. More ministers need to be willing to add their names to that list. . .

Eunice Logan, Harrodsburg
Letter to the editor, *Lexington Herald-Leader*, 1991

• In view of the amount of press coverage concerning the opening of the new Southland Christian Church, it should not go unnoticed that not all elements of the community share the joy.

While churches can be beautiful and inspiring structures, they actually tend to be a financial drain on the community. They occupy property that could be used for revenue-producing enterprises such as stores and gas stations and then, further, they deny us the taxes that the property should produce.

I would think that a group of people who could build a $2.2 million building could pay their fair share of taxes.

It was said that Wayne Smith, pastor of the Southland Christian Church, had been at that job for 25 years. It certainly is commendable for someone to last 25 years in the same job, but perhaps with the proper attitude change and a little vocational training, Mr. Smith could learn a more useful trade, such as firefighting, plumbing, or farming.

Herman Harris
Lexington Chapter American Atheists
Letter to the editor, *Lexington Herald*, Tuesday, September 15, 1981

• The Sunday *Herald-Leader*, March 6,1994, published a section, "Best of the Bluegrass." Best weather forecaster; All time favorite UK basketball player; Best elected official, etc.

• Best local TV preacher: No competition here. The Rev. Wayne Smith.

• When Wayne announced his approaching retirement to the congregation, the *Lexington Herald-Leader* took note on their editorial page, concluding with the following:

The pastor of Southland Christian for the past 40 years has been the Rev. Wayne Smith. In May he will resign. It is a loss for both the church and for all of Central Kentucky.

Smith did something in the last 40 years that's rare. He built a community. In a time when neighbors speak less and life has become fragmented by work and worries, Smith created a place where a large number of people found safe harbor. It was a remarkable achievement, one that will continue long after Smith retires.

On more than one — heck, on more than a dozen — occasions, we've disagreed with Smith on public issues. We've gigged him on these pages and he's chided us from the pulpit. But these disputes pale beside what Smith and the people of Southland Christian Church have created.

Now Smith is leaving a post he's held for four decades. We will miss his vigor, commitment, humor, warmth and leadership. And we can only hope that Smith's retirement will be fruitful and long.

The Southland Story

"I have planted, Appollos watered, but God gave the increase." I Cor. 3:6

YEAR	A.M. WORSHIP	P.M. WORSHIP	SUNDAY SCHOOL	WED. EVENING	NEW MEMBERS	VBS
1956	*	*	170	*	150	*
1957	*	*	195	*	120	*
1958	*	*	201	*	71	175
1959	272	102	251	49	89	199
1960	335	128	290	49	111	217
1961	417	164	350	89	132	300
1962	507	195	381	95	131	285
1963	594	215	433	91	123	335
1964	717	225	487	97	182	*
1965	768	235	534	117	143	435
1966	749	273	551	115	161	447
1967	844	305	608	152	192	530
1968	864	291	626	144	125	530
1969	916	327	630	110	181	538
1970	943	362	637	115	166	516
1971	970	390	663	164	170	513
1972	912	379	641	172	180	526
1973	953	330	619	174	174	601
1974	994	363	648	194	142	429
1975	1,026	349	650	240	155	361
1976	1,105	340	696	199	171	358
1977	1,113	317	677	195	167	400
1978	1,169	350	736	163	187	300
1979	1,214	386	689	193	193	361
1980	1,285	410	681	259	215	399
1981	1,320	512	716	275	236	458
1982	1,221	493	718	261	243	491
1983	1,296	557	713	269	235	409
1984	1,388	642	699	263	248	473
1985	1,522	720	731	294	250	450
1986	1,793	703	835	353	280	594
1987	2,002	612	929	346	322	733
1988	2,011	715	935	284	328	685
1989	2,384	839	979	390	483	786
1990	2,718	911	1,098	532	462	951
1991	3,023	923	1,303	477	447	1,117
1992	3,086	854	1,338	539	382	1,279
1993	3,071	755	1,330	529	417	1,288
1994	3,472	762	1,426	440	469	1,321
1995	3,761	580	1,545	602	414	1,263

31 Things That Contributed to Southland's Growth

By Wayne B. Smith, Retired
After serving 40 years — 1956-1996

Read I Corinthians 3:4-8
Vs. 6: "I have planted, Apollos watered; but God gave the increase."
Vs. 8b: ". . .and every man shall receive his reward according to *His Own Labor.*"

1. **A Rotating Church Board** is essential to growth. Rotation means that you must go off after serving three years. After a year off, you are examined and in most cases, may return. If this plan is not adopted, sooner or later you will have one or two ruling elders. In most cases, this is a matter of tradition; in some cases the issue is power. Growth is limited because church leaders have the mindset they have had for years. Elders should be selected while in their 30s and 40s as well as older men. Maturity is from the neck up.

2. **Term Limits**. A chairman cannot succeed himself — as committee chairmen, treasurer, etc. You avoid cliques this way. Additional elders and deacons are able to use their giftedness.

3. **No limit to the number** of men who can serve on the board. The bigger the better. Many hands lighten the load.

4. **Radio and TV** coverage of service.

5. **Develop a program that is YOURS**. An Easter program, a patriotic service, a Christmas program, etc.

6. **Dual Services**. When you are 80 percent full — you are FULL. Have identical services, and allow 30 minutes between each service.

7. Worship service should be **one hour**. A sermon should **never** be more than 30 minutes long.

8. **Heavy Visitation**. There is no substitute for knocking on doors. "Churches are held together with worthy preaching…they are built by shoe leather and automobile tires." A Sunday visitor would receive a phone call no later than Monday. That week they would receive a letter and a home visit. The needed information would come through a silent roll card. "Go out into the highways and hedges and compel them to come in." Also, purchase a "Newcomers list" — a list of people who have recently moved to your community.

9. **Celebrate Special Days** — Friend's Day, Veteran's Day, special contests, etc.

10. **Join a service club**. I was the charter president of the Breakfast Lion's Club in Lexington. That's where I got our first doctor and first lawyer. If you are fishing for men you must go where the fish are!

11. **Offer Support Groups**. Offer groups to the public (after attending the group they may feel motivated to attend church) — groups like Divorce Recovery; Cancer, Gambler's Anonymous, Alcoholics Anonymous, Depression, etc. We copied support groups from Southeast church in Louisville.

12. **One special offering** — per year — held the Sunday before Thanksgiving. This offering was designated for buses, missions, our building program, etc.

13. Southland was the **largest contributor** in establishing the Lexington Christian Academy. The school is now the fourth largest in the nation

with a 70-acre campus and 1,741 students.

14. Southland **planted** two other churches: Southern Acres (1,000), Hill N' Dale (700) and assisted in several others. They were very generous in giving NorthEast Christian $450,000.

15. I **loved and respected** my peers on the church board and recognized their authority over me.

16. Southland took **a strong stand on issues** in Lexington — issues such as alcohol, abortion, the lottery, etc.

17. Four Southland women created **Women for Life** in 1985. This organization provides shelter and adoption of babies born out of wedlock. God truly blesses a church or organization that stands for the sanctity of life. Proverbs 6:17b "God hates hands that shed innocent blood." Women for Life now occupies a suite of offices in The Doctors' Park and has saved more than 1,400 babies in the past 19 years.

18. Southland provides **excellent salaries and benefits** — staff turnover rate is very low.

19. We always had a big budget for **youth work**. Most years we had two or more youth ministers. If you get the kids, you'll get the parents.

20. **A willingness to hire staff**. Early on, we hired one staff member for every 100 people. If we averaged 500, we would have at least 5 staff members. Notice — we never talked about membership — the important figure is how many are in attendance.

21. **Long ministries** — There is no such thing as a large church without a long ministry.

22. The church was **extremely generous** to me and my family (with

gifts). What does this do for a preacher? Ministers are human. The greatest tool of Satan is **discouragement**. When God's man knows he is loved — (<u>and</u> has tangible proof) he can keep going!

23. Have a clear understanding of **who's in charge**. The staff answers to the Sr. minister, and he answers to the board. Two quarterbacks won't work.

24. If you think you have offended someone, **apologize**. Zig Ziglar said, "People are attracted to a church because of excitement; they stay because of love." You can't hide love. It's obvious.

25. Preaching **that is fresh**. I made a conscious effort to have 5 ingredients in each sermon: Scripture; Illustrations; Humor; Passion; and Application.

26. **The Telephone**: from the *Lexington Herald-Leader* — 9/16/2000 by Tom Schaefer who writes about religion and ethics for the Wichita, Kansas *Eagle*:

> *In this era of cell phones, answering machines, and pagers it's amazing that anyone ever is out of touch. But guess who is?*
>
> *A bunch of churches.*
>
> *This summer, Barna Research group phoned 3,764 Protestant congregations to see whether it could make contact. Turned out it couldn't connect with anyone at 40 percent of churches called, despite repeated efforts. And at half of those called, when no one responded, there was no answering machine. At others, voice messages were left, but no one followed up with a call.*

In this era of instant communication, there's no excuse for a congregation not to respond to someone who calls.

If your congregation hasn't bought an answering machine, it's time to enter the 21st century. And don't forget to return recorded calls.

After all, how would you like it if your call to a higher power went unanswered?

27. **Hard work** — James Byrnes, Secretary of State under FDR said: "Success could be summed up in three simple words...*and then some.*" I discovered at an early age that most of the differences between average and top people could be explained in three words. The top people did what was expected of them...*and then some.* They were thoughtful of others; they were considerate and kind...*and then some.* They met their obligations and responsibilities fairly and squarely...*and then some.* They were good friends to their friends, and could be counted on in an emergency...*and then some.*

The "**and then some**" of the Bible is "**going the second mile.**" The only account we have in the Bible of Jesus being sick is when He said, "I will spew thee out of my mouth." Why? For being lukewarm!! Remember what Paul wrote in Corinthians — God judges our LABORS.

28. **Willingness to change** — METHODS are many. Doctrines are few. METHODS change, Doctrines never do.

Ben Merold explained the paradox of change:
"While the idea of change is usually at first resented, it is enjoyed and appreciated after it is accomplished. He cited a survey of congregations in

southern Illinois that found 84 percent of the members open to change. While only 16 percent of the members would accept no change, 72 percent of the churches' leaders came from this 16 percent." — Mark A. Taylor, in *The Lookout* 14 July 1996.

29. **Prayer** and hopefully being led by the Holy Spirit.
Proverbs 3:6 "In all thy ways acknowledge Him,
 and He shall direct thy paths."
The first six words are <u>our</u> admonition; the last six are <u>God's</u> promise.

30. **Miscellaneous** —
  * I never shared church business with my wife.
  * Have a vision, but keep your feet on the ground.
  * Keep a sense of humor.
  * Never lose your excitement for the ministry.
  * And remember my favorite verse in the Bible — Romans 8:28
    "All Things Work Together For Good To Them That
    Love The Lord." — Even bad things!
  * 16 percent of all income, plus special offerings goes to missions.

31. **Helping Through HIM Ministry** — In the year 2000, the total number of people helped was **16,101**. The number of families helped was **4,839** of which 56 were members and 4,839 were not members or attenders of our church.

Wayne's List of Favorites

Favorite scripture
Romans 8:28 — That keeps me going. If you believe all things — even bad things — work for good then you can tolerate it. Perhaps He didn't will it to be this way, but He can use it.

Favorite hymn
"Blessed Assurance."

Favorite musical groups
The Messengers Quartet and The Vintage Gospel Lads.

Favorite place to pray
My bedroom, when I'm alone.

Favorite sermon text
II Corinthians 4:1-9 — "I'm down but I'm not out."

Favorite UK basketball team
1978 National Champs, and I knew those fellows.

Favorite way to relax
TV: History Channel, *Matlock, Heat of the Night, Colombo, Law & Order, Perry Mason, Monk, City Confidential, the Gaithers.*

Favorite preachers/orators
Dr. B.R. Lakin and Orval Morgan, both now deceased.

Favorite sports program
College football.

Favorite Veterinarian

George N. Gilpin, DVM. Elder in Jessamine Christian Church. Fluff and I like George. Marge likes his prices.

Favorite barber

Frank Mitchell would never let me pay. His wife, Ann, is a great seamstress. She has helped me many times. Frank was called home, and I miss him.

My new barber

Jim Dooley, elder at Northeast Christian Church. Nice guy, but he charges.

Favorite plaque giver

John Presko, minister, Victory Christian Church, Lancaster, Kentucky.

Favorite home away from home

Other than my own home, I have spent more time in the home of Jack and Charlotte Ballard (Atlanta). Unbelievably generous people. Jack retired after 44 years as senior minister of Mount Carmel Christian Church, Stone Mountain, Georgia. Dale and Diane Sikes add to the comfort when I'm there, also.

Favorite soul-winner

Reggie Thomas, White Fields Overseas Evangelism.

Favorite vacation spot

Myrtle Beach. Often several families would go in tandem. However, most of the time it was our family and Bob and Jean Evers, who now live in Greencastle, Indiana.

Favorite jokesters

Manley Pierce, associate minister of First Christian Church, Canton, Ohio; and David Vaughn, senior minister of Whitewater Crossing Christian Church, Cincinnati, Ohio. They have more jokes than I do.

Favorite sponsor

Charles Starky of Washington Court House, Ohio, where he foots the bill to play my old sermon tapes each Sunday morning. I'm honored, and I love Charley.

Favorite fruit man

You've heard of the bread man, milk man, etc. Huff Snyder is a mattress salesman, but he brought me boxes of apples, strawberries, etc., weekly. He supplied the staff with fresh fruit, also. Thank you, Patty and Huff.

Favorite company

A company called Thermal Balance, the founder of which was the late Larry Johnson. Their CEO now is his son, Jay. I use their office equipment, and occasionally seek their secretarial help of Jeanine Blake and Mary Wagner. And, I sometimes steal paper and etc.

Not my favorite

Worship leaders who put preaching on the back burner, and senior ministers who, for whatever reason, lack the ability to insist that the main thing remain the main thing.

Favorite diet

There's no such thing.

Wayne's List of "Mosts"

Most difficult wedding
Gordon and Karen Walls. We received a bomb threat. A good marriage; they are still together.

Most difficult funeral
Larry Johnson, my brother-in-law. There were many others that broke my heart.

Most unexpected honor
Speaker for the University of Kentucky Dental School Commencement in May 1986.

Most appreciated honor
To simply be a preacher. I always have felt honored since my first church that averaged 31 each Sunday.

Most requested speech
Restore Capitol Punishment.

Most repeated sermon
Playing Hurt, and *Joy.*

Most unusual place to preach
Easter Sunrise Service in 1974 after a tornado took the roof off Capitol City Christian Church, Frankfort, Kentucky.

Most impolite people
Users of cell phones.

Most underrated ministry
Jack Ballard led an effort called "The Church Builders" that brings 60 men together twice a year to build a house of worship in 14 days. Thus far they have built 72 churches in 26 states. For information, call 770-979-1069.

Awards and Highlights

1929   Born Scottdale, Pennsylvania.

1931   Smith family moved to Cincinnati.

1939   Wayne accepted Christ as his Savior and was baptized by William S. Boice.

1942   Smith dedicated his life to the ministry while in a Christian Camp (the Oder farm) near Williamstown, Kentucky.

1947   Graduated from Western Hills High School.
- Received the Public Speaking Award.
- President of the Safety Club promoting safe driving, presiding over the seven public high schools in Cincinnati.

1948   Enrolled in Cincinnati Bible Seminary (CBS).

1949   Began preaching every Sunday.
- First place, Oratorical Contest at CBS.
- First place, Annual CBS Inter-Society Debate. Bob Shannon and Wayne Smith were the winning team.

1951   Wayne B. Smith and Marjorie Judy were married.

1952   Wayne graduated from CBS.
- Business manager, school yearbook.

1953   Ordained to the Christian ministry by Dr. Burris Butler, vice-president of Standard Publishing Company, Cincinnati.

1956   Concluded seven-year ministry with Unity Christian Church, near Cynthiana, Kentucky, and moved to Lexington to begin Southland Christian Church.

1957   Judy Lynn Smith was born.

1961   Jana Sue Smith was born.

1963   Wayne became charter president of the first breakfast Lions Club east of the Mississippi River.

1964   Spoke at the North American Christian Convention (NACC) in St. Louis.
- First place in an Idea Fair sponsored by the NACC.

1965   Selected to appear in the 1965 edition of Outstanding Young Men of America.

       • Awarded membership in the Delta Aleph Tau honor society, an award given by CBS for scholarship, outstanding service, or both. "Probably outstanding service," Wayne says.

1968   Asked to serve as trustee of CBS.

1969   Appointed foreman of the Fayette County grand jury in Lexington, voting on 144 cases during 10 days of service.

1970   Honorary doctorate from Louisville Bible College.

1971   Planted Southern Acres Christian Church.

1972   Preached at the NACC in Cincinnati.

       • Won the largest Sunday School contest in recent history: Southland 1,032; Trinity Baptist 997.

1975   Honorary doctorate from Kentucky Christian College, Grayson.

1977   Elected president of the North American Christian Convention.

1981   Southland Christian Church moves to Harrodsburg Road.

       • Hill 'N Dale Christian Church was given birth.

       • Preached at the NACC, Louisville.

1984   Preached at the NACC, Atlanta.

1985   Near fatal automobile accident; hospitalized 29 days; months of recovery.

1986   Commencement speaker, University of Kentucky School of Dentistry.

1987   Preached at the NACC, Oklahoma City.

1988   Served with a core group who merged two Christian schools (total attendance 300) into the Lexington Christian Academy, which is now the fourth largest Christian school in America — 1,740 students, elementary through high school, on a 50 acre campus.

1989   Honorary doctorate from Kerala, India.

       • Christian Bible College Street in Firebrook subdivision, south of Lexington, named "Wayne's Boulevard" in his honor.

1991   Preached "Is it right to go to war?" in response to the Gulf War. Wayne admits half of it came from Russell.

• Former Governor John Y. Brown requested that Wayne deliver this message to the Kentucky House and Senate in Frankfort on February 2. Smith received a standing ovation.

1992   Preached at the NACC, Anaheim.

1993   Awarded Trustee Emeritus for 25 years of service by Cincinnati Bible College and Seminary (CBC&S).

1995   Distinguished Service Award from CBC&S.

• Take Time for Life Award from Lexington's Right to Life Association. "This year's winner is known as a true soldier of Christ. Popular causes do not appear to interest him, only causes which are righteous. He preached the truth without fear, and his efforts have been rewarded. His leadership in Lexington on this issue, and others as well, has been unsurpassed."

1996   Named one of "God's Honored Servants" at the NACC in Dallas.

• Received The Lusby Award, the highest award granted by Kentucky Christian College (KCC).

• Retired from his 40-year ministry with Southland Christian Church.

1997   Wayne was roasted at a banquet at the NACC in Kansas City which raised $30,000 for the convention.

1998   Spoke at the 141st baccalaureate at Berea College, Berea, Kentucky.

2000   Wayne B. Smith Center for Christian Leadership dedicated on the campus of Kentucky Christian College.

• Preached at the NACC, Louisville.

2001   Received the Anchor Award as a Distinguished Alumnus from CBC&S.

• Married 50 years.

• "Welcomed into our home a 2 1/2 pound Shi Tzu, which captured our hearts. Our first and only dog."

2002   Golden Eagle Award from CBC&S.

2003   Preached at the dedication of The Wayne B. Smith Oratorium at CBC&S.

2004   Received the Encourager of the Year Award presented by Barnabas Ministries at its annual winter worship and workshop in Pigeon Forge, Tennessee.

• Prayed at the inaugural ceremonies for Governor Ernie L. Fletcher in the Rotunda at the State Capitol in Frankfort. Wayne says, "Our first Republican governor since 1967."

• Finished this book! Hallelujah!

More to come ...

"Kentucky's Ahead"

There once was a preacher,
As the story is told,
Who preached the great Message
So brave and so bold.

His sermons and his jokes were
The best to be found;
But there was one thing that
He ran in the ground.

As he lifted each sinner
From sin's mire and its muck
He made them confess that
They loved old Kaintuck.

It was "Kaintucky this"
And "Kaintucky that"
And "Kaintucky Hills" and
"Kaintucky Flats."

The plan of salvation,
If you were lucky
Would see you baptized
In the state of Kentucky.

Now some friends grew tired
Of taking a lickin'
And hearing him boast
Of "Kentucky Fried Chicken."

And so late one evening
They asked him to sup —
And they taled of Kentucky —
But sneaked pills in his cup.

Then soon on the table
He fell in deep sleep.
When the men picked him up,
He made not a peep.

Then out to an ambulance
By prearranged plan,
He was taken to the "parlor"
Of "buryin Sam."

Now old Sam, who was in
On the joke, you could say,
Had arranged for a coffin
On that very day.

So into the back room
Where the coffins were kept,
They toted his body while
Preacher Smith slept.

Now into the coffin
And down with the lid,
With just enough air for
The "Kaintucky Kid."

Then out sneaked the men
With nothing undone,
And peaked through the window
To watch all the fun.

They hardly had fastened
The bolt on the door,
When Preacher Smith gave out
With one long, last snore.

Then opening the lid and
With wide-eyed stare,
He saw all the coffins
Around him in there.

He blinked his eyes twice
And then with great speed
He climbed from the coffin
A scared man, indeed.

But much to the surprise
Of everyone there,
A smile came across
His face, so fair —

Then raising his eyes
To the heavens he said,
"Resurrection Day's here,
AND KENTUCKY'S AHEAD!"

— By Grant Layman
October 27, 1972

Afterword

I retired in January of 1996. Soon, a number of people said, "You ought to write a book." To further that suggestion, 10 friends (Larry Johnson, Bill Lancaster, Dr. Clark Standiford, Len Aldridge, Ron Switzer, Bob Turner, Carol Rasmussen, J. L. Lynn, Wayne Wellman and Barney Fitzpatrick) gave $500 each. Susan Nelson, author of a book about Richie Farmer, one of the all-time great high school (Manchester, Ky.) and college (University of Kentucky) basketball players, agreed to spearhead the project and put great effort into the cause.

I averaged speaking three times a week and my plate was full. Something had to give, and I was not in the mood, nor did I have the mindset to give less attention to what I love and felt called to do — preach.

So I called a halt to what seemed like a good idea. My friends have never asked for their money back and I'm hoping with the passing of eight years the statute of limitations has run out.

Rod Huron approached me several times in 2001, and my answer was no. I soon learned that I was dealing with an excellent salesman. I also learned that though another person is the author, the subject must make a serious investment of time. Rod lives in Cincinnati and I in Lexington. Williamstown is halfway between. We met at least 25 times in the Williamstown Christian Church (borrowing a classroom) thanks to the kindness of their minister, Mike McGinnis. Also, some study time was spent over a meal at the Country Kitchen in Dry Ridge, Ky., adjacent to Williamstown. Rod's trips to Lexington were frequent.

Rod loves the writing. I am the opposite. Thus it was not a labor of love on my part. Decisions, decisions. . . what should be written, what should remain unsaid. I have awakened many times in the night, asking myself, "What have I ever done unlike others that merits a book?" I'm not being humble; I'm being honest.

There are more than 500 names in this book and there should be more. The story of my life is the story of people I love and of those who love me.

My fear is that someone will read this book and say, "How could you for-get to include _____?" I can only say, "Forgive me."

The Mitch Coopers, Harold McCartys, Lee Folsters, Jack Metts, Henry Vicks and Ed McKinneys provided lakeside vacations for our fam-ily for many years early in my ministry. Later, our family looked forward to our annual 600-mile trip to Myrtle Beach. One year, seven families met in the parking lot at KFC and drove in tandem. Bob and Jean Evers and children were our travel companions for 14 years. Bob was an elder at Southland until IBM moved him to Greencastle, Ind., and we're still friends.

No one has given more time to this preacher than Barb Turner and Bev Williams. When I was president of the North American Christian Con-vention, they went with me to Cincinnati. When I served as Registration Chairman they traveled to St. Louis and Detroit. If true that we make a living by what we get and a life by what we give, many blessings await these two who eased my burden and advanced the kingdom.

Bob Turner, Barb's husband, greets me each time I see him, "Preacher, what do you need today?" and he means it.

Bill and Wilda Kincheloe have a room in their home which could be called Wall Street. Finance meetings were held there for an extended peri-od of time. Thanks for your love and sharing.

Several years ago I was called to Humana Hospital (currently St. Joseph's East) where a young lady was dying. I knew her mother, Louise Peel. I didn't know Louise's husband, Porter. For whatever reason, he did not attend church. Just before the girl's passing, Porter and I were stand-ing by her bedside and he said, "I want to confess Christ." He did, was baptized, and has been faithful ever since. A decision not based upon his daughter's living, but based upon conviction. I greatly admire a person who remembers a commitment.

Thank you Betty Murphy for many years of free parking at the airport. The Murphys own AVIS, and became members of Southland years ago after her husband, Wendell, heard me speak at Rotary. Wendell was called home, and I miss him.

Marge and I made new friends the past two years by attending a con-ference in Pigeon Forge, Tenn., sponsored by Barnabas Ministries of Gallipolis, Ohio. Denny Coburn, director of this "Winter Worship and Workshop," has served the Gallipolis Church for 30 years.

This year Marge and I were packed and on our way, to be accompanied by John and Nancy Presko, and we stopped at Victory Christian Church, Lancaster, Kentucky, where John preaches. He had asked me to preach that morning.

Toward the end of my sermon I developed a heart blockage and was taken to the hospital in Danville, where I was stabilized, then by ambulance (37 minutes!) to St. Joseph Hospital in Lexington, where they put in a pacemaker. If the Lord tarries, I plan to be in Pigeon Forge next February for the conference. It is a spiritual feast with plenty of time to shop and rest.

I must mention Barry Cameron, Senior Minister of Crossroads Christian Church, Arlington, Texas. Barry and his sidekick, Mel Dietz, have made a portion of my ministry possible. For whatever reason, Barry likes me and he and Crossroads have been there when I had a need. Barry and Mel, you bless me; your new worship center seating 3,500 on 200 acres will bless thousands.

Bill Lancaster is an elder at Southland and an astute businessman and dear friend. At this point in time either Bill or Steve Simmons could be considered my number one chauffeur. Thanks, fellows.

If my accounts are correct, Tony Wash holds the record for the number of trips with yours truly. In 1985, Tony gave me a collage of 41 items he collected accompanying me to speaking engagements; all kinds of memorabilia framed and under glass representing the places we visited. There were no church bulletins because we were always at Southland on Sundays. Thanks for the memories. I hasten to add that Tony and Clara's daughter, Dawayna, is the only girl named for me. Dawayna is now Mrs. Tim Aulick, and the mother of two.

I need to mention the name of Jerry Williams and his wife, Cel. Southland always has had a strong youth program. Quality does not come by accident. The youth program at Southland was built upon the shoulders of the produce manager at Albers. Jerry attended Cincinnati Bible College before deciding that ministry was not his calling. He worked at Albers in Cincinnati, then moved to Lexington when Albers opened a store here.

He and Cel took over the youth for two years without pay. A labor of love. The best use of life is to spend it on something that outlasts it — and they did!

There are many associates in various areas who should have a word of thanks. The early years with fewer people and limited budgets were more difficult. Ron Meadows is now retired from the Lexington Fire Department. However, 50 years ago he used some of his time to lead our youth work sacrificially. Sacrificially means without pay.

Ron Summers was an associate in the early years. Ron now serves as senior minister of a church in northern Kentucky. I appreciated Ron's work ethic.

Al Finch and his lovely wife were never members of Southland; however, they were always ready to lend a helping hand. After a career with IBM, Al became a photographer. I loved to include pictures in *The Voice of Southland*, our weekly church paper. Each time I called, Al would say, "Where and when?"

Thank you, Jess Correll. Jess is CEO of an organization that tithes on all profits generated by his company. What company do you ask? Fasten your seatbelts…First Southern National Bank; home office, Stanford, Ky., with branches in 14 Kentucky cities.

Van Florence has been a big force in my life. Van and his wife are faithful Southland members. He said he worked at IBM, but he spent a lot of time with the basketball program at UK. Anytime I needed something from UK, I dialed Van. After retiring from IBM, Van became head of the United Way because he has an ability for raising money. When duty called, he took a serious cut in salary to manage UK's Basketball Museum in the Civic Center downtown. I don't know how he does it, but he does it, and he has blessed me many times.

I am blessed with great relatives. As stated earlier, my immediate family of Marge, our two married daughters, and their families are well. My growing up family of Mother, Dad, three brothers and sister are deceased. My remaining closest relatives are three sisters-in-law: Emalu Smith, Florence, Ky.; Isabel Smith, Lexington, Ky.; and Nancy Kelsey, Batavia, Ohio. I have three first cousins: Pauline Taylor, Phoenix, Ariz.; Elizabeth Lohr, Somerset, Pa., and Dorothy Westwood, Level Green, Pa.

I have great admiration for Jim Host and his wife, Pat. I baptized this couple and one of the persons in attendance was their good friend, Mrs. Cawood Ledford. Jim felt strongly that this book should be written. Observing my hesitancy, he kindly but firmly suggested I get with the program. I did, and closure is just around the corner.

My good friend, Chuck Lees, minister of First Christian Church, Owingsville, Ky., and I spent a good deal of time making a list of where I have preached or spoken during the past eight years. It included date, place, name of contact person, etc. However, as the printing of the book progressed it became evident that the list would take 30 pages and the print would be small, real small. I regret this omission.

Friendships are dateless and are most important in my life.

There's an old saying, "Out of sight, out of mind." Not true. People like Lewis Fields and Virginia Parker are in my heart, permanently engraved until we meet where "there is no night." Lewis Fields worked for the Gulf Oil Company. However, when I needed something built in the office area, I called Lewis. And another name, Walter Cook, who could build anything and who did so with excellence.

Would any book about my life be complete without the name of Mr. Armstrong? That's all we ever called him. His love and care for the physical needs of the church went beyond the second mile.

Virginia Parker is now 87 and in a nursing home. She would tell you she didn't do much for the church but in my opinion she was a gem. I authored "The Membership Shepherding Plan," which I later sold to Standard Publishing Company. In each worship service we had a silent roll call card. People would secure a card from the back of the pew in front of them, fill in the blanks — name, address, etc. That week Virginia would check these cards against the master list to see how many times people were present or absent. Then our elders and staff contacted these people. Virginia's job had to be boring, but she probably said, "Nevertheless...not my will but thine be done."

There are many more out there like Virginia not mentioned. Their grand reward will be their name in a Book; not my book but The Book of Life. "Well done, thou good and faithful servant. Enter into the joy of thy Lord."

Remembrance is a golden chain
Time tried to break, but all in vain.
To have and hold and then to part,
Is the greatest sorrow in one's heart.

The years may wipe out many things
But this they erase never;
The memory of those good days
When we were yet together.

Thank you for reading this,

Wayne B. Smith